ADVANCE PRAISE FOR
WOMEN HEALING WOMEN

The story of Sister Lucy Kurien and the Maher Project is absolutely thrilling: To absorb everything it has to teach us—about courage, spirit, patience, and loving, non-violent resistance—is to see the world and humanity itself in an altogether new light. With the publication of *Women Healing Women* that story can at last find the global audience it so richly deserves. Let the transformations begin! —**Carol Lee Flinders**, author of *Enduring Grace and At the Root of This Longing*

How can one pay enough or thank enough for pure Gospel? Well, here it is in written and biographical form! I have met Sister Lucy, Cynthia, and Will personally and know their words to be true to life. Read, and let your own life be re-framed and re-gifted for a waiting world.—**Father Richard Rohr, O.F.M.**, Center for Action and Contemplation, Albuquerque

Maher embraces diversity and challenges oppressive stereotypes in Indian society—gender violence, patriarchy, bribery and corruption—with love and truth. Maher is a model that could well be applied in my own and other countries. I hope it will. This book shows us how.—**Nozizwe Madlala-Routledge**, Deputy Speaker of Parliament, Republic of South Africa

Equally heartbreaking and inspiring, this book details the atrocities of how women are treated in India as well as the remarkable solutions offered by Sister Lucy Kurien, and the Maher Project. Keepin and Brix offer an engaging testament to the undeniable effectiveness of love when brought to bear on personal and social challenges. Sister Lucy is a heroine and a shepherd, already living a future longed for in every human heart. —**Hilary Hart**, author of *The Unknown She*

In a world where God is most often still referred to as "He" India stands almost alone in worshipping the Divine as female. And yet, as outlined in this extraordinary book, the position of women in Indian society is still one of profound exploitation and abuse. Sister Lucy Kurien answered a call to respond to the needs of raped, battered and impoverished women and their children. Her work sets an example of the clarity and courage needed to build an alternative for women, and to keep faith in interfaith spirit. If only every young woman in our "emancipated" Western democracies could read this book to gain perspective not only on the real position of women worldwide, but on the many forms of her own exploitation. I thank Sr. Lucy and the authors for what I believe will become an inspirational classic.—**Swami Ambikananda Saraswati**, founder of The Traditional Yoga Association, and translator of the *Katha Upanishad* and the *Uddhava Gita*

Highly recommended for everyone concerned with the quality of life of women throughout the world and especially in Indian society. The authors have looked at the Maher Project with a compassionate heart and a clear mind, listened to the many stories of suffering, pain, and oppression of women in India, and produced a book full of hope.—**Ravi Ravindra**, author of thirteen books including: *Pilgrim without Boundaries, Science and the Sacred,* and *Yoga of the Christ*

This lovingly written book is an inspiring and beautiful story of the practical love of the oppressed, destitute, and downtrodden of India manifested by Sister Lucy Kurien and her supporters. It raises searching questions for missionaries, as well as for those serving in religious communities in countries suffering from centuries of abuse of the poor.—**Father Thomas Keating, OCSO,** founder Contemplative Outreach, Ltd., and author of many books, including, *Open Mind / Open Heart* and *Intimacy with God*

A heartrending yet inspiring account of the triumph of the human spirit in the face of seemingly insurmountable obstacles. These tales of despair and hope serve to remind us of the appalling extent of this abuse directed towards women and children—along with a solution that might possibly work. This book chronicles the unique interfaith organization which passes beyond the narrow boundaries of caste and religion to the shared openness of loving care, faith and mutual respect. It is a wake-up call for us all.—**Jetsunma Tenzin Palmo,** Tibetan Buddhist nun, founder of Dongyu Gatsal Nunnery

Like Sister Lucy Kurien, I witnessed a human being burned to death, which changed my mission in life forever. I watched Patrick electrocuted in the electric chair, and Lucy watched Renuka and her unborn child burn to death after being set afire by her husband. After the tragedy Lucy was driven to begin Maher, and I to abolish the death penalty. I met Lucy in Jaipur in 2008, and I was so impressed by her story. Now you get to read these incredible stories of lives transformed. But watch out. After reading these pages you may well never be the same again. —**Sister Helen Prejean,** CSJ, author of *Dead Man Walking*

The inspired Maher project brings practical and spiritual healing to discarded and destitute women, restoring them to dignity and security. Having personally seen the transformations that occur when people of all faiths, and none, work together for the common good with tenderness and cheer, this book brought tears to my eyes and rejoicing to my soul.—**Ashley Judd**, Hollywood actress, Board Member and Global Ambassador, Population Services International

WOMEN HEALING WOMEN

A Model of Hope for Oppressed Women Everywhere

William Keepin, Ph.D. and Cynthia Brix, M. Div.

HOHM PRESS
Prescott, Arizona

Cover Design: Zachary Parker, Kadak Graphics.
Layout and Interior Design: Becky Fulker, Kubera Book Design.
Cover photograph: Savari (Salim) Muthu Xavier.

Library of Congress Cataloging-in-Publication Data

Keepin, William.
    Women healing women : a model of hope for oppressed women everywhere / William Keepin and Cynthia Brix.
        p. cm.
    Includes index.
    ISBN 978-1-890772-88-8 (trade pbk. : alk. paper)
    1. Poor women--Abuse of--India. 2. Women's rights--India. 3. Child abuse--India. I. Brix, Cynthia. II. Title.
    HV6570.4.I43K44 2009
    362.830954--dc22
                                2008056158

HOHM PRESS
P.O. Box 2501
Prescott, AZ 86302
800-381-2700
http://www.hohmpress.com

This book was printed in the U.S.A. on recycled, acid-free paper using soy ink.

To
the One without a Name . . .

and to
the unnamed millions
of women and girls across the globe
whose similar stories (often with less happy endings)
have never been told.

Contents

Introduction

Maher: Rising to New Life

Listen, my friend, this road is the heart opening . . .
—Mirabai

I (Will K.) first went to Maher near Pune, India, for a brief visit in March, 2003, graciously hosted by Father Francis D'Sa after I attended his powerful training course on the Bhagavad Gita. I was deeply touched and quickly realized that I needed to return to Maher for a longer visit. Having worked since the early 1990s in the fields of gender healing and reconciliation and the development of innovative intentional communities, I had to find out if this place was "for real." So I went back a few weeks after that first visit, and have never stopped going back since. In the intervening years, the authors have visited Maher once or twice each year, sometimes for extended visits, and we discovered that, yes indeed, Maher is a most remarkable community. We have been privileged to watch its growth and witness firsthand how so many women and children are healing and transforming their lives and flourishing in the loving community that is Maher.

Much has been made of the horrific plight of women in India—and rightly so—but Maher is rare in providing a practical response to the appalling injustices suffered by Indian women. Of the more than 1,300 women who have taken refuge at Maher, many would have likely been murdered, committed suicide, or starved to death were it not for this project. As an interfaith community that strongly repudiates caste distinction, Maher unites people and hearts across all religions and castes—making it a rare beacon of light and hope not only for battered and destitute women and children in India, but for oppressed people across the globe.

Maher provides a healing refuge for battered, destitute, and downtrodden women—from all walks of life, all religions, all castes. Every year in India, thousands of women are doused in kerosene and set ablaze. Unwed mothers are abandoned on the streets to starve, and often commit suicide. Teenage girls are brutally raped and forever banished from their families. Many wives are routinely battered by their husbands; other women are rejected for belonging to the "wrong" caste. All such women and girls are welcome at Maher, where they find the warmth and security of a loving home and can begin life again with dignity and renewed hope. Equally poignant stories are recounted by Maher children: preadolescent girls sold to brothels, toddlers who witnessed their mothers being burned alive, and beggar children rescued from squalor who have been groomed at Maher to become national dance performers. For every story told at Maher, thousands of similar stories remain untold in India—most with far less happy endings.

Part of the genius of Maher is that all the housemothers and many of the staff were themselves battered women who once took refuge at Maher. They intrinsically understand the harsh realities from firsthand experience, and thus naturally provide a quality of compassionate care that is unparalleled.

The doors of Maher are open to women of every religion and caste. Maher does not promote any one religion over the others, but instead lives in accordance with the universal divine Spirit that burns at the foundation of all the world's religions. All scriptures are honored at Maher—as reflected by the copies of the Bhagavad Gita, the Qur'an, the Bible, and the Dhammapada in Maher's sanctuary—yet none are taught to the exclusion of the others. Maher upholds universal spiritual values without being beholden to any particular church, philosophy, or sect. As an interfaith community, Maher celebrates major religious holidays from several faiths, including Diwali and Ganesh (Hindu), Christmas and Easter (Christian), Id (Muslim), and Budh Purnima (Buddhist). These interfaith principles are portrayed in Maher's beautiful emblem, which shows the major symbols of the world's religions surrounding a bright flame at the center that represents the universal radiance of love and light that burns at the core of every major spiritual and religious tradition. As a uniting entity, Maher serves as a living example of healing that transcends religious division and strife and thereby offers a model urgently needed in our world today.

It's one thing to create an orphanage for helpless children, each one radiant with bright eyes and shining innocence, portending a promising future. It's quite another to peel off the streets women who have been utterly abandoned by society—women literally rotting in the road who are often raped, robbed, abused, left to starve. Maher rescues these women from the jaws of destruction, takes them in, gives them the first bath they may have had in years, and provides them with a loving home and simple, dignified life at its Vatsalyadham project. This is none other than God's work being done in the lives of these women.

Though originally founded as a refuge for battered women, Maher has grown to address a broad spectrum of interrelated social problems in an integral manner—including urgent social and economic needs within surrounding villages, ecological issues, and the needs of the tribal people and Dalits ("Untouchables") in the region. Maher's program in classical Indian dance provides a powerful vehicle for healing and celebration that draws upon the ancient and profound spirit of India. The Maher dance troupe has performed in prominent venues in India and recently in the United Kingdom. And Maher has done all this without indulging in the corruption that is so rampant in Indian society.

Maher is a shining ray of hope for transforming our troubled world. This book tells its story, and the stories of some of the women and children whose lives have been transformed there. We have been motivated to write this book as an offering to the battered women and children of India—and the world—because we believe that Maher offers a powerful model that can inspire others to create similar healing communities.

Maher is a large project, with many initiatives, facets, and complexities. No one book could do it justice, and this one provides only an introduction to it. No attempt or claim is made to be exhaustive; there are numerous aspects of the Maher project that are not covered here for reasons of space.

As Western authors writing about an Indian project, there are surely many subtleties and intricacies of Indian life and society that we have either missed entirely or distorted in some way—perhaps glaringly in certain passages. We can only ask forgiveness from our Indian friends and colleagues for these blunders, and acknowledge that all failings in the book are entirely ours. We are but the messengers. Maher is the message.

Note to the reader: The stories recounted in this book are all true. The names of the people involved, as well as place names and other incidental details, are changed to protect the identities of the people. The names of Maher staff and board members remain unchanged.

CHAPTER 1

Deliverance from Death

Those who respond to the joys and sorrows of others as if they were their own have attained the highest state of spiritual union.
—Bhagavad Gita (6:32)

The night was dark and ominous, which gave Parubai a strange tinge of comfort as she prepared the children. Her two older daughters were whining for food yet again as Parubai deftly dressed them in the darkest clothes she could find. The babies were sleeping.

Parubai was beyond desperate. She had tried every possible avenue to provide for her daughters, to no avail. Her husband had abandoned the family several months back when Parubai gave birth to their fourth daughter. He was outraged because she had not borne him a son. He had been drinking and beating Parubai almost daily, and finally ran off with another woman. No one had seen or heard from him since. As food and other supplies dwindled, the children's health was steadily deteriorating. Their skin had become dry and scaly, their muscles were weak, and they had increasing diarrhea despite having practically no food—telltale signs of starvation.

The only work Parubai had been able to find was chopping wood. She earned fifteen rupees (about thirty cents) for a hard day's work. This was woefully inadequate to provide even basic needs, and the children's condition was getting worse day by day. Parubai instructed her children to beg for food from local villagers and neighbors, but they were burdened providing for their own children and could spare nothing extra. Even Parubai's own family and relatives had rejected her pleas for help, as they too were desperately poor.

There was no escape, and nowhere to turn. Parubai could not bear another day watching her daughters starve before her very eyes. Better that they move on to their next incarnation, she thought, than be subjected to such trauma and misery every day. They would likely die soon anyway, so was it not more compassionate to circumvent this slow, agonizing death? Tonight the time had come for her to take decisive action.

Parubai's mind raced back and forth as she grappled with the gravitas of her decision. In her haste to get the children ready, her sari caught on one of the sticks poking out from the wall of her mud-and-stick hut. She yanked it free, which shook the rickety wall. The plastic tarp "roof" was rustling in the light breeze, reminding her yet again of the utter lack of funds to ever consider installing a proper thatched roof. She drew in a deep breath of resolution as she continued her preparations, determined this time not to change her mind.

Parubai waited until after 2 AM, when she was sure the village roads would be deserted. Then she slipped silently out of her hovel with the two youngest in her arms, the older girls complaining and asking why they were going out so late. Parubai admonished them to keep quiet, and furtively made her way with her children toward the village center.

As they approached the well, Parubai saw its outlines looming in the darkness ahead. It beckoned as a portal of escape from this miserable world to an unknown solace. Parubai summoned her courage, intending to throw the two older girls into the well first, then jump in herself with the babies.

As Parubai reached the well, she was startled to hear a man's voice call out in alarm, "Hey, where are you going? There's a well there!" Out of the darkness the man suddenly appeared, seeming to materialize out of nowhere. "What are you doing?!" he demanded. Parubai hesitated, frustrated that her plans were being sabotaged by this unexpected turn of events. It was highly improper for a woman to be out alone after dark, especially with children. Parubai began mumbling an explanation, but her interrogator quickly saw through her deception. Jumping into the well is a common way to commit suicide in Indian villages.

The man softened as he realized Parubai's true intent, and he asked her why she was seeking to end her life. Caught red-handed, Parubai felt she had no choice but to justify her intended plan. As the man listened to her plight, he encouraged her to come with him to a place he knew of that provided shelter to women and children in her condition. Parubai was extremely skeptical of this strange man, and she seriously doubted that such a place could exist because she had exhausted every possible avenue she knew to pursue. But the man was adamant, and he insisted that Parubai accompany him, telling her he knew exactly where the place was located because he himself had been helped there to overcome his alcoholism.

Later that morning, Parubai and her four daughters arrived at a small shelter where Sister Lucy Kurien was working, which later evolved into the Maher project. The term *maher* means "mother's home" in the local language of Marathi. Sister Lucy Kurien greeted the new arrivals and listened to the man's story of how he had encountered Parubai, and then he departed. Lucy interviewed Parubai carefully, then admitted her and her four daughters to the shelter. Over the next several days, Parubai and her children received the first proper meals they had had in many months. Within a couple of weeks, Parubai's spirits began to lift as she saw her daughters starting to laugh and play once again and their young bodies begin regaining their vibrancy and health.

Over the next few weeks, the shelter helped Parubai find a children's home that could take her two older daughters and give them proper nourishment and education. Lucy then helped Parubai to find a job as a gardener, which paid her just enough to support herself and her two youngest daughters. Thus was Parubai's life radically turned around. She had been knocking at the door of suicide, determined to take her own life and the lives of her four children. Had it not been for this lone man who suddenly appeared at the right moment, and his personal knowledge of the Maher prototype project, Parubai and her daughters would have joined the ranks of thousands of Indian women and girls who die or disappear each year with hardly a notice.

Today there are many desperate Indian women who choose suicide for themselves and their starving children rather than remain in a world that has rejected and abandoned them. Yet Parubai and her daughters were fortunate enough to avoid this tragic fate, and over the years they have remained close friends of Maher. Recently, Parubai's eldest daughter was married, and Maher provided the space and financial assistance for the wedding ceremony.

THE MAHER PROJECT

Parubai's story is one of many agonizing tales that have come to a happy ending because of the Maher project. Since its inception in 1997, Maher has provided shelter to more than 1,300 Indian women of all religions and castes. Battered, exploited, or abandoned in one of the most oppressive societies on Earth, many of these women would be dead today, were it not for this project.

This book tells the true story of the Maher project and the remarkable difference it is making in the lives of distressed women and children in India. Today there are 115 women and nearly four hundred children living at Maher and its twelve satellite homes, located in several villages about 40 km east of Pune, India. The women come from diverse walks of life—from all different religions, castes, and social strata of Indian society. The children come with mothers who are fleeing for their lives from exceedingly horrific abuse, or else they are found abandoned or battered in the streets, rescued from brothels, or from any number of tragic backgrounds. The women and children are rehabilitated and nurtured back to health and dignity at Maher. The story of Maher is one of profound courage and inspiration—a story showing how the power of love can make a remarkable difference, even in one of the most oppressive, patriarchal, and poverty-stricken societies on earth.

All the stories in this book are true and took place as recounted here. The names of people and various minor details have been changed to protect the identity of the people and places involved and to add substance and local color to the narrative to make it more accessible to Western audiences. However, the dramatic narrative accurately captures the essence of each story as it actually happened, including the foregoing story about Parubai.

One of the key foundational principles of the Maher project is a deep commitment to uphold and honor all religious faiths, and an equally deep commitment to repudiate the caste system in India. The doors of Maher are open to women from every religion and every caste—something that is very rare in India. To illuminate the spiritual essence of the Maher project, this book draws occasionally on quotations from various scriptures. True to the interfaith foundation of Maher, these jewels of wisdom are taken from a broad range of religious and spiritual traditions—East and West. This approach serves to reveal the universality of the spiritual principles upheld at Maher. The authors are students of the spiritual wisdom found in several traditions, and a principal motivation for writing this book is to introduce Maher to wider audiences as a living example of one way in which "universal spirituality" can take practical form in a thriving community.

Recounting the inspiring story of Maher necessarily entails a close look at some of the more disturbing aspects of Indian society, particularly the deeply entrenched, socialized cruelty toward women and girls. Our purpose in articulating these painful realities of Indian culture is by no means intended to foster a negative attitude or ill will toward Indian society or Indian people. On the contrary, this book is written out of a great love for India and for Maher. The intended audience includes both Western and other non-Indian, as well as Indian, readers, and the primary purpose of the book is to highlight something positive and inspiring that is being done to address the seemingly intractable challenges borne by women in India. In order for readers to understand the profound contribution that Maher is making, it is necessary to elucidate the painful conditions endured by women in India. Nevertheless, readers should know that the authors are both avid students of the mystical and spiritual traditions of India, and through our association with Maher and with other Indian colleagues and friends we have come to a deep love for the Indian people and their culture. This book is an expression of that love.

Some further caveats and clarifications are in order. India is a vast country of some 1.13 billion people, with hundreds of millions of loving Indians who do not engage in the abusive or cruel behavior patterns examined in this book. Moreover, India is not alone in harboring oppressive conditions for women, which remains a serious affliction in most countries across the globe. Even in the West, where women are supposedly much more emancipated, profound injustices remain, including widespread domestic abuse and violence against women, and institutionalized inequities for women at every level of society. The official rate of domestic violence is lower in India than in the authors' own country, for example, where, according to UN statistics, a woman is battered somewhere in the United States on average once every fifteen seconds. The United States Justice Department reports that a woman is raped every four minutes in the United States. Moreover, the Justice Department estimates that only 26 percent of rapes are reported, and independent sources place this number as low as 16 percent. So to get a more accurate picture, the statistic above must be at least quadrupled: to one rape every minute. The US National Crime Victims Center stated in 1992 that rape was one of the most frequently committed violent crimes and that the United States had the highest rate of sexual assault of any industrialized country in the world.

Meanwhile, according to statistical estimates, a woman is raped in India somewhere between one and two times every hour.[1] Of course, these figures are also known to be vastly underreported, so comparing these Indian statistics directly with the cited US statistics is not meaningful. Nevertheless, these data clearly indicate that women are certainly not safe from violent sexual assault in the West.

Furthermore, lest it be assumed that the authors are touting a Western model of emancipation as appropriate for women in the East, let the reader be quickly disabused of this notion. Quite apart from issues of overt violence, there is an altogether different kind of oppression and disempowerment experienced by women in the West. To give an anecdotal example, several women colleagues and friends from India and the Middle East who have lived in the West shared with us their perception that many Western women have become "emancipated" at the price of sacrificing or compromising their innate feminine wisdom and autonomy—in a manner that women in the East have never done. Moreover, this takes place largely outside of Western women's direct personal awareness, and it goes virtually unrecognized in a society where the "measure of a woman" is primarily her professional stature and family standing (which are patriarchal metrics in themselves). It is not the authors' place to judge how accurate these reflections might be, but they underscore the notion that women in the West are far from truly free, and they may even be, in certain respects, less empowered and sovereign than some of their counterparts in other supposedly more patriarchal societies.

---

[1] A rape occurs once per hour in India according to Daniel Lak, "Call for Tougher Indian Rape Laws," BBC News Online, 2000, and approximately twice per hour according to the National Family Health Survey, 2007.

Finally, the inspiring lessons from Maher apply not only to India, but to any oppressive culture where women or children are exploited, betrayed, or abandoned by the society. Maher demonstrates how even under highly unjust social conditions a loving community can be created to provide quality care for distressed women and children, and this very accomplishment in turn serves as a remarkable healing force within the larger society. Thus Maher stands as a powerful beacon of hope, not only for India but for other patriarchal societies across the globe.

CHAPTER 2

Dawn of Fire

Out of suffering have emerged the strongest souls;
the most massive characters are seared with scars.
—Kahlil Gibran

It was a peaceful sunny afternoon in 1991 when Sister Lucy answered an insistent knocking at the door of her convent. In the doorway stood a woman who was visibly distraught. She introduced herself as Renuka, from a nearby apartment building. Lucy invited her in, gave her a cup of tea, and listened as Renuka recounted a heart-wrenching tale of physical abuse and harassment at the hands of her husband. He had become increasingly violent toward her, and was now threatening to kill her. Renuka was seven months pregnant, and she was concerned for her safety and that of the fetus she was carrying. Bruises covered her arms and face, bearing silent witness to the veracity of her story. Renuka asked Lucy if the convent could provide temporary shelter for her.

Renuka's story touched a deep nerve in Lucy's heart. She had long been aware of the unconscionable suffering endured by many women in India. But Lucy's superior was away until the following morning, and Lucy did not have the authority to take such an unusual step as offering shelter to an outsider. She asked Renuka how long she had been married, and Renuka said three years. "I was unaware that one night could make such a difference in the life of a woman," Lucy recalled later, "because I had been brought up in a secure family environment."

So Lucy asked Renuka to come back the next day, and assured her that she would work on finding a solution. Renuka departed quietly, and Lucy remained unsettled by the visit.

◇ ◇ ◇

Lucy Kurien had joined the Sisters of the Cross convent thirteen years earlier, longing to do something to improve the plight of the poor and destitute people of India. In her early years in the convent, she had become frustrated with the Western lifestyle of ease and comfort behind cloistered walls that did not seem to touch the lives of the poor. "As a junior sister, many talks and exposure programs were conducted for us. Every exposure visit to the slums and interior villages affected me very deeply. I enjoyed the comfort my religious life offered. Yet something inside me was telling me that the comfort of the religious life was not meant for me, as a person committed to the vowed life. The more I was exposed to the life of the poor, the more I was feeling restless inside. All the time, I was questioning inside me: *For what had I come? What am I doing now?* In my heart, I came to realize that my call to religious life meant serving the poor."

Yet Lucy had been unsure about what to do, or how to go about making a difference. After a few years she was transferred to Pune for religious studies, and it was there that she met Sister Noelline Pinto, who had established a small project called the HOPE Center (Human Organization for Pioneering in Education). The project assisted marginalized women in a low income area to gain modest employment. "Sister Noelline was living a simple life and working for low-income women. This attracted me a lot," Lucy reminisced. "Sister Noelline's simple living and Indian spirituality made me very happy. This lifestyle answered many questions of my thirsty soul. Sister Noelline granted me permission to join her. But getting permission from the religious authorities to join her was not an easy task!"

Lucy appealed to her superiors for permission to join Sister Noelline's social work project. This was an unusual request in a Catholic system that did not normally accede to the wishes of a young nun, even the best intentioned, and she encountered formidable resistance. "My decision was not appreciated by my community sisters, or by my friends. They all left me, and I found myself all alone. There was no one who could see through my eyes. I had even questioned whether I was making a wrong decision."

But Lucy persevered, and she wrestled not only with her religious superiors, but also within herself. "Although inside me, I was very determined to work for the poor, there was also a lot of fear in me. Am I strong enough to be faithful to my vowed life? Will I not be tempted by the complementary sex when I am working so closely alongside them? And giving up the comforts of the religious lifestyle would clearly cost me a lot." But Lucy would not give up, and she finally managed to get the permission. "The bold step was taken on the 18th of May 1989, and Sister Noelline welcomed me at the HOPE Center with open arms." Lucy had been working at the Center for two years on the afternoon that Renuka knocked on her door.

◊ ◊ ◊

Later that evening, as Lucy was at her evening prayers, her reveries were suddenly interrupted by a bone-chilling scream from somewhere nearby. She rushed outside to see what was happening, and followed the sounds of the earsplitting screams. Lucy ran to an adjacent building, and as she darted around the corner she came upon a horrifying sight. Twenty meters away stood a woman engulfed from head to foot in flames. Seeing Lucy, the burning woman started running directly toward her, shouting "Save me! Save me!" Lucy recognized with a shock that it was none other than Renuka, the woman who had sought shelter earlier that afternoon. Renuka's husband had just doused her with kerosene, tossed a lighted match on her, and fled.

Renuka collapsed to the ground, screaming and writhing in the flames. Lucy bolted into an open apartment door, grabbed some blankets and smothered the fire. She carefully wrapped Renuka's severely burned body. Renuka was still breathing, but went unconscious. A small group of onlookers had gathered by this time, and Lucy asked for their help. Renuka was still breathing, and Lucy was determined to get her to medical help as soon as possible. Together they carried Renuka's body into an auto rickshaw, as there was no car available. They drove Renuka to the emergency room at the hospital, which took well over an hour on the narrow, bumpy roads.

The doctors examined Renuka and told Lucy that she was burned over 90 percent of her body and there was not much they could do for her. They did not expect her to live. Lucy implored them to save the baby. The doctors rushed Renuka into the operating room, and a few minutes later emerged with the fetus. "What I received in my hand," recalled Lucy, "was—to put it bluntly—a cooked baby." Both mother and baby died that night.

Renuka met the hideous fate that befalls thousands of women in India every year—murder by immolation. Many of these women are set ablaze by their husband or mother-in-law because they have not complied with the husband's family's demand for ongoing dowry payments or because the wife is deemed to have somehow fallen short of her husband's or his family's expectations. Sometimes, as in Renuka's case, the husband murders his wife because he wants to bring another woman into their home.

DOWRY MURDER IN INDIA

Though prohibited by law since 1961, the practice of giving or demanding "dowry" gifts from the bride's family as a precondition to marriage is still widespread in India. When dowry agreements are deemed to be unfulfilled, or as often happens if dowry demands by the groom's family are insidiously increased in the months or years after the wedding, the bride is often seriously harassed and abused. This can escalate to the point where the husband or his family burns the bride alive, usually by pouring kerosene on her and setting her on fire. The official records of these incidents are low because they are usually reported by the family as accidents or suicides.

Accurate statistics on "dowry deaths" in India are difficult to obtain. Estimates vary widely, but there is general agreement that dowry murders have risen dramatically in recent years. In Delhi, a woman is burned to death almost every twelve hours. Government records for India from the National Crime Records Bureau (NCRB) reveal that 7,618 women were reported killed in dowry-related incidents in 2006, an increase of 12.2 percent over 2005. Uttar Pradesh, with 1,798 cases, had the highest number of such deaths, followed by Bihar with 1,188 cases.[1] Government statistics reveal that dowry deaths have increased significantly in recent years. In 1988, 2,209 women were reported killed in dowry-related incidents, and in 1990, 4,835 were killed. By 1995, the National Crime Bureau of the Government of India was reporting about 6,000 dowry deaths every year. But these are official figures, which are widely regarded as gross understatements of the real situation. Unofficial estimates cited in a 1999 article by Himendra Thakur place the number of deaths at 25,000 women a year, with many more left maimed and scarred as a result of attempts on their lives.[2]

The typical explanation given by the family in these cases is that the gruesome death was caused by a kitchen accident, or a stove that burst. To make this scenario plausible, the victim is doused in kerosene and set ablaze—an exceedingly horrific way to die. If the pretext of an accident seems too implausible, the case is attributed to suicide.

---

[1]   *Hindustan Times,* Jan. 14, 2008.

[2]   Himendra Thakur, "The Chill of Kerosene," 1999, www.himendra-thakur.
sulekha.com/blog/post/1999/07/the-chill-of-kerosene.htm

Either way, it is a relatively simple matter to murder a woman in this grotesque manner in India, without legal retribution.

Police and criminal justice authorities typically do not probe deeply into these cases. As wryly observed by Indu Prakash Singh, author of several books on the status of women in India, "Modern India seems to have at least two parallel legal systems, one for men and the other for women."[3] The lack of official registration of dowry murders is apparent in Delhi, where 90 percent of cases of women burnt were recorded as accidents, 5 percent as suicide, and only the remaining 5 percent as murder. Similarly, in Bangalore in 1997 there were 1,133 cases of "unnatural deaths" of women. Of these, 38 percent were categorized as "accidents," 48 percent as "suicides," and just 14 percent as murder. As activist V. Gowramma from Vimochana in Bangalore explained: "We found that of 550 cases reported between January and September 1997, 71 percent were closed as 'kitchen/cooking accidents' and 'stove-bursts' after brief investigations under section 174 of the Code of Criminal Procedures." The fact that a large proportion of the victims were daughters-in-law was either ignored or treated as coincidence by police.[4] A recent analysis of dowry death by Jane Rudd found that "in cases where violence is threatened, when there are people in the community to whom a woman can complain and ask for help, the incidence of violence is reduced."[5] This directly affirms the key importance of Maher-like refuge projects.

The grotesque brutality of murder by immolation is hard to fathom, particularly in a culture steeped in such a profound spiritual heritage. India is the nation that produced Mahatma Gandhi, and people

---

[3] Indu Prakash Singh, *Women, Law, and Social Change in India*, Stosius/ Advent Books (New Delhi), 1989, p. 158.

[4] Amanda Hitchcock, "Rising number of dowry deaths in India," 2001, *www.wsws.org/articles/2001/jul2001/ind-j04.shtml*

[5] Article by Jane Rudd in *Urban Women in Contemporary India: A Reader*, Rehana Ghadially (Ed.), Sage Publications, 2007.

all across the land revere their beloved *Gandhiji* and his venerated teachings of *ahimsa* (nonviolence) and *satyagraha* (clinging to truth). It is difficult to decide which aspect of dowry murder more blatantly violates *ahimsa*: the widespread practice of burning Indian women alive, or the society's complicit willingness to turn a blind eye to this horrific tradition.

◇ ◇ ◇

Distraught by the horror of Renuka's grisly death, and full of remorse for not having offered her shelter on that fateful night, Lucy was beside herself. Renuka had come to her with an urgent plea for help, and Lucy had not been able to provide refuge. Now Renuka and her unborn baby were dead. "It was a devastating experience in my life," Lucy recalls. "I felt very guilty within me. If Renuka had been my sister or my daughter, I would certainly have taken the risk to help her! Why did I not help?"

Lucy felt a heavy heart and tremendous responsibility for Renuka's death, even though rationally she realized it was not her fault. She felt a growing conviction that she could no longer be content to live a sheltered existence behind the cloistered walls of the convent while such horrific violence and abuse was rampant in the society all around her. Deep down she wanted to do much more for the poor, and for the oppressed women of India.

"This incident convinced me to work for the cause of women. I spoke to many friends about my decision to work exclusively for women," Lucy explained. One such friend and confidant proved to be instrumental: Father Francis D'Sa, a Jesuit priest and professor of comparative theology and philosophy in the nearby Di Nobli College and at the University of Würzburg in Germany. Father D'Sa served on the HOPE board of trustees, which is how Lucy met him. He supported Lucy in taking action, and offered to help her. "Father D'Sa had a great listening ear. He understood me and encouraged me in every step I was taking. He later found donors to help me realize my dream, and raised substantial funds for Maher through his contacts."

◇ ◇ ◇

Lucy Kurien was born in 1956 in the small village of Kolayad in the Kannur district of northern rural Kerala, South India. Raised in a poor but happy family, Lucy was the third of nine children, so she learned early on how to share meager resources. Her mother and father, Marykutty and Kurien, instilled strong moral and spiritual values in their children. As a young girl, Lucy used to put extra food into her lunch bag to give to other children at school who had less to eat than she did. At the age of thirteen, Lucy moved to Bombay, where she lived at a convent and started working to send money home. Whenever she returned home to Kerala, she took back goods and other gifts to her family and friends. The first pair of shoes that her eleven-year-old sister ever owned was brought to her from Bombay by Lucy.

The appalling poverty and squalor in Bombay was a major shock to the young Lucy. Never had she encountered such human suffering and abject destitution in her home state of Kerala. Early on, she determined to make a difference. "When I completed my basic education, I took up a job in Mumbai, as my family back home needed funds. Yet I was deeply shaken by the poverty that I saw around me. It filled me with the urge to reach out to the needy, especially destitute women. The religious life started to attract me, as I was staying with sisters. In my young mind I thought that I would be able to work for the poor if I became a missionary. The slums in Mumbai were a great pull to the religious life. But the normal life of people was also attractive to me. It was a very difficult choice to make. I struggled a lot between the two choices."

At the age of twenty, Lucy Kurien joined a Catholic convent called Sisters of the Cross, with the dream of devoting her life to serving the poor. "I quit my job and became a nun. It was not an easy decision. I had my independence in Mumbai, and the freedom of earning and spending my money as I wished. Now I had to give up my freedom and financial independence—that was very hard."

Lucy went through formation, and she loved the spiritual teachings of Jesus. Yet religious life brought new challenges. "Before long I noticed that my companions were all educated, and I began to feel inferior to them. But when I started to live and work with them, I discovered that I could work and study as equal to them. Slowly my self-confidence started to build up. Many cutting remarks from authorities affected me, and there was a strong temptation to give up and go back to Mumbai to work. The love from my family was also pulling on me. But the spirituality of religious life taught me to be strong, and the spiritual values and teachings were sinking deep into me." Sister Lucy was professed at the age of twenty-four. "The Sisters of the Cross congregation instilled in me the teachings of Jesus and His love for the poor," Lucy recalls, brimming with gratitude. "They also offered me the opportunity to travel, and gave me the benefit of full exposure to the realities of life in India." Cooking had long been a hobby for Lucy, and before long she was put in charge of the kitchen. She enjoyed the job immensely. "The six long years as junior sister strengthened me. The women in the kitchen taught me to be human. Their sharing of life with me opened my eyes to the reality of the life of women. Coming from a secure and sheltered life in Kerala, I couldn't imagine that life could be so hard for women."

Over time, however, Lucy found to her dismay that life in the convent did not enable her to serve the poor effectively. "When I came to the religious life, we were not allowed to eat with the servants," Lucy lamented. "The people who worked with us could not eat with us at our table. I was greatly pained by this. Our congregation had several orphanage projects, or poor children's homes, but in these homes the children always ate separately. The nuns ate better food, away from the children. This was always very painful to me."

Lucy had learned from an early age to treat all human beings as equals. "My mother and father took in the local tribal people and fed them, and they fed the laborers who worked in our field. I must have been around eight years old. We would all eat together, sitting at the table, using the same plates and glasses. This was very rare in those days, and remains so today. My brother is the director of a large, successful quarry company, and to this day he eats with the workers." Lucy's family are Brahmins, the highest caste, who normally never eat or mix with the lowest castes, especially the Untouchable tribals and Dalits. But Lucy's family was different. "Though we ourselves were poor, my parents taught us to share whatever we had. I remember my first Holy Communion white dress—my mother lent it to a poor child. I was sad at first, but my mother insisted that I should let her borrow it, because she was poorer. The dress came back stained, and I was upset, and the girl was avoiding me at school. But my mother helped me to look beyond all that, and before long I befriended the girl. We became good friends."

◇ ◇ ◇

After Renuka's tragic death, Lucy continued to work at the HOPE Center for another six years, while inwardly nurturing her dreams for a project of her own. The HOPE Center provided vocational training for women in tailoring, painting Batiks, and embroidery, and it also ran some kindergartens. Lucy learned a great deal working there. "Sister Noelline was there to guide me in the beginning," she recalls. "She had genuine love for the poor, and she skillfully pushed me into social work. I am not a trained social worker—I didn't have this background. I only had the love, but I did not have the know-how. Sister Noelline was my mentor in social work skills—she taught me so much."

Lucy kept envisioning in her heart and mind the larger project she yearned to manifest. She began thinking carefully and thoroughly through myriad details of how her dream project might look in practice. Meanwhile, Father D'Sa was in conversation with many of his friends and colleagues in Germany and Austria. One such friend was Bernhardt Girardi, a professional musician from Salzburg, Austria. During one of their visits, Bernhardt told Father D'Sa that he wanted to do a project to benefit women in India. Hearing this, Father D'Sa put Bernhardt in touch with Sister Lucy. It was a fateful connection.

Bernhardt Girardi journeyed to India with his son, where he met Sister Lucy Kurien for the first time. "Lucy shared her experience with poor women," Bernhardt recalls. "My mind started working on how I could be involved. I saw in Sister Lucy the desire to do something for the women of India—an idea I liked a lot but did not at that time understand how to implement." Lucy and Bernhardt spent a month together exploring ideas and plans for the project and making visits to potential building sites. Lucy shared the scope of her vision for Maher in detail. By the end of the visit, they had identified a suitable parcel of land in the tiny village of Vadhu Budruk, about 40 km northeast of Pune.

"Like a baby who takes the first step with the help of the mother," Bernhardt mused, "a philanthropic venture needs help from outside to take its first step toward achieving dignity and freedom for all. I think everybody who can help to improve the situation should try it! For me, it was a duty to do everything possible to help Maher take this first step. Although globalization affected the Austrian economic situation, many people in our country did not know or care about the difficult life of the poor in India. By organizing different cultural events back home in Austria with musicians, dancers, artists, or poets it was possible to collect money to support the Maher project."

Bernhardt made a financial commitment to buy the land and pay for the cost of constructing the first building. Beyond that, he informed Lucy, she was on her own, and she would have to raise all operational funds, hire staff, and orchestrate the entire project. Everything else was entirely up to her. Lucy also had to make the difficult decision to leave the HOPE Center, and Sister Noelline. "Living together for eight years, we had developed a strong bonding," Lucy recalls, "and it took me almost a year to tell her my decision." Yet Lucy forged ahead into the unknown. Never having raised money before, and without a clue as to where appropriate staff would be found, Lucy Kurien took a deep breath, and said Yes!

To go forward, Lucy had to obtain formal permission from three different religious authorities, even though none of these organizations provided any funding for her new initiative. Because Lucy insisted that Maher must have an interfaith spiritual foundation, the project was ineligible for funding from any Christian missionary or religious organizations. Some prominent Church authorities opposed the project or refused to support it, primarily for this reason, and no Church authority gave the project official endorsement. Lucy requested and finally obtained written permission to proceed with her project from three sources: the administrative general of her religious order (Sisters of the Cross of Chavanod, France), the Provincial of Pune, and the local Bishop. Lucy's own religious congregation required her to sign a Memorandum of Understanding that effectively disavowed any responsibility for her or her project. She was left to fend for herself—and her cherished dream—entirely on her own.

Father Francis D'Sa was instrumental in brainstorming with Lucy many details of the project, and his fundraising efforts were a primary source of financial support for the project throughout the early years, and remain an important source of funding to this day. As a Jesuit priest and leading scholar of the great scriptures of India, Father D'Sa's lectures and courses in Europe were very popular and well attended. During his public lectures in Germany and Austria he would always bring up Maher and announce that he was charging no fee for the lectures but would accept donations, and whatever funds were raised would go to this cause. His leadership, vision, and fundraising were essential to the project, and he stood by Lucy through multiple challenges.

Thus was the Maher project born. Maher opened its doors on February 2, 1997, in a simple ceremony with blessings given by Father D'Sa and Sister Lucy. That very night, two battered women came to Maher as its first residents.

Within the first few months the nascent project was blessed with the arrival of deeply committed staff, several of whom will be introduced throughout this book. Three are highlighted here because they joined Maher at the beginning and have remained ever since. Anand Ishwar Sagar was Maher's first social worker, and he has worked with unceasing enthusiasm, courage, and dedication to virtually all aspects of the Maher project since its inception. After years of running several village projects, Anand is now expanding Maher's outreach and self-help programs to many villages in the surrounding region. John Soy joined Maher at the very beginning as the driver of Maher's sole vehicle—a small scooter—on which he took Lucy wherever she needed to go. John later served as the driver of Maher's jeep for many years, and today he directs the maintenance department with his characteristic good cheer and steady competence. Anand and John are both married, with two children each, and their families are an integral part of Maher.

Hirabegum Mullah is another social worker who joined Maher in the first year. Growing up as the only girl in her family, with five brothers, Hira learned early on how to share meager resources. After training in social work she gained field experience in emergency earthquake relief before joining Maher. Hira's very life is Maher, and she has devoted herself fully to every aspect of the project. She is a Muslim deeply committed to the interfaith vision of Maher, and she regards the entire project as made possible only through the grace and will of God, whom she believes stands behind and works through all religious faiths. Her father was a social activist and spiritual poet whose devotional poems have been published in Marathi. Hira's impeccable honesty, deep commitment, joyous laughter, and readiness to serve in whatever way is needed at any moment has been a profound blessing to Maher. She served as assistant director for many years, and as Maher continues to expand today Hira is assuming the duties of executive director for Maher's principal facility in Vadhu Budruk.

From these humble beginnings, the nascent Maher began to grow. Challenges presented themselves immediately, several of which are recounted in later chapters. "At first, it was very hard for the local villagers to accept a non-Marathi-speaking Christian, and moreover, a woman director," explains Lucy. Vadhu Budruk was an entirely non-Christian village, and remains so today. The locals were understandably very concerned that as a Catholic nun Lucy had an agenda to convert them to Christianity. Thus there was strong local opposition to Maher in the early days. At the same time, Lucy was continuing to encounter resistance from many of her Christian colleagues, including painful rebuff or cold rejection in certain instances, because Maher was not a Christian project, but was rather interfaith.

"There was fear and rejection from every side," Lucy recalls of the early days, and Maher went through pointed challenges. Lucy and the tiny Maher staff had to conduct their work with tremendous diligence, patience, and sensitivity—navigating tricky waters both with the local villagers and with dubious Christian colleagues and visitors. Money was extremely scarce, and there were times when there simply was no money to buy food. In extreme cases, Lucy and Hira would go to the market just as it was closing and the vendors were packing up to go home. They would deftly snap up whatever few scraps of onions, potatoes, or odd vegetables lay on the ground, having either fallen or been rejected by the vendors as too small or damaged to be worth selling. These meager pickings were taken back home and served with rice for the community dinner.

From the outset, Maher staff put significant energy into outreach to the local villagers, inviting them to visit Maher and learn what it was all about. Maher sponsored festivals periodically, serving free food and putting on street theater performances—always encouraging the local villagers to attend. Over time, trust built up between Maher and the surrounding communities as it became ever clearer to local villagers that it was not pushing any religious agenda. Step by step, Maher continued to grow—sometimes very slowly, other times by leaps and bounds when major new donations came through—gradually evolving into what it has become today.

CHAPTER 3

The Maher Project Today

Whoever says "I abide in Christ" ought to walk just as He walked.
—1 John 2:6

In twelve short years, Maher has grown to become a thriving community of approximately 115 women and nearly 400 children, plus a team of twenty social workers, eight administrative staff, and a board of ten trustees. About half the women and children live at the main facility in Vadhu Budruk, a small village about 32 km east of Pune. The remainder live in twelve satellite "mini-Maher" homes which have been established in surrounding villages, run by fifty-three "housemothers" on the Maher staff. Administrative offices are located in the city of Pune.

The goal of the Maher project is not only to provide refuge from domestic violence and abuse but also to eliminate their fundamental causes in the local communities by making available essential skills, education, and resources to help reduce poverty, violence, social neglect, and superstition.

Transcending religious and caste barriers in all aspects of its work, Maher was founded as an interfaith project. All religions and castes are explicitly honored at Maher, and every woman who takes refuge there is welcomed with open arms, irrespective of her religious faith, caste, or social status. The success of Maher demonstrates the power of interfaith, multicaste collaboration to redress oppressive social conditions in Indian society.

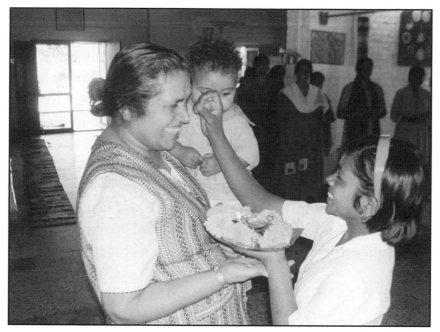

A Maher girl offers a traditional Indian blessing known as *aarti* to Sister Lucy Kurien.

Before reviewing the principal features of the Maher project, we pause briefly to consider the astounding statistics in India on domestic violence, which only recently became a crime with the passage of the Domestic Violence Act in 2006. A recent survey of 10,000 Indian women conducted by India's Health Ministry found that more than half of those interviewed considered violence to be a normal part of married life—the most common cause being the failure to perform domestic duties up to the expectations of their husband's family.[1] Another National Family Health Survey (NFHS), a pan-India survey conducted by eighteen research organizations (including the International Institute for Population Sciences), found that 37.2

---

[1] Amanda Hitchcock, "Rising Number of Dowry Deaths in India" *www.wsws. org/articles/2001/jul2001/ind-j04.shtml*

percent of married Indian women regularly experience spousal violence. In some areas, this figure is much higher; e.g., 46 percent in both Rajasthan and Madhya Pradesh. The worst is in Bihar, where 59 percent of married women regularly experience (often extreme) abuse, and 63 percent of these cases are reported from urban, well-to-do families rather than backward rural ones. Experts emphasize that all these figures are notoriously underreported, and could be higher still. The worst-affected women in the survey are between the ages of twenty and forty. Finally, according to the survey, "74.8 percent of abused women in India are propelled towards committing suicide." Against the background of such widespread social injustice directed at women, the need for projects like Maher cannot be overemphasized.

MAJOR FEATURES AND PROGRAMS OF THE MAHER PROJECT

Interfaith Commitment: Honoring All Religions and Spiritual Traditions

The staff and board of trustees at Maher come from diverse religious faiths, as do the sheltered women and children. Hindus, Muslims, Christians, Buddhists, Sikhs, and Jains all live and work together in harmony—demonstrating Maher's strong commitment to interfaith spiritual values shared by every religious tradition. Residents and staff are supported in practicing their own particular religious faiths, and community meditation and prayers are conducted without reference to specific deities or religious icons. The Maher sanctuary prominently displays copies of key scriptures—the Bhagavad Gita, the Bible, the Qur'an, and the Dhammapada—along with artwork depicting the iconography from each of these traditions. Sacred festivals, feasts (religious holidays), and wedding ceremonies are celebrated at Maher according to the many different faith traditions. At the center of the altar is the beautiful Maher emblem—an artistic depiction of the key symbols for each of the world's major religions arranged in a circle, with a single flame burning brightly at the center, signifying the spiritual unity of all religions.

Maher staff are given ten days of leave each year to attend silent meditation retreats, and children over eight years of age are given ten minutes of nondenominational meditation twice every day, before breakfast and dinner. This successful interfaith collaboration makes the Maher project highly significant in contemporary Indian society.

Caste-Free Zone

The Maher project does not recognize caste distinctions. In all its functions and community activities, people of all castes are mixed together, breaking traditional Indian social taboos. In community dinners, for example, people of the highest and lowest caste sit side by side eating together, which normally they would never do outside of Maher. Maher is thus effectively a caste-free zone, and all who go there learn to appreciate and respect this departure from entrenched cultural norms. As Lucy describes it, "There is no discrimination at Maher, and everyone, including me, gets the same comforts and opportunities. I eat what everyone else eats, and we all practice equality in everything."

Programs for Women

Maher was founded originally as a refuge for women and offers multiple services for battered and destitute women. The various ways in which Maher serves women are presented in detail in subsequent chapters, so only a brief overview is provided here.

Maher's doors are open to women of any religion or caste. Women admitted to Maher are given initial psychological counseling as well as medical care and legal counseling. Ongoing counseling and rehabilitation is provided to all women residents by a team of staff counselors, two psychologists, and a cadre of twenty social workers—assisted by para-social workers and fifty-three housemothers trained at Maher. Maher works with each woman individually, depending on her needs and circumstances. In general, the goal of Maher's work is to help women to reconcile with their husbands or families. If this is impossible, they are assisted in filing for divorce and/or given the skills they need to support themselves on their own. The number of women staying at Maher varies over time, currently ranging between 75 and 120.

Women come to Maher for many reasons, and Maher has different homes and projects to accommodate them, depending on their situation and their goals. The women often bring children with them, and Maher takes them in as well. The majority of women who come to Maher are seeking refuge from abuse or domestic violence in one form or another. They stay for varying lengths of time for their process of rehabilitation, which averages about three months, and then most return to society. Some stay on at Maher and are trained to become housemothers, cooks, or other Maher staff.

Maher has established a special home called Vatsalyadham for mentally disturbed women, many of whom are homeless and found living on the street. Maher staff locates such women, often rescuing them directly from the street, and brings them to Maher, where they are given a decent home and medical or psychiatric care. There are fifty-one such women currently at Maher, housed in a new building that was recently completed.

Another project is a home for elderly women, many of whom are also found homeless on the street. There are currently twenty-three elderly women living in Maher's Sukh Sandhya home near Vatsalyadham. This facility is purposely located adjacent to some of Maher's homes for children, which provides a healing synergy between the youth and the elderly that has proven mutually beneficial.

Maher also serves as a home for unwed mothers. Pregnant girls and women who are not married come to live there until they deliver their babies, who are usually given up for adoption. The expecting women participate actively in all Maher programs during their stay. Such homes are in very short supply in India compared to the need.

Satellite Maher Homes in Surrounding Villages

As Maher grew, the primary facility soon became overcrowded, and a larger, second, facility was built at Vadhu Budruk. The new building was designed with seven separate "mini-Maher" homes, each of which accommodates twenty children and two housemothers. Each home has its own kitchen, bathroom, staff quarters, and a large living/sleeping space for the children. The idea behind this design was that the physical environment should feel like a home, and not a dormitory or hostel.

The division into separate homes with twenty children and two housemothers each is a crucial aspect of the social design at Maher. It

Maher's group home facility at Vadhu Budruk. This building houses seven "mini-Maher" homes, each one having two housemothers and twenty children.

imparts the feeling of family to each of the homes and greatly reduces the institutional feel of the Maher community. Maher's leaders were determined to maximize, for both women and children, the sense of living in a "mother's home," and this is one of the key ways in which that has been accomplished. As Lucy puts it, "When the children are playing, they should hear their housemothers in the next room cooking, and the wonderful smells of the food should waft out to them. This is an integral part of growing up in a nurturing home."

Beyond this, an additional twelve satellite homes (or "sub-centers") have been established in surrounding villages. Each of these homes constitutes a mini-Maher—a small community of self-reliant women and children living together in safety and harmony. Once again, each home consists of twenty children and two housemothers, all of whom are women who took refuge at Maher.

Taken together, these smaller satellite Maher homes scattered throughout the local villages in the region are powerful beacons of light that are having a remarkable transformative effect on the long-standing fabric of patriarchal social conditions in this region. These homes bring the presence and spirit of Maher directly into each of the villages, and they serve as an implicit yet effective deterrent to domestic violence because all the townsfolk are fully aware that any woman who is abused has a place to take refuge. Moreover, if she does so, everyone else in the village will know about it. This effectively shifts the issue of domestic violence out of the household and into the community. Yet, the genius of this approach is that it is accomplished in a subtle manner by simply locating homes for women and children in these villages rather than as a program strategy that would be felt as intimidating by the villagers.

Maher Production Unit

Training women to be economically independent is the primary purpose of Maher's production unit. The women are taught a range of different trades and skills to prepare them to be more economically self-sufficient when they leave Maher and return to their village life.

Several hundred women have been trained, and many are now earning portions of their income working in handicrafts and tailoring. Recently, the program has expanded to include vocational training to area village women in need.

The production unit takes up an entire floor of one of Maher's recently completed buildings, with several rooms dedicated to candle making, greeting card stitchery, tailoring, oil lamp painting, and product storage. Other products made at Maher include incense sticks, curry and henna, crochet products (bags and clothing), decorative gift bags, *utni* (face scrub), and *shikekai* (hair shampoo). The women are also taught how to maintain the account books, keeping record of all orders and sales.

"As word has spread about Maher's products, there is increasing demand for our products both locally and internationally," says Shirly

One of several women's handicrafts teams at work in Maher's training and production unit. These women are making oil lamps to be sold for the Hindu Diwali "festival of lights."

Antony, the longtime director and primary training instructor of the production unit. Maher's production unit has an average earning of 15,000 rupees (340 US dollars) per month. Many products sell at local festivals, such as the full-moon Rakshabandhan festival, where Maher sells several hundred *rakhis*, colorful bracelets that a sister ties on her brother's wrist to symbolize their bond of love. Maher's production unit receives orders from Indian companies as well as international corporations such as HSBC Bank, Quinoxx, Kanbay IT, Pidilite Industries, and many others. Larger sales bring 10,000 to 20,000 rupees in a single order.

Outreach to the Poor, Including "Untouchables"

The Maher project has various programs to provide support to local villages in the region. Maher has also reached out to local communities of Dalits and indigenous tribals, who live in extreme poverty. These are abandoned peoples who are below the lowest rung in the caste system—entirely unrecognized by the Indian government—so they receive no services whatsoever. Maher provides assistance to these people, providing equipment such as water wells and pumps, solar cookers, and basic supplies. Recently, Maher has built day care centers and a small school for their children, who otherwise would have no educational opportunities whatsoever.

Programs for Children

The number of children at Maher has grown dramatically over the years and is now approaching four hundred. Many have come with their battered mothers, but others come from broken homes, or are brought to Maher when their mothers have been injured or killed and the father is unavailable or unable to care for them. Still others are brought in off the streets, often found begging, and are frequently suffering from malnutrition or some other dire health condition. About forty children at Maher are children of prostitutes working in the brothels in Pune or Mumbai, and some are girls who have been rescued from prostitution in the brothels.

Providing homes for these children in groups of twenty with two housemothers gives them a sense of family and belonging. They are educated in local schools—either government run (Marathi medium) or private (English medium), depending on their particular circumstances. Maher has developed extensive programs to provide for the needs of the children and to create as homelike an atmosphere as possible for them. Some of these children's stories are told in subsequent chapters.

Maher has also established several programs for local children in the region who are not part of Maher. There are seventeen kindergartens (called *balwadis*) established in surrounding villages, providing education, nutrition, and day care. Recently, Maher has added day care programs for some of the poorest children from local slums and children of poor laborers who are brickmakers. The slum children come from the squalor of the "rat pickers," the name given to their parents because they eke out a living by picking through garbage—in direct competition with rats and other rodents—to find anything that can be eaten or recycled such as plastic bottles, cans, or other containers. Rat pickers generally must leave home by 4 AM to sort through garbage before municipal trucks pick it up, leaving their children to fend for themselves. The brickmakers' children are similarly left to their own devices. So Maher buses these children back and forth daily to Vadhu Budruk when the Maher children are at school and provides basic day care, education, and a healthy meal to these otherwise exceedingly deprived children.

Community Support and Self-Help Groups

Maher has created 237 self-help groups in more than one hundred villages in the area. Each group consists of twenty villagers who make small donations of money into a community pool. Any member can then request a loan at a nominal interest rate, and the proceeds go back into the community pool. Self-help groups eliminate dependence on unscrupulous loan sharks, who charge interest rates from 60 to 100 percent. Most self-help groups are for women only, but Maher has created thirty self-help groups for men, recognizing the importance of working with entire communities, and not only with women.

The self-help groups also serve as important avenues for raising awareness in rural villages about health, hygiene, domestic violence, alcoholism, and superstitious beliefs. Some typical activities of the groups include micro-finance loan programs in collaboration with local banks, organizing strategies to cover shortages of fuel and cooking gas, planting trees, performing street theater on various topics, presenting seminars on alcohol and drug addiction, building toilets in the villages, and other projects depending on the needs of the village.

Men at Maher

Men are respected at Maher, and there is no atmosphere of male-bashing among the women. Maher is fortunate to have numerous wonderful and deeply committed men on staff and among the social workers who add a great deal to the community. The male staff work closely and harmoniously alongside the women, bringing a protective and healing presence that is crucial to the vitality and safety within the community. In so doing, the men provide a healthy role model and a positive masculine image for other Indian men and boys to emulate. The women and girls also learn that men are able to be caring, loving, and nonviolent. Maher always sends one male and female social worker to co-facilitate the weekly public meetings conducted in Maher's satellite homes in surrounding local villages. The male/female team provides a concrete example of harmonious collaboration between men and women working jointly to transform unjust gender dynamics in the society, which in itself constitutes a valuable element of learning for local village men.

The importance of attending to men's needs and issues in Indian society is recognized at Maher as fundamental to achieving lasting social change and healing. At Maher, gender conflicts in Indian society are viewed not in terms of male versus female, but rather in terms of justice versus injustice. Maher addresses the needs of men in Indian society in numerous ways—first and foremost by providing clinical counseling and psychological support for rehabilitation to men whose wives take refuge at Maher, provided the men will accept this help, which many do. In its village outreach work, Maher's thirty self-help groups for men not only provide a vehicle for addressing economic issues, they also serve as key venues for educating men and helping them to shift their attitudes toward women, and toward each other. Maher's street theater performances and skits are also full of teachings aimed at men, presented in entertaining form to help them see the consequences of their masculine socialization and conditioning and cultivate new attitudes of respect for women. Future near-term plans at Maher call for establishing a home for mentally disturbed men which will provide services to men rescued from the street similar to those currently offered for women at Vatsalyadham.

Health and Education Outreach

In the villages surrounding Maher, competent medical help is often not available. As resources permit, Maher sends out doctors and nurses to these villages to provide free checkups and medical care. Maher children attend nearby primary and secondary schools, but many women of Maher have dropped out or been deprived of education. Maher has created a facility for National Open School and adult literacy classes to give these women and other young adults basic skills and training.

Ecological and Sustainable Technologies at Maher

Maher has integrated ecological technologies and sustainable design throughout its operations. Environmentally friendly technologies are employed to minimize pollution and the consumption of nonrenewable resources. Solar thermal collectors on the rooftops generate most of the hot water, and solar cookers are utilized when possible. Solar lights have been installed in several Maher homes to save costly electricity. No chemical fertilizers or pesticides are used within the premises of Maher. All agriculture and gardening is done with organic farming techniques. Wastewater is saved and used for the organic flower and vegetable gardens.

Maher produces its own biogas for cooking and other purposes. A Total Waste Management system has been implemented under the guidance of Dr. Mhapuskar, a specialist from a leading biotechnology research center in Pune which has developed technologies for producing biogas with a yield of 80 liters/kg of 70 percent methane content.[2] The waste after the production of biogas goes to an open tank and is used as fertilizer for fruit trees. Solid wastes are used as manure, and liquid wastes are carried by separate pipeline to irrigate the garden. Maher's biogas system saves the purchase of at least twenty-five cylinders of liquid petroleum gas each month. One of the Maher social workers is now guiding local villagers in building their own biogas plants.

Food and vegetable wastes are composted using vermiculture systems, which utilize worms to process organic waste into highly effective fertilizer for the fields and trees. The process requires little maintenance and produces no offensive odors. Maher minimizes use of plastics, replacing them with recycled forms of paper and cloth bags whenever possible.

Maher strives for a high degree of consciousness in relation to ecology and the natural environment. Children and women are taught about the fundamental interdependence of all forms of life and are

---

[2]   The biotechnology center in Pune is called Appa Patwardhan Safai wa Paryavaran Tantraniketan.

Maher boys playing cricket. Buildings shown in the background include the original Maher building (right), the new economic production facility (center), and Maher staff quarters (far left).

inspired to develop a deep respect and love for nature. Children are encouraged to take up gardening, and are allotted plots to help maintain and plants to care for. Beyond Maher's premises, there are tree plantation drives in the region that Maher participates in, as well as occasional watershed projects for areas where water shortage is acute. Street theater performances include skits about ecological issues, instructing local villagers how to conserve resources and minimize the use of nonrenewable resources.

STAFF AND STRUCTURE OF MAHER

Maher has a staff of about 120, including twenty social workers and some fifty-three housemothers who run the satellite homes. As mentioned, each satellite home has two housemothers who feed and care for about twenty children. Every housemother was once a battered woman who took refuge at Maher, and her personal healing is augmented by the responsibility of giving love and care to the children.

The battered and downtrodden women who arrive on Maher's doorstep every week are met by compassionate women caretakers who have themselves experienced abuse and violation firsthand, which drove them to take refuge at Maher. Thus the Maher staff and caregivers are especially effective and deeply compassionate, and "women healing women" is integral to the success of the project.

Finding the right professional staff is an ongoing necessity and challenge at Maher. Maher's social workers have all completed postgraduate degrees in social work. During their first month on the job, new recruits are permitted only to observe the functioning of the Maher organization. This extended observation period gives them a chance to perceive and experience for themselves the deeper principles operative at Maher, and to explore the particular role they would like to play in the organization. "Most importantly," Lucy explains, "I tell them, 'You can have advanced degrees, but to work in this place, the highest degree needed is the feeling of love and compassion. Can you look into the eyes of our women and children, and feel their pain? This alone will enable you to help them to the best of your ability.' We have been lucky to find good and committed individuals. Today I need only be consulted for crucial decisions—the staff manages everything else themselves. This way, the organization is able to help more and more people every day."

CRITERIA FOR SELECTING HOUSEMOTHERS

Maher's housemothers are carefully screened and trained for their work. They provide the children a loving, nurturing environment that is as close to a natural home environment as possible. In choosing housemothers, the Maher leadership looks for special qualities among the candidates, all of whom are residents who have taken refuge at Maher. While many women have a natural affinity for the task of mothering, not all are ideally suited for the task. Some of the women are too traumatized or psychologically depressed or damaged to be effective housemothers. Others are better suited to other kinds of work, and Maher's leadership always takes special care to place women where they will best flourish.

Key qualities that Maher leaders look for in prospective house-mothers are, first and foremost, a natural compassion and love for children, and secondly, a strong capacity to fulfill household skills and chores with good cheer and efficiency. The training of housemothers stresses careful attention to many details, as well as basic social work skills, to ensure that high quality care is given and the children are as happy as possible.

As examples of the level of detail involved, housemothers never ring a bell or use alarm clocks when waking the children in the morning. Instead, they put on some *bhajan* music (devotional songs or chants) and go to each child, gently touching a shoulder or arm to wake them up. So the child's day begins with music and a loving touch from the housemother. The housemothers also pay attention to what kinds of foods the different children like. If one child complains that he or she doesn't like a particular food, the housemother explains that on another day she will make the kind of food that child likes. In such ways, the housemothers are sensitive and responsive to the children, who in turn feel loved and cared for on a personal level.

ADMINISTRATIVE STRUCTURE

Maher is a registered charity in the state of Maharashtra and is governed by a board of ten trustees from diverse professional and religious backgrounds. The annual operating budget is around 11 million rupees (or 1.1 crore), which is equivalent to about 300,000 US dollars—a remarkably small sum for all that Maher achieves. Financial support came initially from funds raised in Europe and India, and since 2005 Maher has been raising funds in the United States. Funding in 2007 came from foreign sources (85 percent), local donors (10 percent) and government grants (5 percent), and Maher is working to significantly expand the share of income from Indian sources. Long-term goals for Maher include expanding the proven Maher concept to other areas in India. The potential—and the need—for such replication is enormous. Maher could also serve to inspire similar projects in other countries afflicted with similar conditions of extreme oppression of women, as discussed briefly in chapter 18.

This chapter has provided only a brief overview of Maher. There are a total of twenty-two specific projects, summarized in appendix A, that comprise its programmatic structure. The remaining chapters contain numerous stories and anecdotes that convey the spirit and energy of the Maher community.

CHAPTER 4

Light of Universal Spirit

All religions are glorious! Just as one can reach the roof of a house by means of a ladder, or a bamboo tree, or a staircase, or in various other ways, so diverse are the ways and means to approach God. Every religion offers a pathway to God.
— Ramakrishna

"Bravo!—this is truly God's work you're doing!" exclaimed the priest, bubbling over with enthusiasm. Exuberant after hearing Lucy's presentation on Maher, the impeccably dressed priest had come up to speak with her afterward. It was April 2005, and Lucy was on her first tour of the United States, where she made eighteen presentations on Maher in ten cities from coast to coast over a period of three weeks. Introducing himself, the priest seemed scarcely able to contain his enthusiasm about Maher and asked to meet with Lucy privately.

The two of them met the next afternoon. The priest explained how moved he was by the work of Maher, and proceeded to ask detailed questions about the project. Listening to Lucy's answers, he became increasingly convinced of the importance of Maher's work and began to underscore specific aspects of the project that he found especially inspiring. Toward the end of the meeting he informed Lucy that he was the executive administrator of a charity fund maintained by his church. He then announced, with a radiant smile in his eyes, that his organization would like to make a large financial donation to support the work and further development of Maher.

Lucy breathed a sigh of relief at this welcome news. Maher was at that moment in an especially challenging financial situation, for an ironic reason. Only months earlier, the devastating tsunami of December 2004 had occurred. In compassionate response, many of Maher's long-time donors had decided to substantially reduce their annual contribution to Maher in order to make a contribution to the victims of the tsunami instead. Maher, too, became directly involved in tsunami relief and set up a project in Kerala to support displaced families. These combined factors placed the Maher project itself in a position of significant financial deficit. The financial shortfall had in fact prompted the authors of this book to organize this fundraising trip to the United States—Lucy's first.

Hearing this man's heartfelt enthusiasm for Maher's work—backed up by his offer of major funding for the project—Lucy could feel her gratitude to God welling up. The priest explained that Maher's use of funds was precisely in accordance with the goals of his church's charitable fund, which was committed to relieving poverty in less fortunate societies. Not only was Maher courageously addressing the egregious symptoms of poverty in one of the poorest countries in the world, they were also tackling the entrenched social and cultural conditions that create that poverty in the first place. It was a perfect fit. He finished his congratulatory speech by adding that it would be important for the Maher children to receive Bible education as part of their ongoing schooling program.

A red flag sprang up in Lucy's mind. "I'm afraid we can't do that," she interjected respectfully. "You see, Maher is an interfaith project. This means that we honor all religions," she informed the priest, "and so we don't teach the Bible to the children—nor for that matter, do we teach the Bhagavad Gita, the Qur'an, the Dhammapada, or any other scripture." Lucy went on to explain that Maher upholds the spiritual teachings of all religions, and that although all scriptures are honored, none are taught to the exclusion of the others. "We honor all religions, and all scriptures," she continued, "but we do not and cannot promote any one religion over the others to our women and children. Each person must choose for themselves which particular faith is their heart's true calling. Indeed, Maher thrives by living in accordance with the universal divine Spirit that is at the very foundation of all the world's religions."

The priest was moved by Lucy's eloquent articulation of Maher's philosophy. "What you are doing is such important work," he exclaimed, "and, personally, I fully endorse the interfaith approach you are taking. I share your view that interfaith spirituality is fundamental to healing the conflicts and divisions among the world's major religions. And it's evident that Maher is making a contribution in India that is needed now more than ever, and it needs to be replicated elsewhere." He paused. "But still, you are a Christian . . . a Catholic nun. And these funds require that the children receive at least a modicum of Bible education. It doesn't have to be much, and you needn't teach the women, only the children. And you can still continue to honor all the other religions as you're now doing, and celebrate the feasts (religious holidays) of other religions."

Lucy's attention turned inward to her heart in renewed faith—something she had done so many times before—as she felt this glittering promise of major funding slipping rapidly away. "I appreciate your flexibility and sincerity," she said, "but I cannot do what you're asking." Her countenance softened as she felt an ineffable subtle support coming from within, despite the irony of simultaneously knowing that she was losing substantial financial support. "Please don't misunderstand me," she continued with quiet confidence. "I'm very grateful to you for making such a generous offer of support for Maher. It's clear that you understand the spirit of what we're doing in this project, and I'm very touched and encouraged by that. But we simply cannot accept funding that requires us to teach children the Bible, or any other particular scripture. It would contradict the entire interfaith foundation on which Maher is built."

The priest was visibly chagrined. Here was a project that was clearly doing some of the most important and innovative poverty relief work he had come across. Hearing the details of Maher—how it functioned and the impact it was having—he knew instinctively that every dollar given to Maher would be well spent—indeed more effectively than in several of the other more visible projects his charity organization was funding. Compounding the irony, he was convinced that the spiritual values the Maher children were learning were more aligned with the true essence of Christian faith than what was being taught in the Bible education programs that his charity was funding. He was all too familiar with Bible programs that stressed the words and stories of the scriptures but so often eclipsed their deeper meaning, or violated the spirit of the teachings in the dogmatic way they were taught. Indeed, he had himself blocked the funding of proposed programs to disseminate the Bible indiscriminately in impoverished regions of developing nations because it seemed a shallow and improper way to spread the true message of Jesus. Disturbing reports had come back of Bibles being hastily shoved into mailboxes or literally thrown into people's homes in poor regions throughout South Asia. The priest's conviction was that such haphazard missionary interventions were not only futile, but were positively harmful. The irony at this moment was that partly because he had blocked funding for these other projects, his organization had a substantial surplus of charitable funds, and he believed this money should go to Maher. But his hands were tied by church policy, which required the funds be donated only to projects that specifically included active Bible education.

"Maher was founded on deep faith in two things," Lucy continued, "God, and the inherent goodness of people. That goodness is a reflection of the Divine in each of us, and it doesn't matter which faith we belong to. Yes, I am a Catholic nun, and Jesus is my personal guru. However, rarely do I speak about this, because it is my personal relationship with God, and someone else has her personal relationship with Him. Each person must be free to worship whomever and however they choose. Maher's deputy director [Hirabegum Mulla] is a Muslim. The chair of our board is a prominent teacher of Vipassana meditation in the Buddhist tradition, and other board members are Hindu, Christian, Buddhist, and Muslim. We have many Hindus and Muslims among our staff and residents. The unifying thread is that we all honor the Divine. We pray or meditate in our different ways, but in Maher community gatherings, we never pray to any particular deity, but to 'God' only."

As he continued listening to Lucy, the priest became ever more convinced that Maher's work was somehow truer to the teachings of the gospels than many Christian projects his charity was funding. In a moment of frustration—convinced that Maher would make optimal use of these charitable funds for the relief of human suffering—he proposed briefly that Maher should just go ahead and accept the funding without changing anything whatsoever, and then simply state in their annual reports to the charity that Bible education was taking place. Lucy smiled politely and declined his offer, at which point the priest deftly changed the subject with an embarrassed smile.

The meeting ended at this impasse, with the priest trying to find a way to support Maher and Lucy steadfastly refusing to accept funding with any religious strings attached. It was another victory for Maher's integrity, but it did nothing to help relieve the dire financial situation.

This was not the first time Maher had been in this dilemma. Over the years, tempting monetary gifts from relief organizations of various denominations that came with strings attached to promote a particular agenda had been dangled repeatedly. Each time, Maher had graciously declined these offers. At one point, when Maher had been running for just two years, a financial crisis emerged and there was not enough money to feed the children. Maher leaders approached a prominent Catholic religious leader in the region who controlled very substantial purse strings, but he refused to help because Maher was an interfaith project. Years later, this same official came to visit Maher and was deeply impressed by what he saw and he has since become an ally of the project. Recently, he has even offered occasional modest financial contributions.

Maher has endured these challenges to its integrity, and they have actually served to strengthen the project's interfaith spiritual foundation and commitment. The spirit of trust in the ineffable divine Source is very strong at Maher, and this has never failed to provide what was needed. By giving and giving, and then giving still more, Maher has been given and given, and given still more.

UNIVERSAL SPIRITUALITY EMERGING FROM WORLD RELIGIONS

Love is a unifying principle in all the world's religions. Every swami, priest, or rabbi, lama, sheikh, or shaman espouses love as the true path for each human being. Yet today we see a world beset with more religious conflict than ever before, and the killing on all sides is carried out in the name of God. Religious conflicts tear the fabric of society and gravely imperil global stability and peace. Battle lines of religious difference harden over time to become dangerous fault lines in the harmonious functioning of human civilization, threatening to rupture at any moment with catastrophic consequences.

Perhaps now more than ever, the human heart is crying out for new bridges of love, healing, and reconciliation across differences— not only religious differences, but also racial, social, gender, caste, and class disparities. Enlightened religious and political leaders are calling for greater collaboration across faith traditions, as committed peace activists strive to build new economic and political bridges between warring peoples.

In answer to this call of the heart, the multiplicity of world religions is finally beginning to come together in a new way to acknowledge a universal spirituality and the fundamental unity of essential teachings. Despite the vast and rich differences, the major religions and spiritual traditions of the world can be viewed as different expressions of one living divine truth. In essence, this unitive breakthrough is not new. Saints and sages through the centuries have proclaimed the essential unity of all religions. The Rig Veda put it succinctly thousands of years ago: "Truth is one. Sages call it by many names." The Sufi saint Al Halaj proclaimed the unity of all religions early in the tenth century AD. Ramakrishna, the revered saint of India, proclaimed it again in the late 1800s. During this same time period a new religion that celebrates this essential unity (the Bahai faith) emerged in the Middle East.

In contemporary times, this trend toward universal spirituality is expressed in many different ways, such as the "perennial philosophy" articulated by Aldous Huxley, the Snowmass Conference convened by Father Thomas Keating, the Interspiritual Dialogue initiated by Wayne Teasdale, the integral spirituality of Ken Wilber, the Parliament of World Religions, and the United Religions Initiative. Many other forms of growing interfaith collaboration are emerging as well among spiritual and religious leaders across the globe.

These auspicious developments are taking place despite the continuing widespread conflicts around the world that are constelled along lines of religious difference. There have always been political and fanatical elements within each religion that abuse and manipulate religious teachings to justify persecution, hatred, and war. Yet, despite these destructive religious conflicts, which will likely continue in the near term, the larger overarching trend is in the opposite direction: a gradual but steady shift toward harmonization among the world religions and a growing mutual respect and appreciation of religious diversity. The scriptures of every major religion contain key teachings and injunctions that uphold the spiritual truth and dignity of other religions.[1] There are a number of foundational spiritual teachings that exist in every religion; for example, the "golden rule," a version of which can be found in every major religion.[2] In the end, the human spirit demands this mutual respect and harmony among diverse religions because the only path forward for humanity is for the entire human community to live as one family and one species in harmony with billions of others species on this planet.

---

[1] For examples of religious teachings that encourage respect for other religions, consider the following scriptural passages from various traditions:

Christianity

And Peter opened his mouth and said, "Truly I perceive that God shows no partiality, but in every nation anyone who fears Him and does what is right is acceptable to Him." (Acts 10:34-35).

Islam

Those who believe in the Qur'an, those who follow the Jewish scriptures, and the Sabeans and the Christians—any who believe in God and righteousness—on them shall be no fear, nor shall they grieve. (Qur'an 5.69)

Hinduism

As seekers approach Me, so I receive them. All paths, Arjuna, lead to Me. (Bhagavad Gita 4.11).

The wise person accepts the essence of different scriptures, and sees only the good in all religions. (Srimad Bhagavatam 11.3).

Confucianism

In the world there are many different roads but the destination is the same. There are a hundred deliberations but the result is one.—I Ching (Appended Remarks 2.5)

Sikhism

The Hindus and the Muslims have but one and the same God. (Adi Granth, Bhairo, p.1158)

Buddhism

The Buddha says, "To be attached to a certain view and to look down upon other views as inferior; this the wise call a fetter." (Sutta Nipata 798)

[2] The golden rule expressed in various traditions is widely available in print and on line. For versions in 21 world religions, see *www.religioustolerance.org/reciproc.htm*

An important example of this emerging unity of religious teachings is the work of the Snowmass Conference, a group of spiritual leaders from nine major world religions. Founded by the Cistercian monk Thomas Keating, this group has been meeting for more than twenty years, and is comprised of spiritual leaders from diverse religions, including Protestant, Catholic, Eastern Orthodox, Islamic, Jewish, Native American, Hindu, Theravadan Buddhist, and Tibetan Buddhist. The group created a list of points of common agreement which were recently published in a book called *The Common Heart*.[3] The first of these points affirms the existence of an Ultimate Reality to which different names are given in different traditions—God, Allah, Kali, the Tao, Christ, Krishna, Buddha, and many others. This Ultimate Reality cannot be limited by any name or concept, and it is the source of infinite potentiality and actualization of all human beings. Suffering, ignorance, weakness, and illusion are the result of our experiencing the human condition as separate from this Ultimate Reality. In addition to traditional practices of meditation and prayer, the Snowmass Conference affirms that "Ultimate Reality may be experienced not only through religious practices, but also through nature, art, human relationships, and service to others." The points of common agreement and principal practices are summarized in appendix B.

In the course of articulating universal truths common to their respective traditions, the members of the Snowmass Conference naturally developed close interpersonal bonds and friendships. While this was encouraging and perhaps inevitable, there was a more striking and remarkable attainment by this group. After reaching major points of agreement and articulating them clearly, the group members began to explore their differences in religious beliefs and practices. They embarked upon this task somewhat hesitatingly at first, aware

---

[3]   *The Common Heart: An Experience of Interreligious Dialogue*, Netanel Miles-Yepez (Ed), N.Y.: Lantern Books, 2006.

of major differences among their respective religions and not wishing to disturb the sense of unity and camaraderie they had already achieved. However, to their amazement and delight, what they discovered over time was that they bonded even more deeply over their differences than they had over their points of commonality. Not only did the richness and intricacies of religious differences turn out to be fruitful ground for deep exploration and mutual learning, they also energized the members and brought them even closer together as a group on a human level.

This experience of the Snowmass Conference demonstrates that religious differences, rather than being a source of strife and conflict, can become a source of deep bonding, mutual respect, and love. What the Snowmass Conference experienced in microcosm is now the task for humanity to discover in the macrocosm. Religions in conflict are like branches on the same tree fighting with each other, not recognizing that they are all connected to the same trunk. The branches have their very existence only through that one trunk, which represents the mystical truth at the core of every religion. As the branches struggle with each other, the trunk just stands there, silently supporting and nourishing each branch as it jostles around striving to win a trivial, unwinnable game. In the end, religious conflict will eventually die out, and the plurality of religions will be cherished as a profound resource and blessing to all of humanity.

The emerging spiritual unity of the world's religions does not mean that the different traditions will fuse or unite into a single world religion. This is not the goal, nor is it desirable. Rather, each religion will take its proper place alongside the others, in mutual respect and collaboration, to form a tapestry of traditions that together will uplift humanity in its spiritual evolution—perhaps to unprecedented levels. This process has already begun in earnest. According to Llewellyn Vaughan-Lee, a Sufi teacher in the Naqshbandi lineage that came to the West from the Kanpur region of North India, there is now a certain interconnecting work that can only be done by different spiritual traditions coming together in unique forms of cross-fertilization and mutual collaboration. This is the promise of interfaith or universal spirituality that is now beginning to take root across the globe.

NEED FOR INSPIRING INTERFAITH PROJECTS

In order to ground this inspiring trend of emerging universal spirituality in ways that are meaningful in the daily lives of ordinary people, there is a great need today for practical projects and innovative communities of people who are living these universal principles in practice. Real, on-the-ground examples of thriving interfaith communities and projects that bring people together from diverse backgrounds of religion, class, and caste to live together in harmony and loving service to their fellow human beings are powerful beacons of light for all of humanity. Such communities and projects serve as social incubators where human society is being renewed and transformed; where "the heart's longing meets the world's need" in practical ways that sow the seeds for a new civilization of love. Just as actions speak louder than words, these concrete examples speak volumes beyond religious declarations, academic treatises, or political resolutions calling for peace and reconciliation among people of different religions and faith. These are real communities with real people who actually live in the way of love and selfless service. Yet, such communities remain all too rare in today's world.

Maher is one such community. There is a palpable sense of an invisible grace or universal love "in the air" at Maher—readily felt by all who visit there—symbolized by the flame at the center of Maher's primary emblem. This emblem is prominently displayed at Maher's headquarters and at the main entrance to each of its satellite homes. The central flame represents the fire of universal spirit and love that burns at the core of all the worlds' religions, the love that radiates light and warmth to all, regardless of their religious or spiritual orientation.

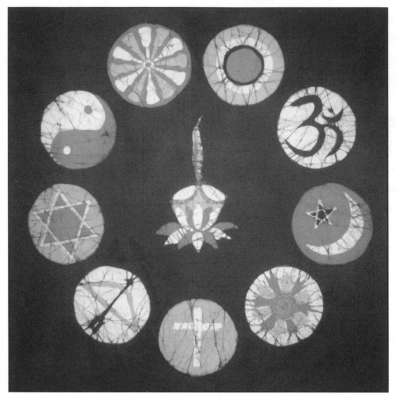

Maher's emblem—prominently displayed in all Maher homes and facilities—honoring the essential unity of all religions. Symbols from various religions surround the flame of universal light and truth that burns at the core of all faith traditions. Symbols shown are (clockwise from top left) taken from Buddhism, Sikhism, Hinduism, Islam, Parsi, Christianity, Indigenous tribal shamanism, Judaism, Taoism.

To a Western sensibility, a close-knit community of religious diversity such as Maher may not seem particularly remarkable. Western cities and communities are full of people from different religious backgrounds, as are Indian cities and communities. But there is a significant difference. In the West, separation of church and state have reigned supreme for a long time, and people often hold their religious values and activities quite separate from their daily public life. For many Westerners, religious activity entails a few hours a week on Sunday, or on the Sabbath for Jewish people. Otherwise, many Westerners are fully occupied pursuing busy lives that entail little if any conscious participation in spiritual or religious endeavor. Moreover, many in the West have no particular religious or active spiritual life at all.

The situation in India is very different. Every aspect of daily life is imbued with activities based on religious faith. People throughout India wake up to religious songs or music, which begins playing on loudspeakers in many villages around 4 AM. Some people chant mantras throughout the day (often silently), others visit the temple frequently throughout the week to make offerings, and still others worship or meditate in ways reflective of their particular faith. Although such extensive involvement with religious activity is changing in India as Western values come more into the culture, it is still very prevalent. Most Indians are generally very aware of themselves and others as belonging to particular religions, and many social and cultural activities in India are segregated by religious difference, or even the awareness of such difference. Children grow up knowing which religions their classmates belong to and often avoid playing or eating with children of other religions.

"We believe in the 'we' spirit!" Lucy beams as she describes the interfaith practice at Maher with her characteristic simplicity and eloquence. "Our residents come from different parts of India, so we do not follow a specific religion. We offer prayers to the Almighty, and we practice meditation twice a day. We read different scriptures—Sufi stories, the Bible, the Qur'an, and the Bhagavad Gita. We also follow the fundamental culture of our land: welcoming guests with *aarti* and touching the feet of elders to pay our respect to them."[4] Regardless

---

[4]   *Aarti* is a simple blessing ritual that entails circulating a ceremonial "Aarti plate" (adorned with a burning ghee candle and flowers) around a person or deity—generally accompanied by the singing of songs in praise of that person or deva. Many versions of aarti exist, but in general the aarti plate itself is supposed to acquire the power of the deity, and the purificatory blessing that was passed from the deva's image to the flame is in turn passed on to the devotee.

of the faith traditions from which staff and residents come, there is a shared commitment at Maher to healing the deep rifts that religious intolerance has forged in Indian society. This is no mere empty rhetoric but is exemplified beautifully by the way Maher staff and residents live in conscious alignment with the oneness of the human family.

RELIGIOUS COMMUNALISM

The term "communalism" denotes the phenomenon of religious intolerance and the attempt to promote religious stereotypes among groups of people belonging to different faith communities. In extreme forms, communalism entails violence promoted by various fundamentalist groups associated with different religions. Hindu-Muslim violence breaks out periodically, perpetrated by terrorists of either religion, such as the attacks in Mumbai in November 2008 that killed over 160 and wounded 300.[5] A spate of anti-Christian violence erupted in Orissa in August, 2008 that claimed thirty lives and displaced 50,000 people who fled the violence.[6] The news media tend to cover eruptions of communal violence and terrorism thoroughly, so there is widespread awareness and information available about these tragic realities; thus there is no need to review them further here. The vast majority of Indians—regardless of their religious faith—abhor the violence of extremist groups and recognize that such violence directly violates the teachings of all religions. Only a very small percentage of the population participate in or endorse the extremist groups, regardless of which religion they belong to. Throughout virtually all of India, most Hindus, Muslims, Christians, Buddhists, Sikhs, Jains, and others live side by side in peace.

---

[5]   *wikipedia.org/wiki/26_November_2008_Mumbai_attacks*

[6]   D. Samuel, "Over 5,000 Christians Take Protest Against Orissa Violence to India's Capital," *Christian Today Reporter*, Sep. 1, 2008, *www.christianpost. com/article/20080901/over-5-000-christians-take-protest-against-orissa-violence-to-india-s-capital.htm*

That said, weaker forms of communalism are prevalent throughout India. Most people are acutely aware of which religious faith they belong to, and they are often cautious about mixing with people of other faiths. This creates widespread divisions and rifts in the social fabric of Indian society, constellated around religious faith. Mahatma Gandhi visualized a great role for women in eradicating the evil of communalism. His appeal to women was to refuse to cook and to starve themselves in protest so long as their men "do not wash their hands of these dirty communal squabbles."[7]

At Maher, communalism is strongly repudiated. All religions are honored and valued, and Maher is an oasis where the rifts of communalism are healed over time. As one Maher staff member recounts, for example:

> I myself have never seen an institution like Maher. The interfaith practice is very genuine here. Throughout my life, in family and in schools and the college where I studied, I used to join in with everybody else, shunning people of other religions. I was a Hindu girl, and so we would never visit a Muslim girl's or boy's house. We would whisper behind their backs, "Oh, she's a Muslim, or he's a Muslim! We should not go to him!"
>
> I've been at Maher for three years now, and I still don't know the surnames of most people here. I don't know whether they are Hindu or Muslim or Sikh or Christian. I don't know what religion they belong to, and I don't care. We are all together, we sit together, we eat together. Maher has changed my view completely. I never have felt or even thought about who is Hindu, who is Muslim here. Never.

---

[7] Usha Thakkar, "Breaking the Shackles: Gandhi's Views on Women," *www.gandhi-manibhavan.org/activities/essay_breakingshackles.htm*

But in school and college, yes. It was everywhere. I was that way myself. I always needed to know what religion people belonged to. I'm telling you the very fact, true things about me! In college, we used to have lunch, and when I saw a Muslim girl, I could not eat her food from her lunchbox. We all avoided her, and she would not eat from our lunchbox. Very rarely did you see friends who were Muslim and Hindu together. Now it's starting to change, but still it's there. But in Maher, I never felt this. It's a very important thing. When we go to our separate rooms to pray, then I'm sure there will be the differences, but we all respect that. All the religions are here.

INTERFAITH SPIRITUALITY AT MAHER

The Sufis have a saying that "the Beloved is with those whose hearts are broken for the sake of the Beloved." This aphorism captures the spirit of love and service at Maher. The staff have allowed their hearts to be broken open by the extensive suffering in Indian society; thus they have become effective instruments of healing for those around them whose lives are broken. In so doing, the staff are themselves blessed by the healing and blessings they confer upon others. This, in a nutshell, is how the interfaith philosophy at Maher is translated into real-world practice.

The commitment to the spiritual unity or oneness of the human family is lived every day at Maher. Reliance on "faith" is strong, understood as trust in a deeper universal wisdom or Being, whether called God, Allah, Brahman, or one of many other names. Regardless of the name or faith tradition, the essence of guidance and stewardship of Maher is through this higher universal grace and wisdom. Despite all manner of ups and downs, financial support and other resources needed to keep Maher afloat have consistently flowed in over the twelve years of its existence.

Interfaith spiritual practice at Maher takes many different forms, including the following:

- **Prayers in community gatherings** are conducted either in silence or are made to "God," but not to any one particular God or deity. In this way the entire community can meditate or pray together, with each person practicing his or her own particular faith or religion. Each morning and evening the community gathers for silent time before eating. These ceremonies last about fifteen minutes and typically begin with bhajans, followed by prayers for Maher's community of women and children, staff, board, and friends in India and around the world. These are followed by focused prayers for individuals who are in particular need and on places of particular suffering in the world. Next comes eight to ten minutes of silent meditation, and finally a closing bhajan.

- **Nondenominational silent meditation** and yoga are taught to the women and children over the age of eight. Maher staff are given repeated leave for ten-day silent meditation retreats, which give them a much-needed respite from the daily intensity and bustle of Maher and support them in cultivating their inner lives. Retreat time for meditation or prayer away from the busyness of the world is intrinsically understood in Indian society as essential—not only for inner reflection, but also for cultivating deeper faith and spiritual realization.

The meditative practice that is integral to Maher has also served the board of trustees in its process of stewarding the entire project. The business of the board quite naturally becomes challenging at times, particularly when Maher is facing a crisis or some difficult decision that needs to be made. Dr. Hamir Ganla, one of the board members who happens also to be a leading teacher of the Vipassana meditation tradition,

Three Maher children in morning meditation.

has often intervened in moments of tension or when a conflict arises. He embodies a deep serenity and calm neutrality that serves the board's process very well, and at times he calls on the board to move into silent meditation as a way to reconnect to the larger spirit and purpose of Maher. After many years of intensive meditation, Dr. Ganla's presence and demeanor bring a powerful blessing to every aspect of Maher, and his leadership and dedication have been exemplary over the years.

• **Major religious holidays and feasts of diverse religions are celebrated** at Maher, including Divali and Ganesh Chaturthi (Hindu), Christmas and Easter (Christian), Id and Ramadan (Muslim), and Budh Purnima (Buddhist). The teachings and rituals of different religions are thus honored for all to partake in as they choose. Many different kinds of marriage ceremonies for women residents have been celebrated at Maher: three Buddhist, six Christian, and eight Hindu weddings have been performed to date. In addition, special interfaith services are held at times of significant world events or tragedies, as in the days and weeks following the tsunami of December 2004.

- **Spiritual songs, called bhajans or kirtan,** are frequently sung at Maher, as is common throughout India. This makes for a lively, rich dimension of singing in daily Indian routine that is largely absent in Western societies. At Maher, staff or residents might break into song at any moment throughout the day—perhaps while driving, or before a meal—engaging those around in a rousing chant or bhajan. During community gatherings and events, bhajans or *kirtans* are carefully chosen to be inclusive so they can be enjoyed by all.

In summary, the interfaith commitment at Maher provides a triple benefit to the residents, staff, and children. First and foremost, each person is supported to practice his or her own particular religious faith. Second, all at Maher are privileged to learn about and witness the religious and spiritual practices of people belonging to other faiths. This provides a kind of built-in education in universal spirituality, with application to community living. This is especially valuable for children, who absorb by osmosis the principal teachings from different religions as they witness daily the practical feasibility of interfaith spiritual community. Maher children cannot help but grow up knowing instinctively that people of diverse religious faiths can live quite happily in peace and harmony together.

Finally, the entire community of Maher provides a strong, concrete proving ground for each resident to practice the tenets of their particular faith against the backdrop of universal spiritual truths common to all faiths. Maher can thus be seen as a microcosm for what ultimately must take place in the world if humanity is to survive this challenging period of global transformation. We must one day learn to live in unity as one human family—honoring and celebrating the vast diversity of faith, religion, language, and beliefs of myriad cultures and races across the globe.

Humanity is ultimately a single large family, and only by learning to live in this essential oneness can we evolve to our highest destiny.

CHAPTER 5

Women Rising from the Ashes

When freedom has been won, women will have an equal share and place with their brothers. Men and women are like two wheels of a big chariot, and unless our movements have been mutually adjusted, our carriage will never move.

—Badshah Khan, the "Frontier Gandhi"

"I was married off at a very young age by my parents in an arranged marriage. Not long afterwards, I realized that my husband's family was not good. They had already killed one sister-in-law." Sameera Sogewad's voice was steady and confident as she began recounting the story of how she came to Maher.

"I became frightened for my life," she continued, "so I left there and returned home. My parents accepted me, but they wanted me to go back to my husband's family. I refused, because they might kill me. So I stayed with my parents and found a job teaching in a high school."

Tears welled up in the corner of Sameera's eyes as she told her story. "My elder sister had committed suicide over the tension of her dowry. Even after her wedding, her husband's family kept demanding more dowry payments, and she couldn't pay. So they abused her and harassed her constantly, and she finally took her own life."

Today Sameera is in charge of the Maher home for teenage boys located in Bakori village, about 43 km from Maher's headquarters in Vadhu Budruk. In this chapter she recounts her story—a story that illustrates the plight of so many Indian women and the remarkable healing and empowerment available to such women at Maher.

Sameera continues her story in her own words:

> While I was teaching [sociology and economics], I met a young man and we fell in love. He was from a higher caste [Maratha] than me. I belong to the Kholi caste of fishermen. After a while I became pregnant, and I thought he would marry me. But he did not have the courage to tell his parents, and he never took me to his house. He came to my house one day, and I showed him I was pregnant. He pulled his feet under his chair, which signaled that he was withdrawing from me. Soon afterward, he disappeared and I heard that he had married someone else.
>
> I couldn't tell anyone I was pregnant. I had to hide it, which was a big problem. I used to tie a sari very tightly around my waist under my clothes, to hold in my growing belly. I ate very little. At night when I untied the sari, everything was very red and sore, and I could barely move. But I had to keep my commitment to the school. And I could never tell my parents. That was unthinkable. My two first cousins had both committed suicide because they became unwed mothers.

As she spoke, Sameera's eyes shown out through angular, delicate facial features, her jet-black hair adorning her attractive face. Her peaceful countenance belied the painful drama of her life. Her golden earrings bobbed up and down in a lively dance as she spoke in animated tones. Her sincerity was marked by spirited body movements, especially the unique side-to-side waggle of the head so characteristic of Indians, which can signify anything from "Yes" or "No" to "I don't know" or "That's life!" or "Well, what do you think?"

During my pregnancy, life was horrible! I was always so tired and needed to rest but I had to work full time. It was so hard not being able to tell my mother. On the weekends she made me clean the house and do chores, because she didn't know. When my belly started to grow more, I had to leave my parents' home. I had to leave the village and never return. So I went away to my aunt, who was very fond of me. She sent me on to a distant relative when I was seven-and-a-half-months pregnant. All my relatives wanted me to abort the child, but I had conceived the child out of love, and I wanted to keep the baby. When labor pains started, I was all alone in the hospital. After many hours in labor, one friend came to visit me. None of my family came; they refused to stand by a woman having a baby out of wedlock.

After the baby was born, I called my father, and he told me to give the baby up for adoption. My friend urged me to do the same. After six days in the hospital, my brother came and took me to my elder brother's house four hours away. Then my father came and forced me to give up the baby to adoption.

I was absolutely miserable without my baby. I took a job at another adoption agency. I tried to live with the situation, but could not. After a few weeks, I started working to get my baby back. It was very difficult, and I had to pay 1,000 rupees, but I finally did get my baby back. But then I knew that my family would disown me, or worse. So I was now a complete outcast from my family, with no place to go.

Sameera was in crisis. She had already lost her sister and two cousins to suicide, and now found herself in the very same circumstances that had pushed her sister and both her cousins to take their own lives.

SUICIDE AMONG WOMEN IN INDIA

Suicide is not uncommon among young unwed mothers in India. The girl's family typically ostracizes her ruthlessly, and the social stigma is severe. The young woman's options are extremely limited, and suicide can seem an attractive out. To address this tragic situation, Maher has launched a project specifically for unwed mothers. The program gives the expecting women a comfortable home in which to bring their babies to term, and supports them in making informed choices regarding their newborns.

Although suicide rates around the globe are about three times higher for men than for women, reliable statistics are beginning to emerge showing a reverse trend among women in India and other Asian countries. According to a study in *The Lancet* medical journal, in a region near Vellore in southern India, over a ten-year period ending in 2001, more than twice as many young women aged ten to nineteen committed suicide as men in the same age group.[1] The study found the average suicide rate for women in this age group was 148 per 100,000, compared with 58 suicides per 100,000 men. So these young Indian women are killing themselves at the appalling rate of twenty-two times the global average of 6.8 per 100,000 for women.

Dr. Lakshmi Vijayakumar, director of the Sneha Suicide Prevention Center in Chennai, offers her explanation: "It could be because of lack of education, conflicts surrounding the issue of arranged marriages, love failures, dowries and things like that." Once the women have children, they become emotionally and psychologically stronger and the suicide rate goes down, she said.

A major difference between suicide in India and suicide in the West is the method used. Women in Western countries often attempt

---

[1]   "Suicide Rising Among Women in India," Associated Press, 2006. Link: *http://www.msnbc.msn.com/id/4647696/from/RL.3/*

suicide by slashing their wrists or swallowing pills, both of which are treatable. In rural India, the methods used include hanging, poisoning with lethal insecticides that are banned in many other parts of the world, setting oneself on fire, and jumping into wells. These methods are far more deadly. Some of the pesticides widely kept in rural homes can kill a person within three hours. For women attempting suicide in the countryside, where there is poor transportation and sometimes no roads, it is often too late by the time they reach a hospital.

◇ ◇ ◇

Sameera continues her story:

> At the adoption agency where I worked, someone had told me about Maher. So I telephoned Maher, but they were full. But there was no place else for me to go, so I went with my baby to Maher anyway. I arrived there late in the evening, and they took me in for one night only. The next day Lucy and Hira interviewed me, and they said they would try to help me. First they sent me for Vipassana meditation for ten days, with my baby. After that, Lucy gave me a chance to be a house-mother in one of Maher's children's homes.

Sameera excelled in her job of caring for Maher children. She exhibited exceptional parenting and organizational skills, and before long, Lucy placed her in charge of one of the children's homes. Then in 2003, when Maher opened a new home for its growing teenage boys in Shirur village, Sameera was named as director. She has a special gift for dealing effectively with the powerful energy and intensity of growing teenage boys.

Reflecting on her years at Maher, Sameera observes:

What was missing in my life was provided by Maher. I learned so many things. I learned how to meditate, which brought peace and joy. I never enjoyed puja or yoga when I was growing up, but here it's different. I enjoy the yoga we do with the children very much. I also learned both English and Hindi. And I did trainings in human health and sexuality, *rangoli* [colored-powder mandalas], singing, art and drawing. As I grow older, I want to learn more and more. I want to learn to dance and play the tabla, and I hope to complete my MA in the arts.

I would also like to give lectures on the interfaith spiritual practice at Maher—how beautifully it works. If you worship a stone, that's not it. The real way is to see God in the human being. When there's a change in the human being, that is the real joy for me. For example, there was a man in the village who was drinking a lot, and I talked to him extensively. Now he isn't drinking and is doing much better. He calls me his daughter.

Even before coming to Maher, I used to think that all religions were true. But after coming to Maher, it is much deeper in me. I believe in all religions, and one God. There is no contradiction in that.

When I look back on my life, it feels almost like a film story. Through the incredible pain came great joy. I went through so much turmoil and pain. But it was all God's plan to bring me out of myself, to know what I am.

WHY DO INDIAN WOMEN TOLERATE SUCH EXTREME ABUSE?

Dr. Anuradha Karkare, president of the Maher board of trustees, is a clinical psychologist with thirty years of experience working with abused and traumatized Indian women. About her work with Maher

The housemothers of Maher (shown with Sister Lucy Kurien and associate director Hirabegum Mullah). These women originally took refuge at Maher from abusive situations, and they now serve as caregivers for the women and children of Maher.

she says, "I became involved with Maher because I saw so many women who were severely abused, and needed to leave their husbands, but would never do it. Maher finally gives these women a way out—not just a place to take refuge, but a pathway to make the changes that are needed in their lives. They never had this before."

Dr. Karkare explains why it's so hard for Indian women to leave their families. "A woman's husband is her very identity, and her security. It is such a totally male-dominated society that she feels like no one without a husband. Most women do not make decisions for themselves; they are not raised to think this way. They believe that they belong to their husbands; she is his property, and if he wants to beat her, he has a right to. And even if a woman does leave her husband, it's very hard for her. Single Indian women are not treated well in society, they have no protection, they are constantly harassed and regarded as women of easy virtue. So her wedding necklace is her protection."

According to Dr. Karkare, in her clinical practice in rational emotive therapy, developed by Albert Ellis, there is a five-fold measure for self-esteem, and Indian women typically come out extremely low on all five criteria. "They are not raised to have an independent existence from their husbands, so no matter how much of a scoundrel he might be, the woman stays with her husband."

Even coming to Maher is no guarantee that the woman will be transformed. Dr. Karkare tells one sad story:

> A woman came to Maher with severe bruises and cuts all over her body, enraged at her husband for his constant beatings. But then he came to visit her, apologized to her, asked her to come back home, and she went, against our advice. In one month she was back—same thing but worse—badly beaten up. This time she was determined to leave him. But again he apologized, and again, after fifteen days, she went back to him, against our strong recommendation. Then about four months later she came back, very badly beaten up. Meanwhile, her husband had become HIV positive, and had given it to her. Then suddenly he committed suicide, because he didn't want to live with AIDS. So now she is HIV positive and rapidly deteriorating. She was not HIV positive when she first came to us. It's very sad.

OTHER CHALLENGES FACED BY INDIAN WOMEN

We pause to briefly consider a few additional challenges that afflict women in India. Globalization and the market-driven economy over the past twenty years have had an enormous impact on Indian women and society. Numerous positive social changes are certainly taking place, but a recent comprehensive review edited by Rehana Ghadially of the Indian Institute of Technology in Mumbai reveals that conditions for Indian women today remain remarkably bleak.[2] The review debunks the notion that urban women are necessarily better off than rural women, although this holds in some respects. Ghadially observes that in the past twenty years, since an earlier edition of the review was published, violence against women continues not only in the same forms (dowry harassment, domestic violence, rape, "eve-teasing" [sexual harassment], declining sex ratios, female feticide), but new forms have emerged in recent years, such as "acid throwing, honor killings, workplace sexual harassment, stalking, and national and transnational trafficking in women, to name a few." Also on the rise are indecent and crass portrayals of women in the news media, on the Internet, and in films and magazines.

Three specific phenomena are reviewed here briefly to illuminate some of the diverse challenges facing women in India: female infanticide, unjust incarceration in mental asylums, and sati.

- **Female Infanticide.** The intentional killing of infant girls is a common practice in India, crossing all castes, from the poorest of the poor to the most wealthy. In a country where female deities are highly revered and worshiped, girl children are often considered a major liability, owing largely to the dowry system, which can place huge economic burdens on a girl's family. Various brutal methods, such as poisoning, suffocation, and utter neglect, are used in female infanticide. Sex-selective abortion is prevalent in India as a means of precluding girls from being born.[3] An infamous billboard blazoned across

---

[2] Rehana Ghadially (Ed.), *Urban Women in Contemporary India: A Reader*, Sage Publications, 2007.

[3] Rachel Arora, "Female Infanticide: The disgrace of and independent India," Merinews, Aug 22, 2007, *http://www.merinews.com/catFull. jsp?articleID=126050*

India read: "Pay 500 Rupees now, or 500,000 Rupees later!" The billboard was an advertisement to sell sex-determination tests (using amniocentesis and ultrasound) to pregnant women wanting to avoid bearing girls. According to an article from Canada's International Development Research Centre, a staggering ten million female fetuses have been intentionally aborted in India since 1985.[4]

The 2001 census showed a rapidly decreasing population of females in India, with 927 girls to 1,000 boys aged 0-6 for the nation overall. Sex ratios vary considerably by region, with only 883 girls to 1,000 boys in Gujarat, 868 girls to 1,000 boys in Delhi, and—the most extreme ratio—only 798 girls to 1,000 boys in Punjab.[5] Female infanticide is a particular form of violence that is deeply entrenched in the social fabric of Indian culture. One consequence is that in many areas there are fewer young women available for marriage, which is creating yet another series of challenges. The infant murders are carried out by both women and men, frequently by midwives or the parents. The Indian government has strict laws against female infanticide, but as with many socially sanctioned atrocities, enforcement has been weak or ignored altogether. However, with the devastating report from the 2001 census, certain programs, such as "cradle shelters," are being implemented to help keep newborn girls alive.[6]

---

[4]   Stephen Dale, "India's Missing Daughters," The International Development Research Centre: Science for Humanity, 2006, *http://www.idrc.ca/en/ev-95719-201-1-DO_TOPIC.html*

[5]   unicef, Child Sex Ratio–India, *http://www.unicef.org/india/CHILD-SEX-RATIOin.pdf*

[6]   Rachel Arora, "Female Infanticide: The disgrace of and independent India," Merinews, Aug 22, 2007, *http://www.merinews.com/catFull.jsp?articleID=126050*

- **Sane Women Incarcerated in Mental Asylums.** There are numerous cases of sane women who have been maliciously declared insane and incarcerated in mental asylums. In 2004 a senior government psychiatrist in the mental hospital at Agra was exposed for falsely certifying sane women as insane. An investigation by the National Commission for Women uncovered the racket that had been going on since at least 1998. The psychiatrist had issued many false certificates of insanity over these years—for a fee between 5,000 and 10,000 rupees—to enable husbands to dispense with their wives, marry other women of their choice, or provide false defense in the case of persons accused of murdering their wives.[7]

  An earlier famous case, during the late 1990s, entailed a perfectly sane young woman from Delhi named Anamika Chawla whose husband and parents obtained a magistrate court order to have her committed to a mental asylum on the basis of verbatim medical certificates issued by two psychiatrists, neither of whom had ever examined her. The case was appealed to the Supreme Court of India, which uncovered the scam and quashed the magistrate court order. Ms. Chawla narrowly escaped incarceration, but most women in similar circumstances are not so lucky. According to one report by medical analysts, "In the many hospitals that have been visited by mental health advocates around the country, there is not a single women's ward where you do not have at least more than a dozen of such like stories, different kinds of scenarios, of what nearly happened to Anamika Chawla."[8] Tragically, once

---

[7] "Investigation into fake medical certificates issued by the Agra Mental Health Institute and Hospital," *www.tehelka.com/story_main4.asp?filename =Ne071004NCW_TEAM.asp&id=3*

[8] *Women and Mental Health: Planning gender sensitive community interventions*, A workshop report, 17-18th September, 1999, YMCA, Pune, *www.camhindia.org/wamh_report.html*

a woman is incarcerated in a mental asylum, even unjustly, "the chances of her being able to access the justice system are next to zero."[9]

- **Sati.** On September 4, 1987, the village of Deorala in Rajasthan was plunged into a furor that focused world attention on the status and treatment of women in modern India. Before a crowd of several thousand people, mostly men, a young woman dressed in her bridal finery was burned alive on her husband's funeral pyre. This ancient practice of *sati*—widows being burned on the funeral pyres of their deceased husbands—was outlawed by the British administration in 1829. Yet the grisly fate of eighteen-year-old Roop Kanwar dramatically proved that the tradition is not dead. About 300,000 people made a pilgrimage to Deorala a few days after Roop Kanwar's death to honor her, and several of her family members and her husband's family members were arrested. About forty cases of sati, mostly in rural areas, have been documented in India since its independence in 1947, but in earlier times the practice was far more prevalent. There were 8,135 documented cases in the fifteen years prior to the British prohibition of the practice. While *sati* has been widely publicized as a telltale symptom of India's patriarchal injustice—and rightly so—the practice is much less common today than many other forms of abuse and violence against women.

ABUSED, ABANDONED, AND THEN BLESSED

Urmila Sawant was fifteen years old when she took her first job in the office of a wealthy political man, whom we shall call Sunil. Urmila was thrilled to be entering the business world for the first time, and to be earning money on her own. She had grown up in a small village with

---

[9] Ibid.

A new arrival at Maher.

her parents and brother—a typical village family that was poor but provided all her needs and a happy childhood. Urmila's boss Sunil was a seasoned politician who wielded considerable political power in the region. Urmila's radiant eyes and youthful attractive figure captivated Sunil's attention, and he soon began to charm and flatter her in the office. Given her sheltered background and naive innocence, Urmila was easily wooed by her boss's affections. Before long, Sunil proclaimed his love for her, and their liaison was "legitimized" in a "marriage" ceremony that consisted of a simple exchange of garlands. Such unofficial "weddings" are not uncommon in India, especially when the circumstances are not entirely legitimate. In this case, Sunil was fully aware that his parents were in the process of seeking a suitable bride for him, and Urmila was not even a remote candidate for that role.

Newlywed bliss was short lived. Urmila soon became pregnant, and Sunil wanted her to abort the baby. She was shocked, having conceived the baby out of love with her husband. When Urmila refused to have an abortion, Sunil began to abuse her severely. He was drinking heavily, and soon became involved with another woman. As Urmila recounts: "My husband became a drunkard, and he started to beat me every day. I had one child, but lost it. He was having an affair with another woman, and he continued to drink and beat me. Then I became pregnant again. Again he wanted me to abort the baby, but I didn't want to."

Meanwhile, Sunil's mother found a suitable bride for him, and he was duly married off to her in a full Indian wedding ceremony. Urmila was left to fend for herself—pregnant and abandoned. "I was living separately, but later, when I became nine-months pregnant, my husband brought me into his house with his other wife. I delivered a baby girl. My husband continued to beat me, and he cared more for his other wife. His mother was also very mean to me, and she supported his other wife more than me. The situation was extremely painful and became intolerable. So one morning I got up early and ran away from there with my baby daughter. She was five months old at that time."

As she spoke, Urmila exuded that special quality of dignity and poise that characterizes so many Indian women—an almost numinous essence that palpably suffuses their mannerisms and gestures. This ineffable grace and strength radiates outward in seeming stark contradiction to the social norms of oppression and inequity to which Indian women are constantly subjected.

"I had nowhere to go," she continued, "so I went back to my parents' house. But they would not accept me, and told me to go back to my husband. I explained to my mother that he was with another woman and that he beat me, but she still said I had to go back. I couldn't do that. My parents wouldn't take me, so I had to leave."

Urmila was an extreme embarrassment to her parents. In their village, an unmarried daughter with a baby was a total disgrace, and Urmila's parents were determined to protect their family's honor and standing in the community. So they shunned Urmila, fully realizing that she had nowhere to go and that they would never see her again. To Urmila's parents, she was as good as dead, quite literally. Immediately after sending her away, they issued an announcement to their village that Urmila had died. They performed the traditional *dhava*, a ten-day mourning ceremony for the loss of a loved one. During this period of mourning the custom is that the family remains inside their home and prepares food for others in the community. When her parents emerged from their home ten days later, Urmila was dead and gone in this village—banished from her family and hometown forever. "I didn't know what to do or where to go. So I went to the railway station. I got on a train—any train. I had no idea where it was going."

After many hours, the train arrived in Pune. "I didn't know where I was, and I had never heard of Pune. When we got there, the conductor asked for my ticket. I didn't have one. He said I had to pay 250 rupees, but I didn't have any money. Other people standing around heard the dispute and came over and talked with him. They told the conductor I must be in a very difficult situation with my young baby and asked him to let me go. After a while, he finally let me go."

Urmila wandered out into the streets of Pune, utterly disoriented and lost. With a six-month-old infant in her arms, she had no time to waste in finding a means to feed her daughter. At this critical juncture in her young life, her entire future was about to be decided.

◊ ◊ ◊

Like Urmila, many a young Indian woman is thrust into precisely such a cruel predicament, often at a very tender age. If she falls victim to any one of many repressive social sanctions against women in this society,

75

her entire future suddenly becomes greatly imperiled. This can happen in myriad ways. Perhaps she becomes pregnant out of wedlock, or falls in love with someone of the wrong caste, or gets raped by a family member and is thrown out of her home to save the family honor, or she is forced to flee for her life from her husband's beatings or her mother-in-law's death threats, only to be turned away at her own parents' door.

Whatever the cause, she finds herself utterly abandoned by family and society—left to fend for herself in a veritable mine field of multiple dangers and sparse opportunities. The future course of her life is often decided by what happens in these next few critical days or weeks, almost as if by sheer fate. Anything could happen to her at this point. She cannot go back to her family or friends, or to her husband's family if she is married. And she is totally unprepared to make her own way in Indian society. She is often uneducated, and even if she has a vocation, there is a very strong stigma against an unmarried woman in Indian society, especially if she has children. If she is lucky, she might find a job, or perhaps a benefactor family who is willing to take her into their home as a live-in maid.

But the dangerous possibilities are myriad. She could be raped or kidnapped, or be seduced into prostitution. Pimps are on a sharp lookout for just such cases. They ply the major railway stations on a daily basis looking for young arrivals just like Urmila, who are often put on trains with one-way tickets after being exiled from their homes or villages for whatever reason. Arriving in a major city, often for the first time, the young girls are extremely vulnerable. The pimps greet them with kindness, offering food and shelter and a chance to earn money, and the disastrous consequences are easy to imagine.

Visitors to India often wonder, as they gaze in shock at the disheveled and destitute women living in the streets with one or two children in tow, how did it come to this? Many of these women were raised in reasonably comfortable homes, with enough to eat and a stable childhood. Yet something happened in their lives that in other societies would not be a life-altering crisis. But in Indian society, it is precisely at these junctures, like the moment Urmila is in at this point in her story, that the young woman's life journey often begins a downward spiral. Abandoned by everyone and everything she knew, and left to the mercy of the streets of India, it is easy to see how a vulnerable, uneducated woman ends up as a destitute beggar living in the streets.

◊ ◊ ◊

Urmila continued,

> I walked around in Pune and found an ashram to sleep in, but it was only for men. They gave me the name of another ashram for women and I went there. By the time I got there it was late in the evening, so the ashram wouldn't let me in. But I pleaded with them, and they let me stay the night. I stayed there and they wanted to write a letter to my husband to come take me back, but I said no. After some time they gave me some work in the ashram, but they didn't pay me anything. I had no money at all, so I couldn't buy any clothes or anything for my child. So after staying and working there one-and-a-half years, I asked the ashram to help me find work. They said no, and then demanded to know the real story about me, and where my husband was.
>
> Then they contacted my husband, and he came to visit. They could see that he was not a good man, but they had a rule that they must send a wife back to her husband. I protested, but they wrote a letter for him to sign saying that he would take care of me and our child, and that he would not drink or beat me. He signed that letter, and they sent me off with him.

We rented a room in Pune. After eight days, he started to drink again, and then he started beating me again every day. So I ran away again and went back to the ashram, and they took me back. Then, after fifteen days, he came there and demanded to take me with him again. This time they told him I had gone somewhere and was not there, and they hid me. He gave them much trouble, but then he left. After that they gave me some work at the ashram, and paid me 900 rupees per month. But after a while that work ended, and they could only give me another work that paid 700 rupees per month.

I stayed there for three years, and then a friend gave me the address of Maher. I came and interviewed with Sister Lucy. She admitted me to Maher on June 1, 2001. When I came to Maher, I felt I had come to my own home. I felt happy here. Didi gave me the work of caring for the pregnant girls, taking them to hospital, and so forth. I liked that work very much, and I got paid for that.

When Urmila arrived at Maher she was deeply disturbed. Psychologically traumatized and despondent, she cried often, and had a difficult time adjusting emotionally. Having been shunted from one place to the next several times, never feeling truly welcome anywhere she had been, it was difficult for her to believe that those around her truly cared or had her best interests at heart. Sometimes she behaved in an abusive manner toward others, including her own daughter. Maher staff separated mother and daughter for a few months, as Urmila slowly got back on her feet psychologically and emotionally. It took more than a year before Urmila's smile began to reappear, and another year for her behavior to transform. Urmila worked in several departments at Maher learning different crafts, and over time she began to heal on a deep level. Her confidence and joyful countenance began to reappear, and her intrinsic smile, sociability, and affable nature surfaced once again.

Today Urmila is a whole new person from the one who came to Maher in 2001. As she reflects upon herself:

> I felt my life turned in a whole new way. I have learned many things at Maher. I learned rangoli [a beautiful form of artistic handicraft using colored powder], and how to make candles and cards. I am now working in the production line making greeting cards.
>
> I am happy to learn difficult things. My dream is to build a beautiful house for my daughter and me. I don't wish to get married again. I would like to give my daughter a good education, and to live with her in our house. At Maher, I found my own intelligence and strength, and came out of myself. I found much love here. I am a new Urmila.
>
> When I had been at Maher for two years, my brother died and I went home to the funeral. There I found out that my husband had met with an accident and died. My daughter sometimes asks why we don't have our own house, and I feel sad. I've told her that her father died in an accident, but I don't tell her that he went off with another woman and beat me, and that I had nowhere to go.

◊ ◊ ◊

Story after story like this one are witnessed at Maher. Each time, the journey that brings the woman to Maher's doorstep is yet another stark testimony to the extreme social conditions endured by women in Indian society. And, each time, Maher does its best to support the woman through her healing process, helping her to take full responsibility for her life and its unique circumstances and to discover her true path forward, taking full account of her particular gifts and capabilities. In this manner, day in and day out they come—one woman after another—arriving at Maher in utter despair, and eventually leaving with a smile on their faces and a new dream in their hearts.

CHAPTER 6

Beyond the Good Samaritan

What the outstanding person does, others will try to do. The standards
such people create will be followed by the whole world.
                                            —Bhagavad Gita (3:21)

It had been a long time since Anulekha had even noticed the maggots
living in her hair. Eking out a barebones survival for more than six
years on Nagar Road outside Pune, the bugs and lice burrowed into
her scalp were the least of her concerns. On this particular morning,
as on so many others, Anulekha was squatting on the side of the road,
picking through garbage that had been dumped by a passing truck,
hoping to find a bite to eat. Amidst the dust, fumes, and traffic noise,
she paid no notice to the jeep that rolled slowly to a stop on the other
side of the road about a hundred yards away. Two women got out and
slowly began walking toward her. Anulekha was used to pedestrians
stepping around or over her, so she paid no attention to these women,
even as they came right up to her. It wasn't until one of them began
speaking to her that she even took notice.

"Hello, what is your name? What are you doing here?" the women
asked. "My name is Lucy, and I noticed you've been in this same spot
on the road the past few days. I wonder if you have a place to stay. Do
you need help? Are you OK?"

Anulekha became suddenly alarmed as she realized these questions were being directed at her. She had no idea who this person was,
and no interest in talking to her. It was unusual for anyone to try to

talk to her. Most people walked right past her and ignored her completely. And if they did pay attention to her, it usually meant trouble. "I'm fine," she replied tersely, keeping her head down.

"We're here to help. We have a place where you can come for some good food, and a warm bed," Lucy said.

"I'm fine. Leave me alone," Anulekha retorted coldly.

"Where is your home?" Lucy persisted. "Why are you here picking through this garbage every day? We have a place for you with plenty of good food and a place to sleep."

"I told you, leave me alone!!" Anulekha stammered threateningly as she stood up and began to back away.

"Come with us. Let us at least show you our place, so you can see if you like it," Lucy persisted. She took a step toward Anulekha, who reacted by swiftly moving further away. Lucy and Hira followed her. As they did so, two more women jumped out of the Maher jeep and crossed the road.

Anulekha broke into a full run, and Lucy and Hira chased her. Anulekha heard Lucy shouting to the other two women across the road, and suddenly they too began running toward her. In total fright, Anulekha veered away from the road to avoid these new pursuers, but she stumbled for a moment, which gave Lucy a chance to catch up with her.

Lucy caught Anulekha's arm, but she wrenched it free, then slammed her fist into Lucy's chest. "Get away from me!" she shouted venomously. Lucy wheeled around and grabbed Anulekha's shoulder. She came back at Lucy swinging both fists wildly.

At this moment Hira and the other two Maher staff members caught up with them. Anulekha was yelling and swinging at Lucy, but Hira grabbed one of Anulekha's flailing arms, which gave Lucy a moment to move in quickly and throw her arms around Anulekha in a big bear hug. "I love you!" Lucy exclaimed, "and I just want to give you a good meal." The foul stench emanating from Anulekha was so strong and putrid that Lucy almost threw up on the spot. But she held her breath and maintained the bear hug.

Anulekha started to dig her fingernails into Lucy's arm. Two of the Maher women quickly grabbed each of Anulekha's hands and held them tightly away from Lucy's body. "It's OK, we're not going to hurt you," Lucy assured her. "We just want you to come with us for a good meal and some rest."

By this point, John, who was driving the jeep, had driven right up to where the women were struggling. Anulekha was still squirming but began to realize she was overpowered as the four women moved her quickly into the jeep. They closed the door, and took off. "It's OK, we're not going to hurt you. You'll be fine," Lucy kept repeating in Marathi. "We're just going to give you some warm food and a bed to sleep in. Come and see."

The stench radiating from Anulekha filled the jeep. Even with the windows open, the reek was so overpowering that it was all Lucy and Hira and the other Maher staff could do to keep from gagging or vomiting. Anulekha began to calm down, wondering if she could perhaps believe Lucy. Nothing like this had ever happened to her before. Lucy continued to console her, and asked Hira to get on the cell phone and cancel her meetings for that morning. They drove straight to Vatsalyadham, Maher's center for destitute street women in Pune, a twenty-minute drive away.

When the jeep arrived at Vatsalyadham, the staff were prepared, having been alerted by Hira that a new admission was coming. Sally and Hira immediately took Anulekha to a quiet spot outside near the garden, and Carmen brought a warm meal of dal, rice, and vegetable curry, with fresh chapattis hot out of the skillet. Anulekha began to eat. Nothing had tasted so good to her in years. This was literally the best meal she could ever remember having, and it was served on a plate. She ate slowly, her system not accustomed to taking in much food at one time.

After lunch, Anulekha became less tense, and she felt a bit more trusting of her newfound situation. The next essential task for the Maher staff was to clean her up. Like most of the street women when they arrive at Vatsalyadham, Anulekha had not had a bath for several years—literally. She reeked so badly that she could not be allowed indoors; the stench was too foul for the other women to bear. Lucy and Sally began the cleaning process. Lucy started with her hair, trying to unravel it. Within minutes she realized the effort was futile—Anulekha's hair was a thick unyielding jungle teeming with maggots, lice, and other bugs of various kinds. It was all Lucy could do to keep from vomiting as she took a pair of scissors and began to cut back the thicket on Anulekha's head. She turned aside to draw each in-breath, carefully timing her breathing process so as to keep the nausea at bay. She knew she dare not throw up, for that would send precisely the wrong signal to her coworkers, who had to follow suit and join in the task.

The maggots had somehow managed to dig small pits into Anulekha's scalp and were burrowed in. The staff treated it with camphor and the maggots came pouring out, some even crawling out of Anulekha's ears. The sight was appalling, matched only by the extreme stench. Sally continued the exacting work, in the face of increasing resistance from Anulekha. Finally, Anulekha's hair was cut back, and most of the maggots and lice had been removed or cut away.

The next step was a bath, and Anulekha flatly refused, so Sally and three other women on the staff used a garden hose to wash her down while restraining her and rubbing her skin with soap. Sally repeatedly assured Anulekha that they were not going to hurt her, which by this point she had begun to believe. Nevertheless, it was a difficult process for her; the only water she had experienced on her body in recent years was rain or gutter splash. The Maher staff completed their wash with a thorough rinse, then applied medicinal ointment to numerous lice-infested areas on her body. They gave Anulekha a simple, clean punjabi suit to wear. She looked a thousand times better, even as she remained totally bewildered by this unbidden turn of events.

A couple of hours later, Lucy and Hira sat down with Anulekha and began asking her questions. She was able to give her name, but not much more information. She could not remember how she came to be living on the street, nor how long she had been there, nor where she had come from. It was not that she was unwilling to share this information but that she literally could not recall her own past. She did mention that sometime in the distant past she had had a husband and three children, but she had no idea of their whereabouts. She could not recall where they had lived, nor how long she had been married, nor how old the children were.

A woman rescued from the streets arriving at Maher.

Today Anulekha remains at Vatsalyadham, where she is doing relatively well. Like many street women in India, she is mentally disturbed and significantly incapacitated—a condition that often results from the exceedingly harsh conditions these women suffered. To this day, Anulekha has not been able to give a coherent account of her story or personal background. She has been at Vatsalyadham for a year and a half, and she is clean and well fed. She works in the garden and likes to dance. Perhaps most telling, Anulekha's eyes shine with a newfound joy. She greets friends and guests warmly and emanates a radiance that reflects her name, which means "the beautiful one."

Anulekha is also one of the lucky ones . . .

WOMEN ROTTING IN THE ROAD

Anyone who has ever visited India knows how the streets are teeming with people of all kinds—middle class, poor, rich—all closely intermingled. Unlike in the West, rich and poor live in close proximity to one another. A posh housing development is often located adjacent to a slum or settlement of itinerant squatters. The reason is simple: the poor serve the rich in India, so they must live nearby. The narrow roads are frequently choked with vehicles of every size and shape, relentlessly honking their horns as pedestrians, often in great numbers, stride deftly alongside and through the traffic. Auto rickshaws weave in and out like bumper cars, with cows, goats, and the occasional elephant or camel wandering about. Belching trucks and rattling buses top off the turmoil as they come barreling through the chaos at breakneck speed—their horns blaring at ear-splitting pitch to clear a pathway.

Amidst the bustle, dust and fumes, one often sees destitute individuals who appear to be sick, disoriented, desperate, mentally or physically debilitated, or otherwise deeply afflicted. Some walk around in a seeming daze, others just sit and stare, and still others lie on the ground—either sleeping, or too weak to stand up. Some are beggars, others have been economically or socially exiled from society for whatever reason. Like Anulekha, they are generally extremely dirty and grungy, not having bathed for months or years. Most pedestrians walk right past these people on the street, paying no attention whatsoever to them or their plight. A small proportion of street people are sannyasins or sadhus who have renounced the world in a spiritual quest. Beggars and sadhus can be hard to tell apart by the untrained eye, particularly since the latter also beg for their food.

Many of these displaced people are women, often accompanied by a child or two, each with her unique story that has brought her to the brink. How do these women end up on the streets? Often through a cruel twist of fate: perhaps they were cast out by their husbands or in-laws, or forced to flee from their homes to escape life-threatening abuse. Their stories are legion. As we have already seen, some women have been discarded by their in-laws for not paying sufficient dowry, or raped and exiled in disgrace. Some have been hideously disfigured—often missing their lips or an ear—by acid having been thrown in their faces, and banished to the streets as freakish outcasts. Others have been widowed and have no place to go; they are neither welcomed back to their families of origin, nor are they allowed to remarry. Many women in this situation commit suicide. Others turn to prostitution. Still others eke out their existence on the streets, where they are susceptible to being robbed, brutalized, raped, or worse—and often become mentally imbalanced or disturbed as a result. The plight of street people in India is more grim than in the United States or other affluent Western countries, where the homeless—tragic as their plight is—typically have access to homeless shelters or soup kitchens. In India, the homeless must fend for themselves.

VATSALYADHAM—ABODE OF LOVE
In 2004, Maher launched a new project to provide service and shelter for these severely traumatized street women who are too disturbed

to mix with the normal Maher community. The project is called Vatsalyadham, which means "abode of love." Because the demand is potentially huge, Maher narrowed its focus by "adopting" the stretch of road between its principal facility in Vadhu village and the city of Pune. Whenever Maher staff see a woman along this 32-km stretch of road who appears destitute or disoriented, they stop to check out the situation. The result has been a remarkable new chapter in the evolution of Maher, and brings with it a new wealth of remarkable stories.

For example, Gangabai was found wandering on the road by Maher staff as they were driving to Pune one day. She was completely naked, and covered with blood. Lucy figured she must have been raped, injured, or otherwise violently assaulted. However, the blood turned out to be her own menstrual blood. Gangabai appeared to be in her early forties. When Maher staff found her, she stank so badly they could barely keep from retching as they transported her in the Maher jeep. Like Anulekha's, Gangabai's hair was knotted into a thick nest. Her nails had not been cut or trimmed for years, her breath had an extremely foul odor, her teeth were covered in muck, and her ears were full of dirt.

The staff brought Gangabai back to Maher, and Sally performed the thankless job of cleaning her up. Gangabai's hair was knotted into such a thick bush that scissors could barely cut into it. When Sally poured water on her, she could not stand it at first, and resisted mightily, defecating on herself in the process. Gangabai could not speak coherently, and to this day she has never said her name. So Maher gave her the name Gangabai.

Gangabai has been with Maher for a year and a half now, and she has improved significantly. For a time she was admitted to the mental hospital, where her condition improved, and then she came back to Maher. For a long time she never smiled, never cried, and ate very little. But now Gangabai smiles, cries, laughs, and eats well. She still has trouble with bathing and only goes through with it when there is direct staff assistance. But Gangabai is unrecognizably transformed. She is happy, and she lives a simple but dignified life in a community where she is loved. She still cannot say her name, or tell her own story, so Maher still doesn't know her background. But Gangabai's eyes smile with the unmistakable joy of a soul at peace.

◊ ◊ ◊

Today there are some forty-three women living at Maher's Vatsalyadham facility for mentally disturbed women. They are housed in a new building that was just completed in 2008, situated on a four-acre parcel of land that Maher acquired in 2002, located about 20 km from the main Maher facilities at Vadhu Budruk. The new building provides enough space for sixty-five women. This is a huge improvement over their former housing in a converted barn with a leaky roof and all of the women cramped together in one big room. Many of the women work on the premises in the garden, which provides a healing connection to nature, and produces a significant quantity of vegetables and fruit.

Despite the extremely basic living conditions, these women are happy here—not only because they have enough to eat and shelter from the elements but because of the community they share with each other. They live a life of comparative dignity and comfort compared to what they experienced living on the street. Most are under psychiatric care, and many are on medication of some kind. Over time, several of them have improved to the point where they can be transferred to Maher's main facility at Vadhu Village.

Most of the women at Vatsalyadham have been deserted by their families or society or both—left to die or starve on the streets. Like Gangabai, they all have their unique stories, which speak for themselves.

Suman was found living in a gutter, covered with filth and carrying bundles of dirty clothes, plastic bags, and bottles. Maher staff brought her to Vatsalyadham and cleaned her up. Her health was failing and her speech was incoherent at first, but her condition improved slowly. After eight months at Maher, she was finally able to give her name and address. Suman was from Uttar Pradesh, and Maher staff managed to contact her family, who were overjoyed to find her. Suman's husband said he had been searching for her for five-and-a-half years. He and his family had no idea how she had disappeared.

When Suman's husband and son came to Maher, Suman recognized her husband, but not her son, who had grown to become a young man of eighteen. The reunion was very joyful and tearful. Suman returned home to her family, where she continues to live happily.

Similar stories abound among the women at Vatsalyadham. Several women have been successfully reunited with their families

Women residents at prayer time in Maher's Vatsalyadham home for mentally disturbed women.

or relatives, often after years of separation. Reunions such as these are deeply touching and gratifying for the Maher community. Just witnessing the radical transformation of destitute women who have spent years begging on the roads or eking out a miserable existence is profoundly healing and inspiring.

◊ ◊ ◊

Kamli was found living under a bridge with her baby, who was a few months old. Kamli was in her early thirties. The baby girl was close to death—unconscious with a high fever and swollen abdomen, a clear sign of imminent starvation. Both mother and daughter stank to high heaven, and ants were incessantly eating away at the baby's eyes. Maher staff took the baby straight to the hospital, where she was placed in the intensive care unit. The baby remained in ICU for several weeks, and her mother was brought to Vatsalyadham.

Today, the baby has grown into a healthy and happy two-and-half-year-old toddler. It would be impossible to tell the difference in health or development between her and any other two-year-old child. Kamli has remained at Vatsalyadham, where she is on medication and is doing well. She works there, and enjoys seeing her child. She has never been able to tell her own story, and she doesn't know where she came from.

◊ ◊ ◊

Sally Samuel rises every morning at 5 AM. She begins her day with meditation, prayer, and scripture reading. Then she bathes and starts work by 6:15. Sally directs the Vatsalyadham project of Maher. Her day begins by checking in on the women and tending to those who need particular attention. She also oversees the kitchen and all the gardening work. Much of her time is spent giving loving care and attention to women who have not received this kind of care in years, if ever.

Sally has a nine-year-old daughter who lives with her grandmother. Sally's husband passed away about two years ago.

Sally explains how she views her work:

> I think of these women as my sisters, or my mother—not patients or residents. These women are not my "work," they are my family. When I reach out to a woman lying on the street, she is my mother. She may be decrepit, reeking, her hair infested with lice, covered with dirt or blood. But she is my sister. So it is not difficult to reach out to her, touch her, comfort her. It doesn't matter how filthy she is, how angry she gets at me for disturbing her. I love her as my own family member, and so it is very natural for me to take care of her needs. It's just that way for me.

Some of these mentally disturbed women have attacked Sally physically. She has been injured more than once, requiring medical treatment or hospitalization. One woman beat her up and then ran away from Vatsalyadham. Another bit Sally deeply on the forearm, creating a bloody gash that has left a large permanent scar. But none of this has deterred Sally. Her eyes shine with the passion and purity of her commitment to serving these women.

Interviewing Sally was so moving we could not keep our eyes dry. The quality and integrity of her service to these destitute women touched us to our core. Sally's attitude was simple and unassuming. To her this service work is the most natural thing in the world. Her attitude is almost as if to say, "These women are in need, so of course we attend to them. What else would we do? What else matters?" For Sally, this work is a matter of bringing her spiritual life and family life together under one roof: "Vatsalyadham is our house. God is staying here. It is a God house. Without God, we couldn't do anything. God is sending the women here. Maher is my second mother's home, my second family."

Sister Lucy surveys the construction site for Maher's new Vatsalyadham home for mentally disturbed women.

The completed building at Vatsalyadham, opened in 2008, shown here along with the small plot of agricultural land that is tended by the women residents.

Sally seemed unaware of the purity and magnitude of the service she is rendering on a daily basis. She repeated several times that she feels herself to be the lucky one, the blessed one, because she feels so close to God, and she feels the divine hand in everything she does. So for Sally this work confers the greatest blessing on those who perform it, and she and the other staff are the lucky ones to be at Maher. Sally ends her day the same way she began, with prayer. She said that she gives the day's work entirely to God, leaving all the challenges, dilemmas, and blessings of the day in the unseen hands of the divine.

Nowhere in any of the Maher brochures or on its website is there a bio of Sally—nothing that reads "Sally Samuel, RN, is a psychiatric nurse with XX years of experience and YY degrees from ZZ university." Nor is there a bio for Hira, Athena, or any of the other staff members. The dedicated staff at Maher and their remarkable accomplishments are not proclaimed in any of Maher's promotional materials. Such are not the ways of these people—just pure, sincere spiritual service, with 1,000 percent commitment. No part of their lives is separate from Maher, and they love it that way. No sitting around in endless meetings talking *about* spiritual activism or "service"—as so often happens in the West—just living it, full on, with no fanfare. These people are utterly devoted to their work, and give their all for it.

Martin Luther King once remarked that "Until you know what you are prepared to die for, and live for that, you have not begun to live." The most committed spiritual activists are those who lay down their lives for their service, in devotion and surrender to the Divine. They sacrifice their lives for the Beloved they serve. Their personal ambitions, desires, and very identity are sacrificed—and replaced with the will of a larger wisdom. Such a person then becomes a purified instrument who can be used by a higher power to implement a higher will and grace in the world. Such is the nature and quality of true spiritual service, and it confers a matchless and universal power upon those who surrender themselves in this manner. The senior staff at Maher exemplify this quality of service beautifully, and nowhere is it more evident than at Vatsalyadham. Indeed, the essence of Vatsalyadham is a profound manifestation of one the great teachings of Jesus Christ, "Whatever you do [or don't do] unto the least of my brethren [and sisteren], you do unto Me."

CHAPTER 7

Paupers to Prodigies

I saw a naked child one day, hungry and shivering by the roadside. I was outraged at God, and rebuked him, "Why do you allow this!? Why don't you do something!?" But God did not answer. Later that evening, relaxing at home after dinner by the fire, I heard God say quietly, "I did do something: I made you."

—Bahai Parable

Four-year-old Vinaya was accustomed to hearing her parents fight. She and her two-year-old sister Vijaya would often be awoken from their sleep when their father Raj came home drunk and beat Kamala, their mother. He would yell and scream and start throwing things, and then start hitting Kamala. She would try to get away from him, which only provoked him further. Kamala would generally sob for hours afterward, and she often had cuts and bruises on her face and arms.

One afternoon, Raj came home early from work. He was in a rage and started yelling at Kamala. She ran out of the kitchen, but Raj followed and caught her, threw her on the floor, and started kicking her. Screaming, Kamala got up, wriggled out of Raj's grasp, and ran out of the house. This infuriated him even more. Terrified, Vinaya and Vijaya huddled together in the corner of the room, crying.

After a while things seemed to calm down, and the girls ventured forth from their corner. Raj was sitting at the table drinking cheap liquor (locally made and common in India, and highly toxic). He just kept sitting there, drinking quietly. Vinaya was hungry and asked her father when dinner would be. He scowled and told her to wait until Mommy came home. Then he went outside and started doing chores, and kept coming in and out of the house.

Two hours passed. Vijaya heard the door open and went running to her mother as she came in. Vinaya followed suit, and both girls followed Kamala into the kitchen, complaining of hunger. Suddenly Raj appeared and ordered the girls out of the kitchen. But they were hungry and didn't leave, so he began shouting at them. Kamala came to their defense, protesting that the girls were only hungry, and she was preparing dinner for them.

Raj bellowed at his wife and stormed out of the kitchen, reeling as he left. Two minutes later he stomped back into the kitchen with a large bucket in his hands. The girls smelled a strong, noxious odor as Raj strode quickly past them to where his wife was stirring a pot of dal on the stove. The girls watched as their father lifted the bucket high into the air and turned it upside down, dumping nine liters of kerosene over Kamala's head. She shrieked and moved to get away, but Raj caught her drenched sari, pulled her back, and threw her against the cabinets. Kamala screamed and again tried to run out. Raj grabbed her with one arm, shoved the pot off the burner with his other arm, and hurled Kamala against the stove, pushing her shoulders down over the open flame.

Vinaya and Vijaya did not comprehend what was happening at first. They heard a loud whooshing sound and saw a brilliant flash as their mother burst into flames before their eyes. Kamala let out an earsplitting scream from within the blaze. Her two daughters froze in horror as their innocent, unformed minds took in what was happening. Kamala's screams were deafening. Raj caught a glimpse of her face, twisted in excruciating agony, as she crumpled to the ground engulfed in flames.

At that moment, Raj apparently had a sudden flash of compassion for his burning wife as she lay writhing and screaming on the kitchen floor. He grabbed a towel and made a pitiful attempt to smother the fire. Leaping flames quickly ignited the towel, along with Raj's shirt. He screamed as he dropped the towel, tearing off his burning shirt and throwing it to the ground. The girls looked on in stark terror as Raj ran to the bedroom and brought out a large blanket and threw it over Kamala's burning body. He succeeded in smothering the fire, but Kamala had stopped moving. She was unconscious and barely breathing. Raj tried to revive her, but to no avail. Kamala had severe burns over her entire body, and her face was almost unrecognizable. Raj grabbed his daughters and ran to the neighbor's hut, where he left the girls while he went to the hospital emergency room and was treated for second-degree burns on both arms.

Kamala died on the floor, leaving behind her two daughters and two-month-old son. A summary police investigation followed, in which Raj reported that the kerosene stove had burst and he had tried to save his wife from the ensuing blaze. With the burns on Raj's arms to bolster his story, the police promptly closed the case as a kitchen accident. Even if they had thought to interrogate the two daughters, it would have done no good. Vinaya was unable to speak after the horrifying incident and, at only two and a half, Vijaya could say nothing coherent.

With their mother gone and their father incapacitated, the two girls were brought to Maher. Both were severely traumatized. Although Vinaya had been a lively and precocious child prior to this event, she lost her capacity to speak for nearly two years. Vijaya spoke rarely. Both girls ran off in terror and locked themselves in the bathroom whenever there was a fire of any kind in the vicinity. This unusual behavior was the telltale clue that eventually led Maher staff to discover what had really happened to the girls' mother.

Vinaya and Vijaya developed predictable symptoms of posttraumatic stress disorder. With the help of intensive counseling, they slowly improved over time. It took more than three years for them to become fully normal children again. Now ten and nine years old respectively, both girls are thriving at Maher. They are active performers in Maher's dance troupe and are a delightful addition to the Maher community. Vinaya still shows a few signs of disturbance, such as a tendency to want to take charge in any group she's in and refusing to participate whenever she is not in charge. Overall, however, the two girls are happy, well adjusted, and faring well at Maher.

◇ ◇ ◇

Stories of other Maher children are equally poignant. Sunny Pawar was eight years old and had been living with his mother, Savita, on the railway tracks for four years when they were brought to Maher three years ago. As Sunny recounts his own story:

> I lived in a village with my parents. They worked as servants in a hospital. They used to fight. Once my father left us, then came back, then left again. Mommy asked him where he went, but he became angry and asked her why she wanted to know. Then he left and didn't come back. [Sunny was four years old at the time]. Mommy took my brother and me on a train. We got on the wrong train, and just as we were trying to get off, the train started moving. Mommy told me to get off so I jumped down from the train, and my mother did too, but my younger brother didn't make it, as he was only two years old. The train left with him still on it. The train was going to Bombay, so we got on the next train to Bombay to look for my brother. We looked everywhere in the station and in the orphans' homes, but we didn't find him anywhere. My mother became more and more upset.
>
> Mommy didn't know where to go, so we stayed in the railway station. We lived there for a year after that. [In fact, it was nearly four years.] Mommy wouldn't let me play with the

other children; she always made me stay with her. She took me with her everywhere. Sometimes, when I cried a lot, she would let me play with the other kids. I used to beg for food. I would give it to my mother and myself. Sometimes people gave me money, and I would buy food for my mother. We lived sometimes at the railway station, and sometimes at the bus stand.

Once, a newspaper reporter came to the station, and interviewed us. Then he published an article about us, but we still didn't find my brother. He also arranged some food for us in a hotel nearby, which we could go to every day. Mommy got worse and worse, and was strange and upset all the time. The newspaper reporter brought us to some institution in Pune. But they locked us indoors. My mother didn't like it, and I didn't either. So we left.

Then a lady told us about Maher. She and the newspaper reporter took us to Maher. They put me in Mogra house [one of the Maher homes]. When I came here, I liked it very much. I go to school, I can play with friends, and I can go to study.

Sunny's mother, Savita, was mentally unbalanced by the time they arrived at Maher. She beat him a few times, so the two had to be separated. The staff soon learned that Savita had beaten Sunny periodically during the years they lived in the railway station or bus stand. She tried several times to run away from Maher with Sunny, but the staff chased them down in the jeep and brought them back. Savita would behave in bizarre ways early on, throwing stones at Maher staff, removing all her clothes, and so on, so she was placed in a mental hospital for three months, where Maher staff visited her often. She improved, and then returned to Maher—initially at Vatsalyadham. As she continued to improve further, she was moved back to Vadhu Budruk, where Sunny lives, and she is now doing quite well. She works in the production unit making cards, and has settled in comfortably.

Sunny is now eleven years old, and he has blossomed at Maher. There was a significant transition period for him to shift from his ingrained habits of begging and living on the street. Now he does exceptionally well in school, and he excels in dancing and singing. "I feel very good here. Everyone loves me. My mother is with me. She is getting better in her health. I feel very safe in my future. I'm learning to dance and to sing."

◊ ◊ ◊

Tisya was six years old when she was brought to Maher by the police. She had witnessed her father kill her mother by bashing her head with a brick. Tisya's older sister was not home that day, so Tisya was the sole witness to the murder. Gazing in shock and horror at her dead mother lying on the floor, Tisya made a firm decision in that moment to tell the truth about what happened. On the basis of Tisya's testimony, her father is now in prison for first-degree murder. He hired powerful attorneys to defend him in the trial, and his parents placed tremendous pressure on Tisya to coerce her into recanting her story. They tried in vain to demonstrate some inconsistency in her testimony. But young Tisya stood her ground, and the police provided protection for her because they feared for her safety. Tisya and her sister were brought to Maher as the trial was still proceeding and have remained there since.

Sunny, Vijaya, Vinaya, and Tisya are all active in the Maher children's dance troupe, which performs frequently both in local venues and at national events in Mumbai. During an interview, I asked Sunny what he would like to be when he grows up. Given his recent stellar dance performance at a national conference in Mumbai where he and the other Maher dancers received a standing ovation, I thought he might harbor a dream of becoming a celebrated dancer or performing artist. Sunny's reply to my question was startling and inspiring, especially coming from an eleven-year-old: "There must be more children

Maher children welcoming a visitor. Note the artwork on the back wall, showing iconography from four different religions (Hinduism, Christianity, Islam, Buddhism).

like me living at the railway station. I have a dream that I will create a place like Maher to look after these children. I would like to stay at Maher and look after these children when they come here."

BORN INTO BROTHELS—FLOURISHING AT MAHER

About forty children at Maher have been rescued from brothels in the cities of Pune and Mumbai. Each child brings a powerful story that closely parallels the deplorable conditions endured by the children of prostitutes as depicted in the 2004 award-winning documentary film, *Born into Brothels*. This film accurately portrays the plight of children of prostitutes in Indian brothels, but it does not propose a viable solution or remedy for the situation. But at least for the forty children from brothels at Maher, their lives have been turned completely around, and they are thriving as happy children in a healthy environment. In some cases their parents come to visit them, and realizing the gift that Maher is giving the children, have not sought to take them back. In other cases, the children's parents have no idea where they are. One disturbing reality for the Maher girls whose mothers are prostitutes is that as the girls mature into their teenage years, their mothers may opt to take them out of Maher to work as prostitutes. Young, attractive adolescent daughters become a major economic asset in the eyes of an aging mother whose own marketability as a prostitute is rapidly fading. Since Maher does not have legal custody of most of the children, there is little recourse to prevent such cruel exploitation short of direct court action, which is a long shot that generally fails.

When these children first arrive at Maher from the brothels, there is generally a difficult transition and adjustment period. Their former lifestyle has to be relinquished and new habits and modes of behavior instilled. Time and patience are required, and even then the process does not always succeed. Particularly in the case of older children (mid-teens and up) who are habituated to the brothel lifestyle, it can be difficult to negotiate the transition. They are accustomed to having plenty of money, indulging in sex, alcohol, and drugs whenever they please, and not being answerable to any authority. Letting go of their attachments to money and giving up their independent, free-wheeling lifestyle is difficult for many of them. Some have left Maher of their own volition to return to their brothel lifestyles. Yet most of them stay, and there are many stories that hearten the Maher staff, such as this one:

Remy was nine years old when a family relative sold her to the brothel in Pune for 9,000 rupees, about 200 US dollars. Her mother had fallen ill and was in the hospital at the time with AIDS, which she had contracted from Remy's philandering father. He had gone to find employment in the city, where he was infected with AIDS from prostitutes. When he returned home to the village, he infected his wife with the deadly virus. This tragic scenario is being repeated with growing frequency throughout rural India. Both of Remy's parents died of AIDS while Remy was in the brothel.

Remy remained at the brothel for two years before she was rescued and brought to Maher. She had to be kept in hiding there for many months because brothel authorities were searching for her. From their standpoint, Remy was their property—bought and paid for like capital equipment—and they wanted her back. She was like many girls sold to the brothel owner. In some cases, the parents have taken out a loan and cannot pay it back so the young girls are forced to earn money by selling their bodies to pay back the loan. The girl has to stay until the amount is paid off. Some were cheated by promises of a job in big cities like Mumbai, but end up trapped in the brothel.

When she first arrived at Maher, Remy continued trying to prostitute herself, as this was the only life she knew. She chewed tobacco, used foul language constantly, spent money extravagantly, and was accustomed to living with no limits placed on her behavior or whereabouts. Yet, over time—with plenty of counseling and the disciplined yet nurturing environment at Maher—Remy gradually became transformed into an entirely different person. She learned how to play with the other children in healthy ways. She began to enjoy learning in school and succeeded in letting go of offensive habits and destructive behavior. As the years passed, Remy became well integrated into the Maher community and relinquished her former lifestyle entirely. She graduated from the twelfth standard (equivalent to high school) and entered college. After a year she became eligible to enter nursing school, where she excelled. Today, at twenty-one, Remy has just completed her nursing training, and she was recently married in a joyous wedding celebration at Maher.

LIGHTHEARTED RELIEF

With all the grief and tragedy in their lives, it is natural to wonder how the Maher children and women could ever recover from their past and lead happy, normal lives. One thing Maher strives to do is not only minister to the needs of the women and children but provide times of fun and frolic to lift everyone's spirits. Mikaela Keepin, a twenty-four-year-old volunteer from the United States, describes one such occasion:

> One day Sister Lucy organized a special treat for the children and housemothers. She took them to the circus! This really touched me. The children always receive nutritious food, clean water, shelter, clothes, education, and lots of love. Maher could easily stop at this and the kids would be happy and healthy. However, Lucy believes that they deserve a little extra fun once in a while. So she arranged to bring all the children and housemothers to a circus—that's nearly 400 kids! They took 200 kids and their housemothers each day, for two days. I went the first day and it was awesome. The kids loved it and the performers' talents were very impressive. It's funny, though—Indian crowds are hard to please. Almost no one clapped for people achieving amazing feats. A dancing midget got the biggest response from the crowd. We were sitting on the outermost seats that cost the least amount of money, about 40 rupees (or 85 cents). They were bleachers made from rough wooden planks. The closest seats were sold for 150 rupees. Sister Lucy explained that people who are able to afford it will give extra money to help out the performers and circus workers who are paid only a pittance. Lucy told me a story of how her mother loved the circus, and she would always give something extra to the performers, who earn so little. One year, when the circus came to Lucy's village in Kerala, her mother made food for all the circus people and sent it by motorcycle with Lucy's older brother. Lucy told this story with overt joy and love for her wonderful mother.

Our final story in this chapter illustrates another set of social strictures imposed upon women and girls in India, and the challenges associated with child marriage in India. Shariyana was born and raised in a region where caste division is very strict. At the age of eight, she was married to a village boy in a wedding ceremony arranged by her parents and the boy's parents. Although officially illegal, child marriages such as this are common in India. After the wedding, the two child spouses generally continue to live separately in their respective parents' homes until they reach puberty, at which time they move in together, usually in the home of the boy.

The consequences of child marriage are often severe, particularly for girls: their education is sacrificed; they become more vulnerable to domestic violence; and they are weakened by early pregnancies. Babies born to girls under seventeen are 60 percent more likely to die during their first year of life.

Yet for every compelling argument against child marriage, Indian parents have a counterargument: it makes economic sense to marry off all the girls in the family at one time in order to avoid the cost of multiple weddings; finding a husband swiftly for a girl removes the burden of feeding and educating her; and marriage relieves parents of the responsibility of preserving a girl's honor throughout adolescence.

◊ ◊ ◊

Efforts to eradicate child marriage in India have been infrequent and ineffective. For example, in 2005 a social worker named Shakuntala Verma who advocated against child marriage was brutally attacked while working in Madhya Pradesh, a state in central India. The state government, eager to improve its poor record on child marriage, had put increased pressure on its grassroots social workers, demanding that they take greater responsibility for underage marriages. Verma had been working with local villagers to prevent about twenty child weddings from going forward on May 11, which was deemed an auspicious day for marriage. In an interview, she explained what happened: "I'd been visiting families in the village, going into their homes and trying to persuade them against marrying their children," she explained. "I was not welcomed by the villagers. Parents hid their children and lied about their ages. There was a lot of anger about my presence there." Verma spent ten days trying to explain to the locals why this could prove harmful to their children. "The youngest child was ten, but the average age was around fifteen or sixteen," she said. "Although the parents were not willing to listen, I kept trying to explain to them that we wanted to help the children have a better future. The response was not very good."[1]

The night before the planned wedding ceremonies in Bhangadh, a remote village in the western part of the state, Verma was home alone when an intruder suddenly appeared and attacked her with a knife, hacking at her head and arms. Both of Verma's hands were left hanging by threads of skin and flesh. Police said there was no solid evidence that the attacks had to do with her advocacy against child marriage, but as she recuperated from a sixteen-hour operation to rejoin arteries, bones, veins and nerves, she said, "I'm quite certain that the attack was connected to the work I was doing."

Verma's case has highlighted the inadequacy of government efforts to eradicate child marriages. Estimates are that 40 to 50 percent of marriages in India involve a girl under eighteen or a boy under twenty-one, the legal ages for marriage. Accurate demographic data on child marriage are difficult to gather, but UNICEF statistics report that 15 percent of girls in rural areas across the country are married before the age of thirteen; and 52 percent of girls have their first pregnancy between fifteen and nineteen. In Rajasthan, where child marriage is

---

[1]   Amelia Gentleman, "India's effort to stop child marriage hits a wall," *International Herald Tribune*, June 2, 2005.

particularly widespread, 82 percent of girls are married by the age of eighteen.[2] UNICEF characterizes child marriage as a "gross violation of all categories of child rights." Yet, according to Jaya Sagade, author of *Child Marriage in India*, published in 2005 by Oxford University Press, Indian people do not take the issue of child marriage seriously. "No political party has taken proper action against it; neither has anyone in the legal fraternity. There's a sense that it won't be possible to uproot such an entrenched custom," he said.

Although the act of marrying below the legal age is, by definition, against the law, the marriage itself is legally valid once performed, even if the child was as young as five at the time. The police do not have the authority to arrest anyone about to take part in a marriage, and the bureaucracy involved in preventing one is so complicated that most weddings have already gone ahead by the time the legal papers are ready.

Premlal Pandey, the inspector general of police in the Indore region, where Verma was attacked, reported that his officers were reluctant to interfere in this case. "We have limited manpower, so we have to decide where the thrust of policing should be," he said. "Mostly we choose to be active in the criminal field. If we intervene in child marriages, we get enemies; relatives get extremely angry. Legally, we may be correct, but we are not welcomed by society because most people do not consider this to be an evil. We can't arrest people, so the only choice is to use force. What does force mean? Well, violence. Yes, beating. It's extremely difficult."

Another high-profile case took place in Rajasthan. A government employee named Bhanwari Devi in the Women Development Program was working in the villages to prevent child marriage. As part of her duties, she attempted to stop the wedding of an infant girl who was less than a year old. Enraged by her actions, five of the vil-

---

[2]   Ibid.

lage elders from the baby girl's family gang-raped the social worker in front of her husband. The case was brought to trial in a Rajasthan court, but the accused were summarily acquitted based on the absurd argument that the men were of upper caste and would therefore not stoop to rape a woman of lower caste. Outraged by the injustice, women's groups across the nation banded together on behalf of the victim and petitioned the Supreme Court of India "to take action against sexual harassment faced by women in the workplace: Bhanwari Devi had attracted the wrath of the men solely on the basis of her work."[3] The Supreme Court issued a landmark decision in 1997, known as the Vishakha Guidelines, that established laws and guidelines on sexual harassment in the workplace for the first time in Indian history. This story is powerfully depicted in an award-winning Bollywood film entitled *Bawandar.*

Some parents argue that girls who are married off very young are not dispatched to the husband's family before puberty, an argument Sagade dismissed. "Even if it's true that the girl remains at home until reaching puberty—which I don't believe is usually the case—puberty is usually around twelve or thirteen, which is still far too young to be ending childhood," he said.

◊ ◊ ◊

Returning to Shariyana's story: Two years after her child marriage, her husband was suddenly killed in an accident. Shariyana was now a widow—at ten years of age! Following obligatory custom enforced by superstitious parents, Shariyana was required to wear only white clothes and to remain indoors in mourning for several years. When, in her mid-teens, she finally emerged from this de facto imprisonment,

---

[3]   Aurina Chatterji, "Sexual harassment: Battling unwelcome sexual attention," karmayog, *http://www.karmayog.org/women/women_1547.htm*

it was very difficult for the exceedingly sheltered Shariyana to make proper social adjustments.

When Shariyana was eighteen years old, she fell in love with a local boy about her own age. Because she was a widow, she was not allowed to marry—all the more so because the boy belonged to a lower class. The two lovers agonized over what to do. Finally, they eloped and went to Pune, where they settled and had two children. However, after three years, Shariyana's husband abandoned her for another woman from his own caste. Shariyana was left alone with their two children. She was now in her mid-twenties, and she had no claim upon her husband because they were never married legally. And because she was a widow who had "remarried" by virtue of having children, she was forever banished in total disgrace from her family and hometown.

At this point Shariyana was in a predicament similar to that of Urmila Sawant (see chapter 5), one that many young Indian women find themselves in at a tender young age. Shariyana did not dare return to her family—they might even kill her if she tried. And she didn't have the option of going back to her husband. If she couldn't find a job or some means of livelihood, there was literally nowhere for her to go. This meant that she and her children would be abandoned to the mercy of the Indian streets, and there was no telling what might happen to her. Such is the plight of many young Indian women, including many who have been well raised and sometimes are even quite educated. Yet many of these women never leave the streets for the rest of their lives.

With nowhere to go, Shariyana and her children were shunted from one temporary shelter to another, struggling to ensure they had enough to eat and unable to stay anywhere for long because Shariyana had no job or income. To their good fortune, a social worker who knew about Maher arranged for them to be taken there for an interview. After relating her story and circumstances in detail, Shariyana and her children were admitted to Maher, where they lived for several years. The children flourished, while Shariyana worked as a house-mother. After some years, she met a man living in the area and was quietly remarried with Maher's help. Her husband adopted the two children, and the family is now living happily together. Shariyana's life was transformed by the existence of the Maher project, as so many other women's lives have been.

These stories are wonderful and heartrending, but they beg the larger question: What about the thousands, or millions, of cases similar to Shariyana's who never hear about Maher or a place like it and never have the opportunity to create a decent life for themselves, simply because they somehow became inadvertently entangled in a web of unjust social norms or oppressive customs that afflict all women of India? Who will care for them? Who will help them to create a life of dignity and simple means?

CHAPTER 8

Casting Aside the Caste System

All those who take refuge in God, whatever their birth, race, sex, or caste, will attain the supreme goal. Divine union can be attained by sinners and those whom society scorns.
—Bhagavad Gita (9:32-3)

People were arriving in droves for the daylong celebration. It was Maher's "birthday," February 2, 2004, marking seven years since its doors first opened. Both Maher jeeps had been ferrying back and forth on the dusty road since early morning. With each trip, another twenty children and several women arrived, as everyone from Maher's satellite communities gathered in Vadhu Budruk for the festivities. The road outside Maher was flanked on both sides by local villagers who came on foot in large numbers from surrounding communities. Maher staff and all the housemothers were out in full force, welcoming people, helping them get settled, setting up the stage, finishing dance costumes, setting up A-V equipment, finding chairs for the elderly and dignitaries. Some guests arrived and sat down in small groups on the ground outside the Maher gates, while hordes of others strode past them onto Maher grounds.

All were gathering for one of Maher's periodic community events, which take place three or four times a year and typically draw between 2,500 and 3,000 people. Everyone knew it would be a wonderful day of fun and frolic, artful dance and singing, entertaining skits and street theater, plus a delicious warm meal offered freely to everyone in attendance. This meant quite a production for the Maher kitchen staff, but the whole community would mobilize efficiently on these occasions to help with cooking and other preparations for the large crowd. The sun was bright but not too hot, children were playing and running around freely. Everyone seemed in the best of spirits, gearing up for a great time.

A young American couple named Peter and Susan were visiting Maher for the first time, having heard about it from a friend back home. They walked around observing the meticulous preparations, wondering how or if they could be of any help, but Maher staff were adamant that they should just enjoy themselves, and didn't allow either of them to lift a finger. So Peter and Susan watched the activities and people, thoroughly enchanted and slightly dazed by the whole spectacle.

Susan peered with curiosity beyond the Maher gates at some of the groups sitting on the road making a small fire with a pot over it. "I wonder why they're making tea out there on the ground?" she asked. "Who knows?" chuckled Peter. "Maybe it's not tea. All I can say is, it's just another of the many strange sights you see here all the time. India is a trip!" They moved on and began admiring the bright colors and strikingly beautiful saris worn by the women. "How do they keep them so impeccably neat and clean?" Susan wondered, as she gazed at several women getting up and down from sitting in the dirt. "It's a marvel . . ." replied Peter thoughtfully. "The whole thing is a marvel."

Lucy and Hira and other senior Maher staff had been busy all morning orchestrating the event and greeting hordes of people as they arrived. Shortly before the appointed hour to begin, Lucy stepped toward the main Maher entrance, and Salim brought her a PA megaphone. "Good morning, and welcome to Maher!!" Lucy's voice thundered through the megaphone, echoing off the walls of the building across the road. The volume was deafening, which sent Salim scurrying to adjust the volume. Lucy resumed, "Welcome to all of you. Today is

Maher's birthday. Seven years ago today we first opened our doors, and two women came to us that very first day. We are now seven years in this place, and it is so nice of all of you that you came to celebrate with us today." Lucy continued with her welcome, thanking Maher friends and well-wishers, and then she led a prayer to open the day's activities and ceremonies.

After the prayer, Lucy outlined the activities planned for the day. She paused briefly and said, "I would like to ask you all to pay very close attention now, because there are just two more things before we begin the day's festivities—very important!" She was beaming. "First, we have a delicious lunch prepared, and you are all invited to eat with us!" The crowd cheered with approval, and Lucy waited a few moments until the enthusiasm died down. Then she turned with deliberation to face the Maher gates and gazed out upon the people sitting outside on the ground. A huge smile warmed her face as she continued, "Second, we are all human beings, aren't we? The blood that runs through our veins is equally red . . . and equally pure . . . in every one of us! So here at Maher, we will all eat together, sitting side by side! Please, come!" With that, Lucy stepped outside the Maher gate and began to usher in all the people sitting on the ground outside. "Come, please come!" she kept insisting, with her characteristic broad smile.

Peter and Susan were standing next to Hira, and they whispered to her, "What's happening? Why were they sitting on the ground out there?" Hira explained to them, "These people are Dalits and tribals— which means they are 'Untouchable' people. Normally in India, they are not allowed to mix with people of higher caste. They cannot come to the same places, or be in the same buildings, or sit in the same chairs. And especially, they must never eat the same food or in the same establishments as higher-caste people. That never happens." Hira's eyes beamed with joy. "Except here!"

Peter and Susan recalled how they had often noticed groups of people sitting on the ground outside of major public events, but they

Maher celebration drawing thousands of villagers from surrounding communities. Maher hosts these festive occasions a few times each year. All guests are fed a delicious meal without charge, and then treated to a show of Maher dance and theater performances.

had never guessed the reason. They watched with keen interest as Lucy kept ushering in the tribal and Dalit people—seating them alongside the people of all the higher castes, including Brahmins, Kshatriyas, Vaishyas and Shudras. A broad smile adorned Lucy's face as she was cheerfully breaking one of the most entrenched taboos in Indian society. And she did it all with such an irresistible grace and charm. So here at Maher, on this beautiful February day commemorating Maher's seventh birthday, the Untouchables and the Brahmins, tribals and Kshatriyas—and people of every caste and color in between—sat down next to each other and ate their meal as equal brothers and sisters of this great land that is India.

APARTHEID IN DRAG: THE CASTE SYSTEM OF INDIA

More than one sixth of the population of India—some 160 million people—eke out a bare-bones existence as "Untouchables" in India.

They are called Dalits, which literally means "broken" people, and their social status is below the lowest rung of India's caste system. Alongside them—equally dispossessed—are another 84 million people known as "tribals" or "Adivasis," who comprise India's indigenous populations. Dalits and tribals are routinely discriminated against in myriad ways: denied access to land and water, forced to work in abominable conditions for extremely low pay, and routinely abused at the hands of the police and higher-caste groups that enjoy the state's protection.

The caste system is India's "hidden apartheid," and entire villages in many areas of India are completely segregated by caste. "Untouchability" was abolished under India's constitution in 1950, yet the practice continues, especially in rural India. Untouchables may not cross the line dividing their part of the village from that occupied by higher castes. They are prohibited from using the same wells, visiting the same temples, and drinking or eating from the same utensils in public places. Dalits are prevented from laying claim to land that is legally theirs, and their villages are often located several kilometers from a permissible water source.

Most Dalits live in extreme poverty, without land or opportunities for better employment or education. The higher castes strive to maintain these deplorable conditions in order to keep a steady supply of cheap labor and indentured servitude. Most Dalits are relegated to menial work, including agricultural labor, manual scavenging, leather working, street sweeping, cobbling, and removing human waste and dead animals. Tens of millions work as agricultural laborers for a daily wage of a few kilograms of rice or 15 to 35 rupees (between 30 and 80 US cents). Dalit children are routinely sold into bondage to pay off debts to upper-caste creditors.

Conditions for Dalit women are especially severe, with the triple burden of caste, class, and gender. Dalit girls are forced to become prostitutes for upper-caste patrons and village priests. Sexual abuse and other forms of violence against women are used by landlords and the police to inflict political "lessons" and quell dissent within the community. According to a Tamil Nadu state government official, the raping of Dalit women exposes the hypocrisy of the caste system, because "no one practices untouchability when it comes to sex."[1] Like other Indian women whose relatives are sought by the police, Dalit women have also been arrested and tortured in custody as a means of punishing their male relatives who are hiding from the authorities. In India's southern states, thousands of Dalit girls are forced into prostitution before reaching the age of puberty. The girl is not allowed to marry, is made a prostitute for upper-caste community members, and is eventually auctioned off to an urban brothel.

◊ ◊ ◊

One nineteen-year-old volunteer from the Netherlands, Andrea van der Leeuw, described an experience when she accompanied Maher staff to a Pune slum.

> Maher is wonderful and amazing, but sometimes it was hard to be in India. To see how the poor live, and the position of the women, made me feel very sad. The stories from the women and children at Maher were hard to accept. To think that these things are really happening in the world, right in front of you!
>
> I recall one incident very vividly. We went to donate clothes in one of the slums in Pune. As we drove into the slum, I got a strange feeling. When we got out of the jeep it was unbelievable what we saw. I was speechless to see people so poor, and totally covered with filth. When the people realised we were

---

[1]   *Human Rights Watch* interview, Madras, February 13, 1998, *http://www.hrw. org/reports/1999/india/India994-02.htm*

offering clothes to them, they started grabbing and fighting over them. We and the Maher staff had to push them back, and the children started begging for food. It was heartbreaking.

To see the sadness in their eyes made me cry. I was feeling so sorry for the children and people there. And to realize that they will probably never go to school, never have a home or nice place to live, was very hard. When we were finished and driving back to Pune, none of the volunteers said a word.

◇ ◇ ◇

Legal reforms granting Dalits and tribals special consideration for government benefits, including jobs and education, exist, but so far have reached only a small percentage of the beneficiary populations. The Indian government established categories of "scheduled caste" for Dalits and "scheduled tribe" for indigenous peoples, with laws guaranteeing equal rights and protection, but these laws have seldom been enforced. Dalits who dare to challenge the social order have been subject to abuses by their higher caste neighbors. Police regularly refuse to register Dalits's complaints about violations of the law, and rarely prosecute for abuses ranging from murder and rape to exploitative labor practices and forced displacement. Dalit activists are jailed under preventive detention statutes, or charged as "terrorists" and "threats to national security." Court cases drag on for years, costing impoverished people precious money and time. Dalit villages are collectively penalized for individual "transgressions" through social boycotts, including loss of employment and denial of access to water, grazing lands, and ration shops.

In the southern districts of Tamil Nadu, clashes between Pallars (a community of Dalits) and Thevars (a marginally higher caste community) have plagued rural areas since 1995. New wealth among the Pallars, who have sent male family members to work in Gulf states and elsewhere abroad, has triggered a backlash from the Thevars as the Pallars have increasingly been able to buy and farm their own lands or look elsewhere for employment. The Thevars have responded by assaulting, raping, and murdering Dalits to preserve the status quo.

Between 1994 and 1996, a total of 98,349 cases were registered with the police nationwide as crimes and atrocities against scheduled castes. Of these, 38,483 were registered under the Atrocities Act for the sorts of offenses enumerated above. A further 1,660 were for murder, 2,814 for rape, and 13,671 for injury.[2] Given that Dalits are both reluctant and unable (for lack of police cooperation) to report crimes against themselves, the actual number of abuses is presumably much higher.

An estimated forty million people in India, including fifteen million children, are bonded laborers, working in slave-like conditions in order to pay off a debt. According to Swami Agnivesh, a leading Hindu reformer, the bonded labor system is "one of the most virulent and prevalent contemporary forms of slavery."[3] The money-lending system, coupled with usurious rates of interest, sometimes as high as 200 percent, creates the phenomenon of sustained debt bondage. The employer entraps a laborer by offering an advance to be paid off through future earnings. But since the wages are low and the employer frequently makes deductions for accommodation and tools, the worker cannot repay. As the debts mount, the employer insists that the debt be passed on from parent to child or even grandchild. Cases have been found of people slaving to pay off debts eight generations old.

---

[2] National Commission for Scheduled Castes and Scheduled Tribes, *National Crime Records Bureau (M.H.A.), Statement Showing Cases Registered with the Police Under Different Nature of Crimes and Atrocities on Scheduled Castes and Scheduled Tribes from 1994 to 1996* (New Delhi: Government of India, 1997).

[3] Rajiv Malik, Interview: Swami Agnivesh, Hinduism Today, March/April 2001, *http://www.hinduismtoday.com/archives/2001/3-4/14_swami_agnivesh. shtml*

There are national heroes among the Dalits, most notably Dr. B. R. Ambedkar, born in 1891 into an Untouchable caste of Maharashtra. He was one of the most ardent and outspoken advocates of Dalits's rights in twentieth-century India. At a time when less than 1 percent of his caste was literate, he obtained a PhD from Columbia University and a DSc from the University of London. Ambedkar established a Dalit movement by founding newspapers, organizing political parties, and opening colleges and educational institutions for the welfare of Dalits. He led campaigns for religious rights for Dalits, including lifting prohibitions on allowing Dalits to enter temples. Eventually he advocated conversion to other religions, most notably Buddhism. Ambedkar is perhaps best known for improving the status of Dalits through the drafting of relevant articles in the Indian constitution. He served as law minister in Nehru's cabinet in independent India, and chaired the drafting committee for the Constitution of India.

A Dalit woman cooking in her one-room hut. Heavy smoke from the wood fire thickens the air to the point of obscuring visibility, as shown in the photograph.

MAHER AS A CASTE-FREE ZONE

The Maher project was founded with a commitment to recognize all human beings as inherently equal in the eyes of the Divine. Hence, the divisions of Indian society into a hierarchical caste system are not recognized at Maher. Human beings are viewed as inherently equal on a spiritual plane, regardless of their myriad differences in terms of race, caste, gender, social standing, and so on. This is not to deny the glorious diversity of human beings and their resplendent spectrum of personalities, perspectives, and innate gifts or talents. Rather, it is a categorical rejection of the idea that people are inherently inferior or superior by virtue of the particular caste or race or indigenous tribe into which they were born.

Maher is thus effectively a "caste-free zone." In practice, this means that it routinely mixes people of different castes in all its gatherings and events, public or private, as described in the above example. Maher's public events go a long way toward cultivating and sustaining harmonious relations with the local people in surrounding villages. By mixing people of different castes and religions, these events not only serve as important bridge builders with the surrounding communities, but also provide significant opportunities to share Maher's values with all the local people. Maher also repudiates traditional prohibitions against mixed-caste marriages, and several such weddings have taken place there.

After life-long social conditioning in Indian society, new residents and staff at Maher sometimes require an adjustment period to fully adapt to Maher's high ideals of religious pluralism and repudiation of caste. One staff member describes her experience at Maher:

> In my family there was caste-ism all around. I tried to hide my feelings about it, but they were there—especially around eating. We would never eat food with lower caste people.

I would try not to have these feelings, but there was a feeling of disgust. Before coming to Maher, I was like that, which I don't like to admit.

Now, at Maher, I don't know what caste anyone is from. Caste is never in one's mind when you're at Maher. It's forgotten—really I've forgotten about it. No one is bothered about who is from what caste.

MAHER'S OUTREACH TO DALITS AND UNTOUCHABLES

As Maher's work began in the early days, some of the women taking refuge there were from nearby tribal villages and communities of Dalits. Through these women, over time, Maher staff began to learn about the living conditions in these villages. For example, in the nearby tribal village of Thakarvasti, the people had no water source. They had to walk nearly 5 km just to obtain water, and this trek was a major part of their day's activity. They had to walk even further, about 7 km, to obtain basic supplies. In tribal families, both parents had to work full time in the fields to scrape out a barely survivable living. Men were typically paid 35 rupees per day (about 87 US cents) as agricultural workers, and women about 25 rupees (about 62 US cents). Their children had to go with them to the fields because there was no one to look after them at home during the day. This meant that the children never went to school, and not receiving an education, they were destined to the exact same lifestyles as their parents and their parents' parents down through the generations.

Maher started looking into ways to help these communities. They began by visiting those villages from which the women at Maher had come and began to make friends with the Dalits and tribal people. Over time, it became clear what the most pressing needs in these communities were, and then Maher began to make some judicious interventions. First, they drilled several wells in these communities so the villagers would have their own water source. The cost of the wells varied depending on how deep they had to drill to hit water, and funds for this purpose were donated by Maher benefactors from Italy and India. This one change alone has revolutionized life for these villagers. Now, instead of spending four hours a day walking back and forth to obtain water, they have their own water source right in the center of their village. It makes a huge and welcome difference in their community.

Maher also established miniature outposts to provide a convenient local outlet for villagers to purchase basic foodstuffs and supplies, including grains, vegetables, and simple hardware. Each outpost consists of a small wooden shed about two meters wide on four wooden legs, with locking doors. The outposts are tended by one of the villagers. Deliveries are made once weekly, and now the communities manage the outposts on their own. This innovation saves the village women an average of fifteen hours per week, because they no longer have to walk the full 7 km to obtain basic necessities.

Perhaps the most significant intervention Maher has made in these Untouchable communities is that they have constructed buildings for kindergartens in the villages. This innovation serves several key purposes. First, the kindergartens provide a safe place for the children to be educated while their parents work in the fields. Maher pays for teachers to come in and teach the children fundamental skills, including English, arithmetic, and writing Hindi. Maher has also provided bicycles for the older children to ride to the public school several kilometers away. This basic education will support these young people, as they grow up, to interact far more knowledgeably with the power structures in Indian society and to stand up for their rights and their communities in ways that their parents and earlier generations have never been able to do. Maher is thus making an investment in these communities in ways that the local and federal government as well as society at large have systematically refused to do.

Sister Lucy Kurien joyously breaks the ribbon at the inauguration of a small playground built by Maher supporters for children in the nearby tribal community of Thakarvasti.

Maher has initiated a profound service of uplifting the oppressed
classes in its vicinity near Pune, where the local people have come to
know and respect that Maher is one place where the traditional norms
and rules of Indian society do not apply. Whether it is women, Dalits,
tribals, or whoever else Maher serves, as these people begin to build
their lives back up in dignity and self-respect, the unmistakable light
of love and joy begins to shine through their eyes ever more brightly.
This joy and love is the primary reward for the Maher staff, and it is the
fundamental key that keeps the project growing, vital, and thriving.

CHAPTER 9

The Magic of Maher

We make a living from what we get.
We make a life from what we give.
—The Buddha

Every Monday afternoon a delivery of 15 kgs of fresh vegetables arrived at Maher. This produce was sent from the home of a wealthy man living in a nearby town. At the time of the first delivery, more than five years ago, Maher staff were naturally grateful for the donation of fresh food, and so they sent a thank-you note to the rich man. The note was never acknowledged, but the vegetables continued to come. More thank-you notes were sent, but none were ever acknowledged. Still the vegetables continued to come faithfully every Monday.

Finally it was decided that something more than mere thank-you notes was called for, so the Maher staff paid a visit to the house of the rich man in the city. When the man answered the door he was very friendly, but when the Maher staff began to thank him profusely for the vegetables, he protested. "Oh, don't thank me! The vegetables don't come from me. I'm just the conduit. Those vegetables are sent by someone who wishes to remain anonymous."

"We only want to thank the donor," responded the Maher staff, but the man was adamant, and would not give the name of the donor. Over the next few months, the vegetables continued to arrive every Monday without fail. As the seasons changed, the vegetables too would change, but they were always fresh, and some 15 kgs came every week. The Maher staff wanted to find a way to acknowledge the goodness of the donor, but the rich man refused to divulge his or her identity.

Over time it became progressively more awkward for Maher to continue to accept this generosity, and the issue was raised during a Maher board meeting. Soon thereafter, a group of Maher staff and board members went together back to the rich man's house. Under friendly but firm pressure, with repeated assurances that Maher's only purpose was to give proper thanks to the donor, the rich man finally relented and disclosed the identity of the donor. He was a man named Anil Kamble.

It turned out that Anil Kamble lived in a neighboring settlement, so a visit to his house was arranged. It was an unforgettable moment. "When we arrived at his house—or rather a hovel—and he opened the door, I was absolutely shocked!" recalled Sister Lucy later. "There stood before us a humble man from the lowest caste—living with his wife and four daughters in a tiny one-room hut." The entire hut was the size of one small bedroom. "When I saw his situation, my first impulse was that we should give *him* 15 kilos of vegetables a week!"

Anil Kamble made his living riding a bicycle around the village, carrying a basket on his head full of vegetables which he delivered to restaurants and private homes. One sees these vendors periodically in the dusty streets of the towns and cities of India. But Anil was a man of a remarkable caliber. He looked upon what he did for Maher as his duty toward others less fortunate than himself, and he refused to be thanked for it.

Lucy and Hira were at once taken aback and deeply touched by this man. "How can you possibly afford to make such a generous gift to Maher each week," they stammered, "when you have your own wife and four children to feed and care for?" Anil turned and pointed to his daughters, who were vibrant and bubbly, giggling with each other and peeking out with shining eyes from behind their mother, enthralled to have visitors at their door. "Look at them," he said, smiling, "They are doing fine. They have plenty to eat. But you are caring for women and children who have not had enough to eat." He paused, smiling at his daughters' mischievous grins, then looked up. "I learned about Maher in the newspaper a few years ago. What you are doing is very important. Your children and women need to eat too. I am merely doing my part."

Here was a man of the lowest caste, giving in the highest spirit of integrity and service. Anil Kamble not only wanted nothing for himself, he did not even want to be recognized or thanked for his generous giving. Indeed, he had actively sought to prevent his identity from being discovered by anyone. He simply wanted to give what he could to nurture the women and children at Maher. The staff at Maher were enchanted and deeply moved by this man. All the preaching and sermons of great philosophers and spiritual teachers were somehow vibrant and alive in this simple person. The Maher staff were eager to find some way to properly acknowledge what this man had done, and before too long, that opportunity arose.

⋄ ⋄ ⋄

A related story concerns an anonymous money order that arrived every month at Maher. The money order was for 100 rupees (about 2.20 US dollars), which came in the mail shortly after the first of each month. Like the vegetable deliveries, this too went on for months— which eventually became a couple years. Again, the Maher staff tried to send thank-you notes, but there was no return address, so they went to the post office but the postal officials would not reveal the address the money orders were coming from. Finally, Maher politely but firmly wrangled the donor's name from the post office. They then tracked down the woman who was making the donations and paid her a visit. Her name was Lakshmi Singh, and she was from a very poor family (though not as poor as Anil Kamble). Lakshmi's husband gave her a small fixed allowance every month with which to buy all the household food and supplies.

When Hira asked Lakshmi how she could afford to send Maher monthly donations of 100 rupees, she explained: "When I go to the market, there are potatoes for ten rupees, and potatoes for eight rupees. I buy the potatoes for eight rupees, and put two rupees in the tin for Maher. There are carrots for six rupees and carrots for five rupees, so I buy the cheaper ones and put one rupee in the Maher tin. At the end of the month, I always have something around 100 rupees in the tin, and I send that to Maher." Like Anil Kamble, this woman refused any gifts or gestures of thanks from Lucy and Hira. She wanted to support what Maher was doing, and this was how she could do it. Lakshmi's story is reminiscent of the story in the Gospels about the woman who had but one coin to give, yet her gift was worth far more than the contribution from another who gave callously and ostentatiously, even though a much greater amount in monetary terms.

Over the years, Maher had received many gifts of many kinds from many people, but few had been quite so touching and meaningful as these gifts from these two humble people. On the face of it, they were modest gifts in material terms, but in terms of the spirit of true giving—the manner in which they came, the meager means of those who gave—these gifts were some of the most valuable Maher had ever received. And both Anil Kamble and Lakshmi Singh had tried everything in their power to remain completely anonymous.

The Bhagavad Gita, one of the great scriptures of India, contains a beautiful passage that describes in elegant simplicity this pure spirit of true charity: "Giving simply because it is right to give, without thought of return, at a proper time, in proper circumstances, and to a worthy person or cause." The Gita further promises that those of the lowest caste, women, and others whom society scorns can attain the highest spiritual goal if they take refuge in the Divine. Anil Kamble and Lakshmi Singh are quintessential examples of this true spirit of India, shining brightly through the forms of a peasant housewife and a humble vegetable vendor.

◊ ◊ ◊

Some months later, Maher was planning an inaugural celebration to mark the opening of a new building to house Maher staff. This was another big community event for Maher, with at least 1,500 people expected to attend. As usual, the program included dance and theater performances, bhajans and speeches, plus a wonderful Indian dinner for all who came. In the planning process, one of the many questions that emerged was who should be invited as the honored "Chief Guest," the person who would give the keynote talk at the inaugural dinner.

There were several obvious candidates for Chief Guest, including prominent businessmen in the area, some of whom had given five lakhs or more toward the construction of the new Maher building (one lakh is 100,000 rupees, or about 2,600 US dollars). There were also the foreign donors from Europe and America, some of whom had made equally large donations. Then there were the Maher staff themselves, some of whom had been serving Maher nonstop since the early days, and deserved to be recognized for years of devoted service. And then there were the members of the board of trustees, some of whom had slaved tirelessly to bring the Maher project to fruition, often spending long hours for months on end navigating through the morass of Indian bureaucracy and red tape to get planning permission without ever paying a single bribe—a monumental achievement in itself!

At one point in these discussions, Lucy interjected the novel idea of inviting Anil Kamble and Lakshmi Singh to be Chief Guest(s). "Why not?" she beamed as she envisaged the possibility. "They could share the stage, and each could give a short keynote speech for the gala affair!" After brief deliberation, the Maher staff unanimously and enthusiastically elected Anil Kamble and Lakshmi Singh to be Chief Guests. Lucy had been wracking her brain for months to find an appropriate way to thank each of them, and neither would accept any material offering from her. But here was a way Maher could finally give proper acknowledgment and recognition to Anil Kamble and Lakshmi Singh.

At first this decision created quite a stir among the Maher trustees, who were legitimately concerned because there were several prominent donors and wealthy businessmen who had given large sums toward the cost of the building. Some of these individuals were long-time friends and supporters of Maher, and thus seemed to be the most obvious and appropriate candidates to invite as Chief Guests. There was concern that one or more of them might be offended if not asked. Moreover, neither of Lucy's choices for Chief Guests had any experience whatsoever in public speaking. And the final clincher was that although Maher was a "caste-free zone," Anil and Lakshmi were both from the lowest castes, and it would be highly irregular for wealthy, high-caste Brahmins and well-to-do merchants who had given so much to the building project to be sitting in the audience listening to keynote presentations delivered by simple people of the lowest caste who had donated virtually nothing to the building project in material terms.

But the staff of Maher held their ground. Their general conviction was that all considerations of caste must be firmly and entirely disregarded, in this as in all other Maher matters. It was precisely this kind of situation in which Maher's commitment to its deep values was truly tested. Several Maher staff pointed out that it was easy to mix people of different castes in a dinner gathering, but that was not a true test, whereas this case was. Sentiments expressed in the board/staff deliberations were strong and impassioned. Hira stammered at one point, "Are we going to yield to our major donors' potential prejudices about the low caste of our Chief Guest(s)? Or are we going to stand by Maher's principles and commitments and do what is right—come what may?!" Still, there was legitimate concern that some donors could take offense, and this could potentially hurt Maher significantly. After further deliberations, Lucy finally interjected, "Let them take offense, if they do! If that happens, it should demonstrate to them firsthand their own betrayal of Maher's values, and this will be Maher's gift back to them." The board sympathized with Lucy's and the Maher staff's position in principle and narrowly approved the decision, but some trustees were still concerned that significant damage might be done in the minds of some of Maher's prominent friends and supporters.

Quite apart from the caste issue, there was yet another reason that Lucy wanted Anil and Lakshmi to be the Chief Guests. These two individuals had given from their very scanty means in the purest spirit of charity, seeking no reward or even recognition for themselves. As such, they exemplified the highest integrity of giving from the heart, and this would serve as a particularly important lesson, especially for the children, most of whom came from very poor households. "No matter how little you have, there is always someone who has even less," Lucy exclaimed. "You can always find it in your heart to give to them. But how many of us actually do this? How many of us go out of our way and set aside our own troubles and turmoil long enough to provide for the less fortunate on a regular basis? Anil and Lakshmi have both done this! So it is right for them to be the Chief Guests, and we can all learn from their example."

And so it came to pass. The guest appearances by Anil Kamble and Lakshmi Singh as Chief Guests are now part of the tapestry that makes up the "magic" of Maher. Neither one had any public speaking experience, so they were not comfortable giving talks. They were brought up on stage and their stories were recounted to the audience, who were deeply moved. The inauguration came off beautifully, with deep gratitude to these two wonderful souls, who had so little, yet gave so much.

Plenty of love and laughter go into the meals prepared at Maher.

IMPACT OF MAHER ON VISITORS AND INTERNS

"Glad to see you, glad to see you! Glad! Glad! Very very Glad!" This verse comes from the upbeat song of welcome that the Maher children sing to each and every visitor to Maher. Afterwards the children rush up, throw their arms around the startled visitors, and give them a gigantic group hug. This is followed by a simple aarti blessing, in traditional Indian style. The experience is something one does not soon forget.

"Even the breeze is consoling at Maher." This lyric comes from a song written as a tribute to Maher by one of the women who took refuge at Maher. She was in an abusive marriage, and after a series of periodic visits to Maher over two years' time, her marriage was transformed, and the abuse ceased. Her lyric aptly describes the psychosocial environment of Maher, which is exceptionally positive and healthy. Visitors are always impressed by how happy the children are, and by the joy of the women and staff. As Dr. Ganla observes, "The radiant smiles, laughter, and joy of the Maher residents tell the real story—this is not something that could be staged!"

Another Maher trustee, Dr. Sharma, describes it this way: "My job is easy, because Maher sells itself. The positive, healing spirit is contagious, and the smiles and joy are genuine. On the whole, I find the children at Maher to be happier and more fulfilled than many children in ordinary families. All it takes is one visit to Maher, and your heart is touched." He paused, and added with a mischievous wink, "And if not, there's nothing wrong with Maher, but perhaps you should consider psychological counseling!"

Students from India as well as from other regions of the world come to Maher as interns for their academic, professional, or religious training. Many of these interns are completing advanced degrees or clinical requirements for field experience.

Alexandra Gramps, who is twenty-one, has visited Maher twice. She is currently completing her undergraduate degree at Smith College, and is applying for foundation grants to serve as a research intern at Maher for one year. If awarded, Alexandra will work alongside Lucy to produce detailed documentation of the specific practices and components that make up the Maher project. This work will provide a basis for future research and much-needed training documentation that Maher will use in its training program. Alexandra describes her experience of Maher:

> I have been inspired by the Maher project since I first visited it at the age of seventeen, and have promised myself and Sister Lucy that I would return to do further work. When I stayed at the shelter I felt as safe and cared for as though I were at home, and the light in the eyes of the women and children there told me that they experienced the same sensation. I am highly motivated to do whatever I can to support the Maher

project. Sister Lucy has much to offer to the world through her philosophy and practices, and I would be honored to support her in working toward realizing her dream of re-creating as many similar environments like Maher as possible.

Twenty-four-year-old Mikaela Keepin, a volunteer from the United States, visited Maher for a few weeks and was so inspired that she returned a year later to volunteer for four months. She shares her experience:

> Reuniting with the children was so joyful. They were very surprised to see me, and for me it was like living a dream, one that I had dreamt every day since leaving Maher nearly a year earlier. I returned for a four-month internship to help in whatever way was needed. I was saddened to learn that two of my best friends, Seema and Shoba, are no longer here, but glad that they are pursuing other jobs and living on their own. This is one of Maher's goals, to encourage and support women to re-enter society and find ways to be self-sufficient.
>
> Manda is another woman I really miss. She had lived at Maher for ten years and worked as the head cook. She divorced her abusive husband many years ago. Manda brought such joy to Maher and to everyone who came to visit. Her laughter filled the kitchen, as did the love that she poured into the delicious food she made. A few months ago she married a man named Anthony, a widower, who has two teenaged boys. Manda invited me to visit and stay at her house for two days. We had a great time in her tiny two-roomed home. Anthony is a kind, playful man. His eyes are innocent and sweet, and he helped Manda in the kitchen a lot. I learned that Anthony had remarried just seven months after his wife's death; Indian society works in very practical ways sometimes. He remarried so soon

out of pure necessity. The culture has a sad double standard—for a widow to take another husband is totally unacceptable. A widow and her children are considered damaged, a bad omen and a burden to society. Manda really wanted to be married, and Manda and Anthony seem very happy together.

Two other students, Johanna Ober and Roswitha Ertl, from Vienna, Austria, both twenty-four, completed a four-month internship at Maher as part of their masters program in social work. They share their reflections on "the magic of Maher."

We were welcomed with arms wide open when we arrived at Maher on November 1, 2006. The children greeted us with songs and the staff did everything to make us feel comfortable.

Soon, we were interacting with the staff, women, and children on a regular basis. Most who seek refuge at Maher come from a very poor background and never had the opportunity to attend school, so they do not speak English. We did not speak Hindi or Marathi. Nevertheless, we became very close to everyone and we were pleasantly surprised by how much could be communicated nonverbally.

One of the most memorable times during our stay was when we first saw the dance-drama performances that reenacted some of the true stories of the children and women of Maher [described in chapters 13 and 14]. Two scenes in particular had a significant impact on us—first, when a young girl was raped on her way home from school, and second, when the woman was burnt alive with kerosene by her drunken husband as their little girl watched. We were shocked when we saw these performances! However, we also deeply admired and respected Sister Lucy and the Maher staff for being so courageous to show such brutal and life-threatening scenes. Maher is not afraid to bring the most taboo subjects out in the open, and in doing so they help to encourage society to become more self-reflective.

It was also a very important learning for us to experience how little a person really needs in order to live. At Maher, there were times when we had no electricity, or even water. This could have been very distressing; however, it proved quite the contrary. During these times, there were many wonderful moments, like when we sat down together as a community for prayers before dinner, and the whole room was lit just by candles or moonlight.

For meals, we sat on the ground and used our hands to eat instead of knives, spoons and forks. There was no TV, no fridge, and no cupboard full of clothes. Quite different than our European lifestyle! We really enjoyed the slower pace at Maher. There's much more time for self-reflection, because time doesn't run so fast, like in our busy Western world. It was a bit challenging for us to get used to the Indian customs. The children and women were very patient teachers and they valued our attempts to learn daily habits of their culture. At the end of our stay they said, "Thank you for living with us like sisters and brothers."

We still are overwhelmed by the power and strength of the Maher staff's steady work for the poorest in India. Never before have we seen a group of people with such strong character and deep belief in human beings. When we came to India we expected to gain life experience and a better understanding of the Indian culture, but above all these, Sister Lucy and the Maher family gave us a new family and a new feeling of coming home. There is a real pure and honest love and acceptance at Maher that is palpable to anyone who enters through their doors. Maher is dependent on donations from all over the world, but it gives a thousand times more than it takes. Maher will always be deeply in our hearts and minds.

GIGGLE-BYTES GALORE AT MAHER

In the intensity of all that Maher deals with, laughter is an essential healing balm. Peals of laughter spring up at any moment in the Maher community, sparked by anything from the absurd to the sublime. Many a time there will be something quite serious taking place, and then someone says something or something happens that suddenly sparks one or another of the staff into bouts of laughter, which quickly spreads to the others. Maher staff seem to find many things to laugh about throughout the day, which provides a powerful relief from the intensity of their work and helps maintain perspective and a healthy detachment.

As one volunteer observed, "What I find remarkable about Maher is that such poignant and often heartbreaking social service work is being done here, and yet there is so much joy and laughter all around. It's as if the profundity of the service being done for society confers a special kind of grace at Maher." He added with a chuckle, "If happiness could be measured in terms of the frequency of laughter per capita, then I would say there are more 'giggle-bytes' per hour at Maher than anywhere else I've ever been!"

CHAPTER 10

Dowry, Dharma, and Karma: Women's Healing Stories at Maher

I measure the progress of a community by the degree of progress which women have achieved.

—B. R. Ambedkar

"Stop it!" Lila screamed, yanking her arm loose. Her husband Ishan was beating her with a broom and trying to hold her down. Lila wrenched herself free and scrambled quickly beyond his reach.

"I'm telling you—one last time!" Ishan roared. "You get that money to us—or you will die!" His eyes blazed fiercely. "Do you hear me?! There's nothing I can do to prevent it!" Ishan slammed the broom against the wall, and pieces went flying everywhere as it shattered. "You will go up in smoke!!" he bellowed.

Lila ran out of the house into the black night. It was 2 AM, and she knew instinctively that she dare not return home that night. She ran to her friend Meera's house a short way down the road and knocked urgently on the door. In recent weeks Lila had been confiding in Meera, who had assured her that she could come to her house at any time, day or night, especially if the threats became more ominous. Difficult as it was to disturb her friend at this hour, Lila had no other choice.

"What happened?" Meera asked, opening the door and rubbing her eyes to wake up. Lila explained in hushed tones how Ishan had just come back from his parents' home, and he was more insistent than ever that she deliver the dowry money. Otherwise they would kill her. "We must leave quickly!" Meera said, "in case they come looking for you. His parents will be enraged when they find out you left the house." Meera woke her husband and asked him to drive them to Vadhu Budruk, about 8 km away.

Meera had told Lila several weeks earlier about a shelter in the nearby village of Vadhu Budruk where she could take refuge if need be. Neither Meera nor Lila had ever been to this place, called Maher, but Meera knew exactly where it was located because she had driven past it many times in her husband's auto rickshaw.

It was 2:45 AM when the tiny auto rickshaw sputtered to a stop in Maher's driveway. Meera let out a sigh of relief when she saw that the gate was open, but she was concerned that there would be no one to greet them at this hour. She did not know that Maher's doors are always open—day and night—every day of the year. She rang the bell, and in a few moments the lights came on inside. Mina greeted them at the door. Meera briefly explained the plight of her friend Lila. Mina ushered them in and told them to have a seat while she went to put on the teakettle and summon Hira.

Soon they were drinking tea with Hira, and Lila began to recount her story. Hira listened intently, quickly assessing the situation. After a few minutes she interjected, "It's very late, and I know you've been through a lot in recent days. Why don't you take some rest now. I'll show you to your room. Tomorrow you can tell us the whole story." Lila expressed tremendous relief and gratitude to Hira for taking her in. As Meera and her husband were preparing to depart, Lila bent down and touched Meera's feet as an expression of her deep gratitude. In India, touching the feet of another person is a gesture of deep respect, reserved primarily for elders or spiritual masters.

The next morning, Lila was introduced to Lucy, and she recounted her story in detail to Lucy, Hira, and Athena. Athena is the current director of the women's program at Maher, and she readily understands cases like Lila's because she, too, originally came to Maher seeking refuge. Lila told the three women that her husband Ishan had begun beating and threatening her in recent weeks. He was under strong pressure from his parents and his brother to force Lila's parents to make full and immediate payment on a promise Lila's family had made two years earlier to give a sum of money to Ishan's family as part of her dowry. Ishan's family had become very impatient to receive the money because they were eager to buy a motorcycle. In the meantime, however, there had been a serious drought in the region, and the crop had failed on Lila's parents' farm two years in a row, so they were now in dire financial straits. Ishan's parents and his brother were demanding that the dowry be paid regardless, and they were becoming aggressive and threatening about the situation. They had been mistreating Lila and pressuring Ishan for months, and recently they had begun making thinly veiled threats to Lila.

Lila said that she loved her husband and that he was a decent man and generally a loving father to their two children, but lately he had changed. He was starting to beat her regularly, and his family was urging him to dispense with Lila altogether and get a new wife who would be more lucrative for the family. The tension was mounting day by day, and Lila was now fearing for her life, primarily because of threats from Ishan's parents and brother rather than from Ishan himself.

Lila was admitted to Maher and went through the standard intake procedures, including a medical checkup, psychological assessment, and initial counseling. Ishan was unable to care for the children because he had to work, so the two children were also brought to Maher.

Over the next two weeks, there was a series of meetings between Lila and Ishan and his family members. Lila's parents did not attend the meetings because there was so much friction between them and

Ishan's family. Maher staff and counselors facilitated each of these meetings. It soon became clear that Ishan was not operating on his own, but within a powerful family system that was pressuring him to secure the dowry money from Lila's family. Ishan's parents, and to a lesser extent his brother, were pushing Ishan to kill Lila if the dowry payments were not forthcoming, and find a new wife. As the meetings continued, Ishan became increasingly remorseful for his abusive behavior. At one point he apologized to Lila and asked her to come back home. Lila too wanted to go back home to her family.

Maher counselors insisted on certain conditions for Lila's possible return home, and negotiated a contract between Ishan and Lila that included the following points: (1) the physical and verbal abuse of Lila must stop immediately and completely; (2) all threats to Lila, from either Ishan or his family members, must stop; (3) Ishan was to impress upon his family that he was happily married to Lila and that he intended to remain with her and would not tolerate intervention from them; and (4) henceforth, no future dowry payments would ever be demanded from Lila's family, and Ishan would continue to explore avenues for the earlier dowry agreement to be honored, if possible.

After fifteen days at Maher, Lila and her children went home to rejoin her husband, and Maher staff checked in at least once a week to ensure that all was going well. At first it did, but before long, when the dowry payment was still not forthcoming, Ishan's family began to pressure him again, and he in turn renewed his insistence that Lila's family produce the dowry money. The tension in the household once again started to rise.

During a visit to Lila's parents' home, Ishan took Lila's father aside and asked him privately, "Regarding the dowry money, when do you think you could pay that to my family? They keep asking me about it." Lila's father frowned as he drew in a slow breath. "You are aware that we've continued to have a serious drought again this year," he began. "It has been disastrous for us, and the dire conditions have not let up.

It's been very tough for us since two years back. Actually, right now we are barely scraping by ourselves. And my wife needs some medical attention for her hip and her eyes, but we haven't been able to afford that either. So, I don't know . . ." His voice trailed off.

Ishan tensed up as he listened, and his jaw tightened. "That will not be acceptable news to my parents and brother, who brought our family into this marriage with a clear understanding about the dowry," he replied tersely. "I'm very concerned about what might happen if this agreement is not fulfilled," he warned, his face contorted in a menacing expression. "I strongly advise you to find a way to make good on this payment!" At that moment Lila and her mother walked into the room and the conversation shifted abruptly.

When Lila and Ishan returned home from visiting her parents, things took a turn for the worse. "You need to make your parents give over that money!" Ishan barked at his wife, and he began harassing her again. Up to this point, Ishan had honored the terms of the contract he had signed, but now he once again began calling Lila names and shoving her around. It was not long before he hit her, and one night when she defended her parents' case and her mother's need for medical attention, he flew into a rage and beat her. Lila cried herself to sleep that night.

The next morning, after Ishan had left for work, Lila called Maher to inform them that the harassment and beating had begun again. Lucy called a meeting at Maher with Lila, Ishan, and Ishan's family. As Lila recounted how the abuse had begun again, Ishan denied it and insisted that Lila was making it all up. Lucy interrupted the game of "he said, she said" and asked them all to go back home, telling Lila that if the harassment began again, she should write it up in a letter and send it to her at Maher. The letter would provide the documentation they would need to take further legal action. Things were patched up once again, and Lila and her family all went back home.

Within a few days, the abuse resumed, and Lila realized this was a clear and dangerous pattern. She was in tears as she wrote the letter to Maher documenting the latest episodes of abuse, as Lucy had asked her to do. She posted the letter and went about her day's business, and when Ishan returned home from work that evening, she confronted him. "You signed a contract affirming that the abuse would stop!" Lila began, but Ishan interrupted her. "Oh, forget all that," he said, scowling. "Your family hasn't kept up your part of the bargain." A cold, painful silence settled between them.

When Lila's letter arrived at Maher, Lucy instructed Lila not to run to Maher immediately but to wait a few days to see if the abuse let up. "If the tension or threats begin to feel dangerous, then run away to your friend Meera's house and call us. You can always return to Maher," Lucy assured her. Lila had packed the children's clothes and made preparations to leave on short notice.

The pattern of abuse repeated itself the next evening, and Lila knew she needed to take action. When Ishan left for work the following morning, she packed up the children, and with Meera's help she left her home and returned to Maher.

When Lila arrived at Maher for the second time, she was very distraught and not sure what to do. She feared for her life, and was seriously considering leaving Ishan and getting a divorce. Maher counselors advised her to take some time and not feel a need to make any decisions immediately. She needed some space and peace of mind before such an important decision could be made.

Within a couple of days Ishan and his parents were back at Maher, wanting to take Lila and the children back home. Ishan again offered apologies for the abuse, and promised that it would not happen again. But this time Ishan and his family met a much less accommodating response. The Maher team took a strong stance of challenge and protection for Lila.

"Why should Lila come back home with you, when you violated your promise to stop the abuse?" Hira demanded. "Forget it! You committed yourself—in writing—to stop this violence toward your wife, and you broke that promise. What guarantee do we have that you won't start up the abuse again? Forget it, Lila stays here for the time being. It's not safe for her to return to your home."

Ishan and his parents went home empty-handed. Within a few days, they were back, and Lucy joined the meeting this time. Listening to the arguments back and forth, she was becoming increasingly incensed, but she sat for a time quietly, in deep prayer. Then suddenly she interjected, "How dare you come here wanting to take Lila back, when you just took her back a few weeks ago, promising to treat her right, and you violated her again! Why should we believe that you won't do the same yet again?" Ishan began to mumble a reply, and his parents shifted uncomfortably in their seats. "Why should we trust you ever again?" Lucy demanded.

Then, with piercing eyes, Lucy turned to Ishan's parents. "Who are you—tell me!—that you can stoop to such a low level as to think of murdering your own daughter-in-law? How could you?" she implored. "And for what? Just for money?" Lucy's face twisted into an expression of absolute disgust in a characteristic manner that only she can make when she is totally abhorred by something. "I know exactly what you have been thinking and plotting!" she thundered. "You thought you can just burn Lila to a crisp, be done with her, and get a brand new wife for your son—one that pays you handsomely!" Lucy glowered. "What sort of people are you?!" she roared. "How can you even sleep at night with those hideous schemes in your mind? You tell me!"

There was a long, poignant silence as the room reverberated with Lucy's thundering words. Her indignation imparted a power and authority that drove her point straight home. Lucy trains all the Maher counseling staff to deal with each person and each situation uniquely and precisely, according to the need of the moment. In this moment, Lucy did not flinch from naming the demon head on. Ishan's parents hung their heads in silent shame, knowing full well their culpability. Never before had anyone challenged them directly on their behavior and reflected their despicability back to them with such devastating clarity.

Lucy challenged them in this manner because she could see inwardly that Ishan's parents were not evil people; they were basically decent people who had become fully entangled in the greed and cruelty of India's insane dowry system. By mirroring back to them the absolute horror of what they were contemplating, Lucy was marshaling the inner forces of their own morality and dignity and demanding that they come to their senses and recognize, in sorrow and remorse, what a profound injustice they were contemplating. By this means Lucy was calling forth the highest in them, and helping them to forego a ruthless and criminal course of action.

It was a risky tactic, and one that hinged on a precise assessment of Ishan's parents and their likely response. With other people, in different circumstances, Lucy would take other approaches. Lucy is always in prayer when she intervenes, and her words pour forth with a force and clarity not her own, but empowered by the purity and intensity of her prayer. In this case, it was a powerful illustration of the teaching in Proverbs, "Well meant are the criticisms of a friend, but profuse are the kisses of an enemy." Rather than indulge Ishan and his family with social niceties or friendly seductions, Lucy chastised the lot of them, thereby befriending the good within them, and strengthening their resolve to do the right thing.

And it worked—this meeting was the turning point. Over the next few months, Lila and her children remained at Maher as negotiations between Ishan's family and Lila continued. Ishan's parents' scheme having been exposed, their strident stance weakened. They shifted their tactic, and one day Ishan announced that he wanted a divorce—a decision that again was made under pressure from his family. The new strategy was self-evident—a divorce would enable Ishan to marry another woman, who would hopefully bring in a greater dowry, while Lila and the kids could remain at Maher. Maher staff responded that Ishan was of course free to pursue a divorce, but they informed him that Maher would strongly support Lila's divorce settlement in court, demanding that Ishan provide financial maintenance for Lila and their two children. This slowed Ishan down, and it also led to a series of confrontations between him and his parents. Over the course of these challenges, it became ever clearer to Ishan that he was being manipulated by his family for their own material gain. And throughout the process, Lila's character as a genuine and compassionate person became evident to everyone involved.

Maher offered counseling to Ishan and his family, and Ishan agreed to it. Maher counselors helped him explore what he really wanted, and why he was so determined to divorce his wife. Lila still wanted to remain married to him, even after all that had transpired between them, provided they could mend their relationship. As Ishan realized the extent of his family's meddling in his personal affairs, and the magnanimity of his wife's character, his attitude began to shift. He recognized that he had been happy with Lila for several years, and the primary problem between them had been stirred up by the unresolved dowry payment. A new wife would very likely mean similar tensions around the dowry issue, beginning all over again with another family, and Maher counselors asked Ishan why he was so sure that a new wife would be an improvement. Ishan could see how much Lila had grown to be loved and appreciated within the Maher community, and Maher staff observed how Lila had resisted attention from other men because she was ever faithful to Ishan. This touched Ishan's heart, and he acknowledged to himself and to the Maher counselors how much he was missing Lila at home.

Ishan and Lila began to meet privately at Maher without his parents or brother, who had always accompanied him in earlier meetings. The two began spending more and more time together, under the watchful eye of Maher counseling staff. The love between Ishan and Lila was rekindled, and the two began to repair their broken relationship. There were many moments of tears and tenderness as they sought to heal all that had transpired between them, and Maher counselors supported each of them throughout this process. It took a few months, and also required Ishan to stand up to his parents and brother. He insisted that they allow him to come to his own decision about whether to divorce and remarry or to remain with Lila.

Lila and Ishan came to a place where they wanted to go back together and reestablish the loving family they had once shared. Ishan announced this decision to his parents, and asked for their blessing. In consultation with Maher staff, a new contract was drawn up to support the couple, and to protect Lila. Given the earlier experience with the violation of the first contract, this second contract carried significantly more "teeth," and was explicit about the consequences if the abuse should start again, or if any harm should come to Lila.

The political leader of the local village was summoned to preside over the new agreement and provide his personal assurance that he would support legal action in the case of any wrongdoing against Lila. Relatives of Ishan's family were from his same village, so his support of the contract added a certain political leverage over and beyond Maher that extended directly into the village where Ishan's family resided. Like most Indian families, Ishan's family was very concerned about their social image and status, and this step ensured that any legal difficulties the family might get into regarding Lila would quickly become common knowledge in their village. Maher staff insisted that the village leader provide his signature on the contract before they felt comfortable releasing Lila again.

A special clause was included in the contract to cover the contingency of a suicide or accident involving Lila. A suicide would be assumed to be foul play, and Maher would instigate a full investigation and ensure that any guilty parties be prosecuted to the fullest extent of the law. An accident would also be thoroughly investigated, with foul play presumed as highly likely. This was an important element in the contract, because dowry murders in India are often covered up and dismissed as suicides or accidents. The contract stated that in the case of a reported suicide, legal action would be immediately taken against the family for suspected murder, because there was no plausible reason for Lila to take such a drastic action. If Lila were unhappy or desperate for any reason that might precipitate such a drastic measure, she would never commit suicide, but would instead simply return to Maher, which was always open to her as a refuge. Therefore, there was no conceivable scenario in which a suicide would be credible.

After long discussions between Lila and her parents, Lila's father came forth to say that if the marital situation for Lila was resolved and she enjoyed a peaceful home life, he would begin making payments to Ishan's family toward the previously agreed upon dowry arrangement. Ishan's family accepted this good faith gesture, and Maher staff insisted that the contract stipulate no further dowry payments of any kind, once this prior agreement was fulfilled.

Lucy attended these negotiation meetings whenever possible, and she was very direct with Ishan and his parents. "As Lila makes her decision to return home, we are hoping that all troubles between you have now been resolved, and we wish the best for all of you. Nevertheless, you need to know that we at Maher will stand by Lila, and we will protect her. We will stay in close contact to keep abreast of how things are going. If the harassment or hitting or beatings start up again, we will take legal action and put you behind bars. We have done it before, and we will not hesitate to do it in your case if necessary. We already have all the evidence in writing and testimony we need. Such mistreatment of Lila, or of any woman for that matter, is absolutely unacceptable, and it will not be tolerated. Do you understand?"

"Yes, I understand," Ishan replied, "and I assure you this will not happen again."

"We understand, and Lila will be well cared for," Ishan's father added.

"We've heard those assurances from you before," Lucy said. "How do we know that this time you mean business?"

"Because Lila and I have made up, and recommitted to our marriage," replied Ishan. "And because my family has agreed to leave Lila and the dowry situation alone, and stop pressuring me. And because I love Lila, and we both want our marriage to last, and to rebuild our family." Tears welled up in Ishan's eyes as he spoke.

"We too want it to last for your sakes," said Hira, "and we want the best for your family and children." Lucy pulled out the contract which the Maher staff had prepared, and it was duly signed by Ishan, both of his parents, his brother, the village leader, and the Maher staff. By this time, Lila had been at Maher for five months. Now she left for the second time and went back to her home with her husband.

Maher staff checked in with Lila every few days at first, then once each week, and then every couple of weeks for the first several months. Things went well overall, with a few inevitable adjustments at first. Maher kept checking in at least once a month over the next two years. Its strong support for Lila served as a deterrent to any intimidating behavior toward her from Ishan's family, and they stopped pressuring Ishan as well. In time, the family began to bond with Lila, and the tensions dissolved. Lila's life changed dramatically for the better. She and her husband were able to heal their broken relationship, and they are now thriving. Five years have passed, and Lila and Ishan are happily raising their children, who are now six and eight years old. Ishan's parents have grown to like and accept Lila fully, and Lila's family made the payments in fulfillment of the earlier dowry agreement, which has long since been completed.

Maher served in at least four specific capacities on behalf of Lila. First, as a refuge—a safe place where she could go at any time to get herself out of harm's way. Second, it provided a clear and unwavering mirror of integrity and justice—helping Ishan's family recognize the full horror of dowry murder and turn away from any such action.

Third, it provided counseling services to Lila, and also to her family members, which was essential in their healing process. Finally, Maher provided a de facto extended arm of law enforcement by facilitating a contract between the parties that guaranteed Maher's commitment to doing whatever it could to bring the family to justice, should they cause any harm to Lila.

◊ ◊ ◊

Thus was the life of Lila spared, and today she is thriving. Were it not for Maher's intervention, she almost certainly would have become another dowry murder victim, easily dismissed as a suicide or kitchen accident, and quickly forgotten. There are literally hundreds of similar stories of women like Lila who came to Maher fleeing for their lives and who were saved by Maher's intervention. In each case, Maher served in various capacities according to the woman's particular needs and circumstances—providing a mixture of refuge and sanctuary, psychological counseling, medical treatment, legal support, vocational training, counseling for the woman's husband or family, and a vibrant community to which she can return anytime she needs to in the future.

It may be hard for people of Western sensibility to imagine how Lila could possibly move back in with a husband whose family had been threatening to kill her. It's perhaps even harder to imagine that her marital relationship would work out in a fulfilling way after such an ordeal. It is important to understand that Indian society operates in a different manner, and this family was caught up in an unhealthy social system that is in profound need of healing and transformation. Once it became clear that Ishan was sincere in wanting to mend the relationship with Lila, and vice versa, it went a long way toward healing relations between the couple and thwarting the coercive manipulations from Ishan's family.

A joyful healing moment for Maher women with Sister Lucy Kurien.

The file records at Maher are very revealing. One can read page after page of entries showing the name of each woman who took refuge there—why she came, how her case was handled, and what became of her. Lila's case is a representative example of someone whose life was in immediate danger when she arrived at Maher. There are many other kinds of cases as well, as a few more examples will illustrate.

A STRANGE ODOR

A mysterious odor wafted through the doorway as Purna introduced herself. She had just arrived on Maher's doorstep with her two young children, her mother, and a woman friend. It was almost 11:30 PM as Athena and Lucy sat down to interview these new arrivals. "My husband has been abusing me," Purna began slowly. "I heard about Maher from my neighbor, and she brought me here." She motioned toward her friend. Expressions of deep sorrow were carved into the faces of both women. Sitting next to Purna was her mother—wizened, yet resolute, with her jaw set tight, and obviously distraught.

151

Athena offered the women tea, and inquired where they had come from. They had traveled for more than an hour in an auto rickshaw from an interior village more than 25 km away. As Athena returned with the tea, both she and Lucy got another whiff of the mysterious putrid odor. It must be her foul breath, Lucy thought to herself, mindful of the unsanitary hygiene that typifies many poor households.

"I have no place to go," Purna continued, "and I would like to take refuge at Maher." Her mother added quickly, "The children need shelter also. We have no place to keep them." Lucy and Athena listened to the details of Purna's story, and continued to ask questions to learn the particulars of the case. As with every woman who comes to their door, Maher staff have to carefully assess the situation to discern whether she is genuinely in distress or simply looking for free shelter or otherwise trying to take advantage of the services offered by Maher without being in true need. In this case, both Athena and Lucy had a sense that Purna was hiding something, but they could not discern what it was.

After some time, Purna suddenly asked if she could see Lucy alone. This was an unusual request, but Lucy complied without hesitation. She took Purna into the adjacent room, noting another waft of the foul odor as they entered. Purna sat down facing Lucy, and tears began to well up in her eyes. "Let me just show you," she said quietly, lowering her eyes and lifting her sari. Lucy got a sudden shock. Purna's body was covered with several open wounds and burns. The rancid odor emanating from her festering wounds, some of which were infected, was strong and caustic. Purna explained that the burns were from cigarettes. Her husband would tie her down with ropes and burn her body with cigarettes while he had sex with her. Her ankles, wrists, and lower calves had several bruised, weeping gashes where the ropes had chafed and torn into her flesh.

Lucy choked back her impulse to vomit and immediately admitted Purna and her children to Maher. She later learned that Purna's husband had been abusing her in this manner for more than three years. The couple had been married for six years, and the abuse started in the third year of their marriage and had become steadily worse. In her desperation, Purna had convinced herself that her husband would stop or change, and she pleaded with him to stop on many occasions, only to discover that this further fueled his abusive behavior. She hid what was happening from her friends and family, and she always made sure to bathe alone so no one would see her wounds.

The situation continued to deteriorate, and one day Purna's mother caught sight of a burn on her arm and asked her about it. Purna dodged the question by mumbling something unintelligible, and this evasion incensed her mother. She grabbed at her daughter's sari and unveiled several more burns and festering flesh wounds. When her mother demanded an explanation, Purna broke down and confessed her plight. Mother and daughter melted into tears together, and Purna began to wail in agony, finally beginning to release the extreme pain she had been suffering at the hands of her husband.

Maher staff took Purna to the hospital the next morning, where she embarked upon a course of medical treatment for her wounds. They initiated intensive counseling for her, during which it became apparent that she was feeling tremendous guilt for having left her husband and her household to come to Maher. She held a deep-seated belief that a wife should always be subservient to her husband's will, regardless of what happens. This conviction, which is widespread among Indian women, had prevented her from leaving her husband sooner, despite the torture he was inflicting upon her. Maher counselors worked with Purna to help her see that such cruel behavior was pathological and required clinical psychological or psychiatric treatment.

In the meantime, Purna's husband, Ashok, had found out where his wife had gone, and he showed up at Maher's doorstep demanding that Purna be released to go back home with him. The staff refused to let Ashok see Purna unless he agreed to meet with their staff counselors. He agreed, and several meetings were held in which

Purna, supported by Athena and other Maher staff, confronted Ashok about the abuse. As a precondition for Purna's return home, Ashok was required to receive psychiatric treatment (outside of Maher) for his condition, and the staff provided referrals for him. He followed through with the treatment.

Purna remained at Maher for three months, during which time her wounds healed and her counseling sessions continued. Ashok remained in psychiatric treatment throughout this period, and beyond. After three months, Purna returned home on a provisional basis, with the clear understanding by all parties that she could return to Maher at any time if necessary. Athena and Hira kept close tabs on Purna for the first few weeks after she went home and remained in frequent contact with her over the next several months. The clinical treatment Ashok received was effective, in part because he was determined to get beyond the behavior that would otherwise cost him his marriage. Maher followed up with Purna periodically for two years afterward, and she and Ashok were able to mend the broken trust between them and build a new life together.

◊ ◊ ◊

We might pause here to ask: why do women put up with such abuse, often with little or no protest, even in extreme cases, such as Purna's? According to one report, entitled "Women and Mental Health,"[1] there are several factors that contribute to the problem.

- Women internalize gender roles and the prescribed morality of "what is good for us women," making them feel guilty and anxious about transgressions;

---

[1]   *Women and Mental Health: Planning gender sensitive community interventions*, a workshop report, 17-18th September, 1999, YMCA, Pune, India, *www.camhindia.org/wamh_report.html*

- Privacy is considered to be a "virtue," and so the disclosure of family violence is taboo;
- The perpetrator's mood-swings between extreme violence and extreme affection are confusing to women;
- A woman's life (and that of her children) has typically been one of dependency, leaving her with few options;
- A women's emotional life is built around caring and giving support, so breaking family bonds is very difficult.

Experience at Maher bears out these factors in many cases. Beyond these are the grim facts of widespread illiteracy, poverty, lack of education, caste and religious conflicts, and a lack of awareness among women of their rights and options for legal recourse. A significant portion of Maher's work is educating women about these matters and supporting them to take decisive steps on their own behalf that they would otherwise be unlikely to take.

◊ ◊ ◊

Reena was a young widow who arrived at Maher in very bad shape. She was barely able to lift her head and say her name. She had been married at a very tender age, and shortly before she turned nineteen her husband died. He had cirrhosis of the liver, exacerbated by heavy drinking.

Once she became a widow, Reena's life in her home village was basically ruined, despite her young years.

The plight of widows in India is bleak indeed (as depicted, for example, in Deepa Mehta's film, *Water*, which was banned in India but won an Oscar nomination in the West). Widows are not socially accepted in Indian society and are regarded as a bad omen wherever they go. A widow cannot participate in the forefront of any public or family function but must always remain in the background. Otherwise, if anything should go wrong, the blame is automatically placed on her. She becomes a heavy burden to her dead husband's family, as well as to her own. A widow is not allowed to remarry and must spend the rest of her life in mourning, whereas a widower can remarry the moment his wife dies. As Mahatma Gandhi wryly observed, "Men have ordained perpetual widowhood for women, and conferred on themselves the right to fix marriage with another partner on the cremation-ground itself."

Reena was given extensive counseling as well as training at Maher. She became a kindergarten teacher for some of the Maher children. Later she was trained to be a housemother. In this role, she continued to improve and gain confidence, and her courage began to grow. After a year's time, Reena wanted to work outside Maher, and the staff helped her to find a job in Pune. Within a few months she met a man in Pune who was a security guard, originally from Mumbai, and they fell in love. While he had some concerns early on that Reena was a widow, after he spoke to Maher staff his reservations were cleared up. Reena wanted to marry him, and Maher helped that to happen in a very quiet way because of the incredible stigma associated with a widow's remarrying. She would not likely have dared to take such a bold step were it not for Maher. She and her husband have a court (legal) marriage, but they couldn't hold a large public ceremony, as they would have done had Reena not been a widow.

Reena had brought two children from her previous marriage with her to Maher. After her marriage, the children remained at Maher for several months to give the newly married couple time to adjust to their married life together. After this period they took the children back, and now the family of four is living happily together in Pune. Her past as a widow is no longer a factor in her life. Her new friends and community accept her as a married woman without the stigma of being a widow because they know nothing about her past.

Reena was at Maher for a total of nearly two years, and she keeps in frequent touch with her many friends and supporters there.

CHALLENGES FROM IRATE HUSBANDS AND FAMILY MEMBERS

"I can have you disappeared within thirty minutes' time!" the man thundered at Lucy, his eyes blazing with fiery rage. Lucy and Hira stood together in the doorway, blocking the man's entrance. His wife had taken refuge at Maher two days earlier, and he had been outraged by her disappearance. He found out where she was, and it was 11 PM when he arrived on Maher's doorstep—drunk—demanding that his wife come home with him. It was not the first time that an irate husband had threatened to kill Lucy, or one of the other Maher staff.

The putrid-sweet odor of alcohol was strong in the gentle breeze that wafted through the doorway. "Yes, I know you can," replied Sister Lucy firmly, without flinching. "And if you kill me, three things will happen. First, it will not bring your wife back. Maher will go on without me, and shelter for your wife will continue here unabated. Second, I will die a peaceful death, knowing that I have lived a worthwhile and meaningful life. And third, you will go on living in even greater misery than you are already in right now."

Flabbergasted, the man shifted his feet uncomfortably. He remained speechless for several difficult moments, unused to having his threats and attempts at intimidation thwarted. Lucy and Hira stood motionless in the doorway, holding their ground. After a few moments, the man suddenly scowled, turned briskly on his heels, and disappeared into the night. Lucy encountered him on several other occasions over the next couple of years as negotiations between him and his wife continued during the time his wife was staying at Maher. But after that night he remained always nervous and uncomfortable in Lucy's presence, and he never threatened her again.

Irate husbands or other family members showing up on Maher's doorstep has been a frequent occurrence over the years. The staff has dealt with these situations in various ways, usually by talking the person(s) down out of their anger to a point where they leave of their own accord. At times it has been necessary to call in the police, who have been quick to respond. Lucy took special care early on to form good relations with the local officials, and Maher maintains a healthy relationship with all the law enforcement agencies in the area. This has proved very beneficial at those times when outside force has been needed. For the most part, however, as Maher has gained a greater reputation in the area and a high level of respect from the locals, such incidents have been less frequent than they were in the earlier days.

FOLLOW-UP AND SUPPORT FOR WOMEN AFTER THEY LEAVE MAHER

The average length of stay at Maher is three months, but it varies widely, depending on each woman's particular needs and circumstances. When they arrive at Maher, the women are typically depressed, angry, and frustrated. Many are also quite shy and not willing or able to speak in depth about their situation. An Indian woman leaving her home and family entails a strong social stigma and often a sense of personal failure. Even when her case is totally justified, the woman often feels embarrassed or ashamed that she could not make her marriage or family life work. Many Indian women are under tremendous pressure from their own families, parents, siblings, and friends to simply endure the abuse. So it can be a big step just to break away and come to a place like Maher.

When it comes time for women to leave Maher, they typically depart with courage and determination to do something meaningful with their lives. They have the benefit not only of the healing work they have done and the personal empowerment that comes from having lived among empowered women, but also the examples of other women who came to Maher and have gone on to make better lives for themselves.

Maher staff generally keep in touch with women who have left Maher for about two years, depending on the particular situation. Its social workers visit their homes periodically and stay in contact with them by telephone and/or letters (or e-mail if it's available). The long-term follow-up gives women an important safety net of support and helps them to build and maintain confidence as they reenter their family unit, community, and society.

Perhaps most important, Maher's follow-up and support for a woman after she leaves sends a clear message to her husband and in-laws that she has strong backing from the Maher organization, and serves as an ever-present reminder that she has somewhere to go should things take a turn for the worse. This fact alone goes a long way toward preventing potentially destructive behavior from her husband and in-laws because she has a practical and effective resource to fall back on should it become necessary. Moreover, if she chooses to exercise this option, her village and community will generally come to know about it. Thus, if things go awry, the family's abuse of the woman will tend to become community knowledge, and this alone serves as a strong deterrent.

Nevertheless, there are cases in which the abuse repeats itself after the woman leaves Maher to return home, and when this happens she often returns. Maher always takes these women back, of course, and the staff try to determine the factors behind the return and what practical steps can be taken to address the continuing problem. Sometimes the fault lies with the woman rather than with her husband or other family members, in which case Maher works to correct her behavior.

There are also cases of women who left Maher prematurely and returned to abusive situations, even though they were strongly advised by Maher staff not to leave out of concern for their safety or their weak condition. In some instances this has led to an unfortunate turn of events. One woman had a mental breakdown when she was not able to cope with the tensions she encountered at home after leaving Maher.

Maher is not a panacea, and there are never any guarantees of healing or resolution in any given case. The staff do the best they can in each case, and every case is unique. But for women who can rise to the occasion and are willing to help themselves, the results of their time at Maher are often nothing short of miraculous.

◊ ◊ ◊

This chapter barely scratches the surface of the multitude of stories of the courageous women who have found their way to Maher. And for each story there are millions of similar stories of Indian women who have never heard about Maher and have not had the benefit of support from such a project. Although their stories remain untold, perhaps their plight can be glimpsed through the stories recounted here, and perhaps the healing stories of women at Maher can be the beginning of their healing as well.

CHAPTER 11

No *Chai Pani* Here!

If you stand straight, do not fear a crooked shadow.
—Chinese Proverb

"What do you know about these people?" asked Sunil as he drove with his colleague, Anil, through the hot bumpy streets of Pune in their company's shiny air-conditioned automobile. "Not much. But I guess they must be pretty eccentric," Anil replied, as he honked the horn repeatedly to pass an auto rickshaw, then veered sharply at the last minute to avoid an oncoming truck. "With a name like 'Mother's Home,' it seems they should be very accommodating," Sunil chuckled.

Sunil and Anil were employees in the local government planning office, and they had been dispatched on a mission to complete the inspection and approval process for a proposed new building at an organization called Maher. "I understand they have a bit of a reputation for these kinds of problems," said Anil thoughtfully, "but let's see."

The car screeched to a stop at a major intersection in Pune behind a large bus spewing plumes of black exhaust fumes directly at their windshield. Beggars appeared, knocking on the side windows, extending their hands and arms with pitiful expressions on their faces. Some of them had only a stub or perhaps a single finger where their hands used to be because they had been cut off when they were young by their parents or beggar ringleaders to make them more compelling beggars. Anil waved them off in habitual disdain, but one beggar woman at his window was especially tenacious. She was short and of slight frame and held a sickly looking baby on her arm. Her stare was determined, and aimed directly at Anil's eye level. She knocked gently on the window, then made gestures of feeding the baby with one hand while holding out the other toward Anil. He shook his head vigorously and exclaimed "No! No!" through the closed window. He looked away from her, but she knocked on the window again and repeated the hand gestures, at which point Anil rolled down the window in anger and rattled off a sharp reprimand in Marathi. "Get away from here! Nothing for you!" He rolled the window up as the car lurched forward, leaving the woman and her baby in a swirling cloud of dust and vehicle exhaust.

Lucy and Hira were engrossed in a conversation about how to handle a challenging new case that had just arrived at Maher that morning when the slick government automobile pulled up. Sunil and Anil got out of the car and came up the steps, brushing the dust off their impeccable clothing and glossy shoes. Seena greeted them warmly and confirmed that they had arrived at the right place. She asked if they would like some tea, and then gracefully excused herself to summon Lucy and Hira. As they waited, the two gentlemen walked idly around the front office, looking at the notices and artwork on the walls. Lucy and Hira came in, greeted them heartily, and invited them to sit. Manda disappeared into the kitchen to prepare the tea, and Seena began assembling the children in the sanctuary to welcome the visitors.

As Manda brought the tea and cookies, Lucy and Hira began outlining the Maher project and its different programs. The men asked a few questions, and then Seena reappeared, announcing that the children would like to welcome the two distinguished visitors to Maher. Hira shot a knowing smile at Lucy as the men were led into the sanctuary in the adjacent building.

The children began singing the customary Maher greeting song. Both visitors were taken aback when mobs of children ran up to each of them and threw their tiny arms around their legs and waists in hugs of love. Sunil glanced over at Anil, who was laughing nervously as he tried to gingerly wrest his arm free from three boys who were fascinated by the large digital watch on his wrist. The boys were punching the small buttons on the watch with great enthusiasm, shrieking with delight each time it made a beeping sound. Hira and Seena began peeling the children away from the startled men as two Maher girls approached, one with red aarti powder and the other holding a butter lamp. The first girl placed a dab of bright red powder between the eyebrows of both men, and the other girl ceremoniously moved the butter lamp in circles as a blessing. Then two boys came up with garlands of flowers and motioned for the visitors to bow their heads while they carefully draped the garlands over their heads and rested them on their shoulders.

The men smiled, thanked the children, and bowed to them, saying "*Namaskar,*" a respectful blessing expressing thanks. Lucy offered them a tour of Maher's facilities, but Sunil politely declined, explaining that their time was short and they should complete their business meeting so they could get back to their office. "At least come and see the new building site for which we applied for planning permission!" Lucy beamed. This was, after all, the purpose of their visit. Sunil consented and the four of them went out to see the plot of land that had been surveyed for the new building. Lucy showed where the building would be located according to the architects' plan, and explained how this building would make a big difference in Maher's ability to provide its daily services to needy women and children. Sunil and Anil were impressed and expressed their approval, thanking Lucy for showing them the site. Sunil then suggested they go back to the office.

Smiling, Lucy ushered them into the Maher office. The men sat down as Manda brought in another round of tea. "We are pleased to

163

inform you that the planning process is nearly complete," Sunil began. "The architects' plan, building site, septic system and soil quality, and proposed utility connections have all been reviewed and approved. The only remaining item is due consideration of 30,000 rupees to expedite the process."

"Due consideration? What is this? Some sort of *chai pani*?" Lucy asked, knowing full well the answer. *Chai* literally means "tea," and *pani* means "water," or some other cold drink, and *chai pani* is the vernacular term used throughout India for petty bribes. "I understood that building permits are issued entirely free of charge by the government!" Lucy exclaimed.

"Of course they are free!" Sunil stammered indignantly. He drew in a deep breath and exhaled slowly before continuing. "It's just that the process can take a very long time." Sunil let his words sink in. Anil sat next to him, silent and stone-faced. Lowering his voice, Sunil continued in a slow, condescending tone. "With all due respect, Sister, do you have any idea how many building permit applications our office receives every month? Unless there is a way to expedite the process, the approval can be delayed so long that the permit application expires." Sunil uncrossed his legs and leaned closer toward Lucy, his face taking on an expression of feigned concern. "The work you are doing here is such noble and important service. Surely you don't wish to delay the construction of this new facility, do you? That would deny the destitute women and children the vital services you are providing to them." He sat back again. "Can you understand what I'm saying here?"

Lucy understood all too well what Sunil was saying. He was demanding a bribe, but not willing to call it such. Maher had already applied for this same building permit three times, each time complying fully with all applicable regulations and deadlines. Each time the permit application period expired before the approval was granted. In effect, Maher was consistently denied the building permit. After three rounds of this, the local authorities had seen fit to dispatch Sunil and

Anil to make a personal visit to Maher in order to coerce or manipulate Lucy into complying with their illegal demand for a bribe.

Lucy had always adamantly refused to pay any bribes. Over the years, this policy had already created a number of practical challenges for Maher. It took more than two years for another Maher building to have its electric utility service connected because Maher refused to pay a bribe. Moreover, Maher itself had developed something of a reputation in the region for refusing to play the bribery game.

◊ ◊ ◊

Corruption and graft are rampant in Indian society. According to Ramesh Thakur, author of *The Government and Politics of India,*

> People are forced to pay bribes for securing virtually any service connected with the government, even that which is theirs by right and law. Graft is said to lubricate the wheel of government in India, to bring the costs of services in line with market prices . . . Political interference, reduced attractiveness of service, and declining morale have all combined to whittle away officials' will to remain honest. India is notorious for its influence-peddling politicians, money-seeking bureaucrats and bribe-dispensing entrepreneurs. Bribery is so thoroughly institutionalized that most people engaged in the transactions are fully aware of the scale of the charges, and the lateral and upwards percentage shares in the illicit rent.

Thakur reports that in one state of India police officers dislike being posted to districts with low crime because their earning power is directly related to crime levels. Officers extract bribes from victims before registering crimes, and from criminals on pain of arrest. Some officers deliberately foment lawlessness in order to line their pockets with bribes.

The India Corruption Study 2007, published by Transparency International and the Centre for Media Studies, found that about one-third of Indian households that were below the poverty line had bribed officials to avail themselves of eleven basic services—ranging from water and electricity supply to hospital and police services. According to the survey, which covered 22,728 households in all states of India, an estimated 8,830 million rupees (about 240 million US dollars) was paid as bribes in 2007.[1] A corruption watchdog group called Transparency International in Berlin ranked India as the worst performer on its global Bribe Payers Index, which is based on the propensity of companies from the world's thirty leading exporting countries to pay bribes abroad.[2]

In Maher's case, refusal to pay bribes has been a source of tension for the organization. Trusted and well-meaning business advisors have counseled that Maher should accede to pay bribes under certain circumstances. Their argument is that bribes are simply part of the routine cost of doing business in India, and everyone does it because it's the only way to get things done. Otherwise, these well-meaning advisors have warned, Maher will not only delay or preclude the provision of vital services, but it will not be able to grow in the future. "Fine!" Lucy would reply to these arguments. "Then Maher will not grow. If Maher cannot grow without paying bribes, then Maher need never be any bigger than it is today!"

◊ ◊ ◊

Lucy gave Sunil a long, searching gaze, and replied, "Ah yes, I certainly do understand." Her face lit up with a smile, and she said, "Please come with me." Both men stood up, and Sunil shot a pregnant glance to

---

[1]   www.expressindia.com/latest-news/BPL-households-paid-Rs-8-830-mn-as-bribe-in-2007/329282/

[2]   www.dnaindia.com/report.asp?NewsID=1056700

Anil, feeling pleased with himself for having "talked sense" into Lucy and confident that he was about to receive the money. Lucy walked briskly out of the building and crossed the road, with Sunil and Anil in tow. She led them to the large room where the women's production circle and children's study classes were conducted.

Lucy drew Sunil and Anil to one side, and began whispering to them. The men leaned forward to listen. "I'm sure you understand that at Maher we have to be as frugal as possible," she began. "The women and children have enough to eat and a roof over their heads, but nothing extra." In the corner a small group of children erupted into peels of laughter, and Lucy paused until they became quiet again. "The women stay here for an average of three months," she continued, "and our monthly cost for four women and four children is more than 10,000 rupees. So in order to pay your 'due consideration' I would have to pluck out four of these women and four of these children, and put them back on the street." Lucy turned to face Sunil and Anil directly. "So, now I would like you to choose which ones are to go. Please, you decide. Walk around the room and take a good look at all these women and children. Then come back to me and point out which four women and which four children are to be put out on the street!"

Sunil and Anil were speechless at first, as Lucy's words sunk in. Then Anil started to mumble something, but Sunil interrupted. "That's ridiculous!" he blurted with a shudder. "How could you be so callous?!" Lucy replied calmly, "It's neither ridiculous nor callous. It's the simple reality. You are asking me to pay you a bribe of 30,000 rupees to have you grant us a building permit, which by all legal rights should cost us nothing. And I'm asking you to take personal responsibility for the practical consequences of paying such a bribe—were I to pay it, which I will not!"

"Let's go!" Sunil muttered to Anil, and the two men turned on their heels and strode quickly out of the room. Lucy followed and called after them, "I'm glad to see that you can no more stand to put these women and children back on the street than I can. That gives me hope!" Sunil glanced back at Lucy, half scowling and half intimidated, then spun around, jumped into the car with Anil, and they sped off.

Two weeks later, Maher received the building permit.

One might well make the same observation about Lucy Kurien that was made of the great Christian mystic, Saint Teresa of Avila: "Men encountered in her a woman who was more fully a man than they were, while she was also fully a woman."[3]

---

[3] J.G. Bennett, *Sex: The Relationship between Sex and Spiritual Development* (York Beach, Maine: Samuel Weiser, 1981).

CHAPTER 12

To the Dancer Belongs the Universe

Praise the name of God with dancing!—Psalm 149:3

"You won't last more than two weeks!" Ila's mother thundered. "It's an interior village you're talking about. You have no idea of the harsh conditions under which these poor people live!"

Ila Tiwari had just announced to her parents that she was considering moving to Maher to serve the women and children there. This meant not only that she would have to move more than a thousand miles away from her comfortable home in a modern upscale neighborhood of New Delhi but that she would have to resign her coveted post as a lecturer of Indian classical music at a college in Firozabad near Agra.

"I have to go," Ila responded. "It's something I know I must do." A friend had recently shown Ila the Maher nine-minute video and she had been so inspired by what she saw and what her friend told her about the project that she felt a strong inner calling to go and experience it herself. She wanted to teach the women and children at Maher classical Indian dance.

"What about your students here in Delhi?" her mother demanded. "What about your dance performances? What about your own master training?" Ila's mother's concern was eminently understandable. This was a radical change her daughter was contemplating—turning away from a glamorous career, full of promise, to teach dance to the poor. Ila was in her late twenties, and she was already both a successful dance performer and a lecturer in Indian classical music. She and her family knew full well what a unique and coveted position she held at the college in Firozabad, a position not to be abandoned lightly. It was something for which she had worked hard throughout her life; Ila had been committed to dance and music since childhood. Now she would be turning away from this bright career path—and from her sheltered upbringing in a well-to-do educated urban family—to move into a poor community in rural India to give dance lessons to battered women and destitute children. To Ila's family, the idea was preposterous.

"Dance is not just an art form reserved for the cultivated and the elite," Ila protested. "It is for everyone. Dance inspires the soul, and through dance, the human body becomes transformed into a temple inhabited by the gods!" Ila was articulating one of the great secrets of the Indian classical dance tradition. "We are in grave danger of losing the depth and true purpose of our profound dance heritage in India," she continued. "As the Western dance forms and attitudes gain ever more prominence here, our own tradition of classical dance is eroding and vanishing, or else it gets watered down into some glamorous performance spectacle."

Ila's passion had always been one of her stronger qualities, and her parents realized as she spoke how determined she was. Ila was motivated by a profound conviction about the deeper purpose of Indian dance. "It is through our dance heritage that the true spirit of India comes fully alive," she continued, her eyes shining fiercely. "We must preserve this tradition and pass it on so it can sustain and inspire all those who embrace and practice it! Dance belongs to the people as an ecstatic practice that expresses the Divine, and not just to the universities or art schools as a cultivated art form to be performed by the few."

Ila went on to explain that the Western dance forms themselves are not the real problem, but rather the Westernized values in relation to dance. "Indian dance is not meant to be assessed and evaluated according to precise artistic categories or observational criteria, like ballet," she insisted. "Indian dance is not an outer discipline of cultivated poise and performance—it is an inner discipline of spiritual transformation. The true purpose of dance is not to show off oneself or one's talents, but to allow the Divine to reveal itself, using the human body as its instrument. For that, the dancer's self-importance and personal ego have to go. Yet much of what's happening today in professional dance is just the opposite—building up the dancer's ego. Indian classical dance is thus in danger of becoming an outer spectacle of artistic glamour and technical virtuosity, rather than an inner communion with God."

Yet, much as her family admired her idealistic principles, they were aware that Ila had been born and bred in a privileged, sheltered family of the highest Brahmin caste. She was highly educated and living in a sophisticated, modern urban context. It was the only life she had ever known. Her parents were understandably concerned about how she would manage, being suddenly thrust into a poverty-stricken rural village community of abused women and destitute children who themselves had just been rescued from the clutches of violation and starvation. It was a daunting proposition. "It took over two months to convince my friends and family that I was serious, that I really was moving to Maher," Ila recalled. "For the first time in my life, I was doing something. Before that, it was always my life, my goals—I always felt, I have to go high, perform widely on stage, become somebody. I only thought about myself. I was a lecturer with a handsome salary, and also did acting and some modeling on the side. Maher gave me a new way of life—it changed my thinking, my personality. Now I'm a true person. Now I can face myself. Now I'm living life."

INDIAN CLASSICAL DANCE

In the cosmology of Hinduism, the entire universe is a manifestation of the dance of the Supreme Dancer, known as Shiva Nataraja. As Lord of dance, Shiva is said to have created the universe with His

Ila Tiwari, founder of Maher's dance program.

Ananda Tandavam, or the dance of joy. It is He we see dancing in the rise and fall of the waves in the oceans, in volcanoes and earthquakes, in lightning and thunder, and in the revolving planets and galaxies. All movements within the cosmos are said to be His dance.

According to Indian mythology, dance was created in ancient times during a period when the world was steeped in anger and jealousy, greed and anguish. The people went to Lord Brahma to seek an end to this misery, and Brahma created the Natya Veda, the fifth scripture, to save humanity from deterioration from moral values. Brahma created this Veda by taking elements from the four principal Vedas and revealed them to the Sage Bharata, who wove them into a grand Vedic drama. Sage Bharata took this to Lord Shiva, who added dance movements to the drama, and thus were dance and drama created. The resulting Natya Shastra, written by Sage Bharata (and probably subsequent contributors) is the oldest and most exhaustive scriptural text on dance and drama in the world. It covers stage design, music, dance, makeup, and virtually every aspect of stagecraft, and forms the common basis for the Indian classical tradition of music, dance, drama and iconography.

Every deity in the Hindu pantheon has a particular style of dance, and there are twenty-three celestial beings, called *apsaras*, who express the supreme divine truths through the magic of movement. Dance is a sacred movement of the physical limbs while being infused with deep divine presence and feeling. The accompanying music is purely devotional, with the dancer as the devotee and God as the beloved. When the dancer becomes infused or taken over by the divine beloved, not only is (s)he transported to a higher plane of consciousness, but the audience is also transported to this higher spiritual plane.

Dances were originally performed in the temples as the highest form of worship to God. The temple dances gradually evolved into what is known today as Indian classical dance, which still preserves many ritualistic elements of Hinduism. There are many specific forms of Indian dance, such as Bharat Natyam, Odissi, Kathak, and others, that developed in different regions. Some of the classical Indian dancers are believed to be incarnations of apsaras.

Down through the ages, dance has always symbolized the best and noblest aspect of India's glorious cultural heritage. A renewed interest in Indian dance forms over the past fifty years has helped to develop the contemporary styles. Many glories of past traditions have been uncovered, and are sometimes presented in new forms and technique. The purpose and spirit of Indian dance is beautifully expressed by Sudha Chandrasekhar, a leading teacher of Indian dance for more than fifty years: "With the Lord's name on my lips, and my heart singing His glories, and my feet ever dancing to His rhythms, I shall abide . . . He will be there always, till the end and beyond . . ."

◊ ◊ ◊

Ila Tiwari packed her bags, left her post at the college, and made her move to Maher with her parents' hesitant but sincere blessing. She began teaching dance to the women and children at Maher, holding classes for the children early each morning before they went to school. She also managed to find a master dance teacher in Pune with whom she was able to continue her own training discipline and practice. "When I moved to Maher, I did have some problems at first," Ila confided. "I used to cry suddenly at times, and I missed my family, friends, and the city life terribly. I missed going out for dinners, outings, television, entertainment, and all that. At Maher there was nowhere to go. But then I fell in love with the children and the women, and this made all the difference."

It was not long before the children and women fell in love with their dance classes. Ila taught them many different forms and movements from Indian classical dance as well as folk dance of North India. Soon the children began performing at Maher's informal celebrations, street theater productions, and religious festivals. Before long, the children were performing in Maher's larger public gatherings, which are well attended by people from surrounding villages. Special costumes were designed and created for this purpose, and the Maher dancers began to take their craft ever more seriously.

After a couple of years, the Maher dancers began to gain a bit of a reputation in the area. They were invited repeatedly to perform in Pune, and then in Mumbai. A major performance opportunity for the troupe came in December of 2006, when they were invited to give a performance at the opening of a large national conference in Mumbai. The conference was organized by the National Regeneration Movement of India, led by Swami Sachidananda Bharath from Kerala. Several hundred professionals and laypersons from all over India came to address pressing questions of social change and development throughout India.

Classical Indian dance is taught daily at Maher for children, and weekly for women.

The Maher dancers piled into a bus for the four-hour journey to Mumbai, where they delivered a beautiful performance of three dances as the opening to the conference (see photo on p. 185). The authors were privileged to witness this auspicious moment for Maher, and the resounding applause afterward gave hearty assurance to the children that their efforts were appreciated. As Cynthia Brix later described it, "Tears ran down my cheeks as my heart filled with immense joy. I felt an overwhelming sense of pride, as any mother would for her own children. My mind flashed with images of where these children had come from—what their lives must have been like before Maher. Now, to see these kids on a national stage, lifted up and revered for their beauty and their dance, was a very sacred and holy moment." The conference organizers announced to the audience afterward that these were poor children of battered women, beggars, and prostitutes who had been rehabilitated at Maher. That night the children stayed at a local hostel in Mumbai, and they left to go home to Maher the next morning.

Shortly after they arrived back in Vadhu Budruk the next after-noon, there was a telephone call from the conference organizers, who told Ila they were so impressed with the children's performance they would like to invite them to return to Mumbai to give the same dance performance at the close of the conference—in just two days' time. Ila was gratified to hear their enthusiasm, and a bit taken back by this second invitation. She paused to consider what it would mean for the children's school schedule and their other lessons. After consulting with Hira briefly, the two quickly decided that the children could indeed return for another performance, except this time they would perform different dances. Ila explained this to the conference organizers, who were pleased but said they wanted the exact same performance the children had just completed. Ila con-firmed that they would come back, but she didn't promise that the performance would be exactly the same, knowing full well that the Maher community would want to prepare a fresh performance for the occasion.

The next two days were a flurry of activity as Ila choreographed a new dance and the children worked tirelessly with her to rehearse it and to prepare the props. The theme chosen for this dance was some-thing dear to everyone in the Maher community: the essential unity of all world religions. The Maher staff, women, and children all felt this theme was a vibrant expression of the heart of Maher and a key message to convey to a conference on the regeneration of India. There was much to be done to get ready. Large, colorful, round placards were made for each major world religion depicting the primary symbol(s) of that religion. The placards were carefully designed, crafted, and painted, then attached to beautifully decorated handles so the dancers could display them prominently as part of the dance.

Once again, the Maher dance troupe piled into the bus to make the journey back to Mumbai. They arrived and prepared their cos-tumes. By this time the audience was primed, and eager to see their new performance. The children opened with one of the dances they had done for the conference opening. Then they announced that they had prepared a special dance just for this occasion, which was both an important expression of the Maher community and the blessing they wanted to offer to the conference.

The Maher dancers then began performing their new dance, and it was exquisitely executed. As the women and children danced and crisscrossed the stage—weaving the placards in and out—the world's major religions were symbolically interwoven into a grand unified tapestry. The Hindu *OM* symbol, the Christian cross, the Muslim Crescent moon and star, the Buddhist wheel of dharma, the Taoist yin-yang, the Jewish Star of David, and the symbols for Jainism, Sikhism, Zoroastrianism, and indigenous and other religions were all choreographed into a glorious unitive dance.

The effect of the dance was at once enchanting and spellbinding. The audience was deeply moved watching these women and children— many of whom had suffered or witnessed some of the most brutal violations and degradations imaginable—now dancing in ecstatic joy and celebration of the Divine in all religions. When the dance concluded, there was a moment of deep silence, then a resounding round of applause and cheers. The audience gave the Maher dancers a standing ovation. It was a triumphant moment for Maher, for the dancers, for Lucy and Ila, for the Maher staff, and for the unitive spiritual vision that Maher stands for.

DANCE AS THERAPY

Dance serves not only as performance art, but as a powerful adjunct to healing and therapy for the women and children at Maher. For example, there was one girl who came to Maher after having been raped continually over a period of two months when she was ten years old. While dancing, at times she would suddenly become very agitated and wild and start hitting her head against the wall, fiercely pulling at her hair. Tremendous rage and violence would pour out of her, and then she would collapse, crying bitterly.

Ila had no idea what was going on, and at first did not know how to respond. After it had happened two or three times, she pulled the girl aside and asked her what was causing her agitated behavior. The girl replied, "When I dance, all my body shakes, and then I remember when my cousin used to rape me. He used to lock the door when no one was home, and I could not say a word!" The girl had been living with her grandmother, and the rapes took place when her grandmother went to work. Once Ila knew what was disturbing this girl, she was able to help her process and release her strong emotions through the dance. "Over time we saw a miraculous change in that girl," Ila said with great joy. "She is much better now. Dancing really helped her to heal."

Ila continued, "I have seen similar healing effects with several of the children and women. There was one boy who had a reputation for being a bit of a bad kid—he was quite aggressive and often used foul language. I worked with him in dance, and over time he really took to it. His mother had AIDS, and one day we learned that she had died. We had an important dance performance that day, and the sad news came in shortly before the performance was supposed to begin. We debated about whether to tell him, but we had no choice. The boy was shocked, of course, and very sad. But then, when he noticed how we were scrambling to redesign the choreography to adjust for his absence, he suddenly announced, "No, I will dance." We were all surprised, thinking that he could not possibly dance after just receiving such painful news about such a huge personal loss. But he pulled himself together and insisted that he must dance. "The whole performance will be wrecked if any one of us is not there," he explained in earnest. "I'm fine, and I must do this dance!" So he danced, and very beautifully, and we all felt such admiration and compassion for him. I was so moved by him this day, and could not keep from crying.

I felt he was teaching me, as I watched this young boy of eight or nine dancing out of a deep sense of duty. Afterward, he sank into his grief and cried bitterly about his mother's passing, but not before he had upheld his commitment to the Maher dance troupe.

"The women are so happy when they dance," Ila exclaimed. "You can see how they burst into laughter, and they want to show each other what they can do. They realize their dignity and grace as women, and it helps them to realize they should never have been thrown about and abused like they were. They feel, *we are women, and we are graceful.* They are excited—we have classes on Mondays and they look forward to it all week. After dancing, they are much more relaxed and calm. It provides an important release for them, and a needed change."

Dance at Maher has also served at times as a kind of therapeutic balm for healing relationships. For example, there was a young woman named Urvasi and her six-year-old daughter Tarini who had come to Maher. Urvasi's story was tragic. She had been brutally raped when she was sixteen, and became pregnant as a result. She was then totally shunned by her family and ruthlessly expelled from her village community for bearing the child out of wedlock, despite the fact that all of this was entirely beyond her control. Urvasi was bitter about this double twist of cruel fate, and she took it out on her daughter Tarini, whom she despised as the rotten fruit of the rape that had ruined her life. Urvasi wanted to kill Tarini, and in her early days at Maher there were times when she had to be separated from her daughter for the child's safety.

Over time, relations gradually improved between Urvasi and Tarini, and the dance classes helped immensely. As luck would have it, both mother and daughter were very talented at dance, and Ila took advantage of this and worked diligently with each of them separately to cultivate their respective talents. She took every opportunity to express to Urvasi how skilled and beautiful her daughter was as a dancer, and she frequently pulled Tarini aside to tell her how magnificently her mother danced, quietly whispering that she was better than Ila herself. Ila also made sure that Urvasi attended all of Tarini's performances, and vice versa.

It took time, and there were some awkward adjustments for Urvasi as she struggled to step into her new role as a dance performer. Ila confided in an interview with the authors that she was quite nervous the first time she asked Urvasi to dance at a major performance, with more than a thousand people attending. But Urvasi rose to the occasion and performed exquisitely. As time went on, Urvasi developed a new confidence and sense of self that she had never known. Of greater importance, a new bond emerged between Urvasi and Tarini. This bond grew ever stronger as the two began to perform together. In several Maher performances mother and daughter performed magnificently together on stage, and this had a major healing effect on their relationship.

Ila remained at Maher for three years—living and working to bring dance and music to its residents and staff. During her tenure, the Maher dance troupe grew from its humble beginnings into a professional group performing in numerous prominent venues in Pune and Mumbai. After three years Ila left Maher to be married and join her new husband in Delhi, but the dance program she founded continues to develop and thrive. "The children have developed real confidence at Maher, and the dance program has helped a lot," Ila said. "Before coming to Maher, many had a kind of inferiority complex, feeling that they were poor and downtrodden. Now they radiate a wonderful sense of prosperity of the spirit, which they share with enthusiasm and grace in their dance performances."

NEW DANCE TEACHERS AT MAHER

The large community room at Maher reverberated with chatter, laughter, and an occasional baby's cry as Sheetal stood in the middle of this unfamiliar territory, not exactly sure why she was here. Knowing that Sheetal was interested in volunteering with some project, a friend had recommended that she visit Maher. This isn't exactly what I had in mind, Sheetal thought, looking around reluctantly and trying to find a place to sit on the floor among all the women and children. This was the first time she had ever shared a meal with people of a lower caste than she was. She was a "city girl" from Pune and not accustomed to the rural, village ways of Vadhu Budruk. Sheetal tried to push away the discomfort she felt in every cell of her body and let herself trust the larger unknown wisdom that had brought her to this place called Maher.

Over the next several months Sheetal returned time and time again to Maher, never quite knowing what the attraction was, but continuing to trust whatever was unfolding. She was not a particularly religious person, and her life seemingly had little to do with "spiritual things." She spent her days working at a bank as a financial analyst and her evenings and weekends with friends going to the clubs and movies or shopping. She loved to shop and buy nice things to wear and to decorate her apartment. Being single and without children, Sheetal had the money and time to enjoy the material advantages that life offered.

Dance instructor Satish Sakinal (left) and choreographer Sheetal Kharka (right).

Over the previous year, however, all of this had become less and less fulfilling—life was a bit drab and routine. Sheetal longed to do more for others, to share some of her good fortune. She had thought of helping destitute women and children before, but being in this new environment and interacting with people so radically different from herself was challenging. Inwardly, She wondered why she kept returning to Maher. Her friends and family certainly didn't understand this desire she had, and they questioned her spending so much time with destitute women and children. Yet Sheetal couldn't deny how good and uplifted she felt each time she went to Maher. Everyone was so accepting of her and so happy when she visited. She was also aware that whenever she went away, her mind was flooded with thoughts of the children and women.

Like Ila before her, Sheetal answered the strong call from within her heart to serve others, and she too turned away from the familiar comforts of her relatively posh lifestyle. Both took a leap of faith, and in so doing discovered unknown depths within themselves and found a mentor and a friend in Sister Lucy, who guided them in their call to serve. "It took some time for me to adjust to being here," Sheetal said. "Thankfully, Sister Lucy saw my potential and encouraged me to volunteer despite my own personal reservations."

Knowing that Sheetal liked to dance and had a background in stage performance, Lucy approached her one day and said, "I need your help. We have our tenth anniversary coming soon, and we want the children to perform their dances for the celebration. I would like you to choreograph the dances for the program." Lucy had observed Sheetal's love for the children grow over time, and she believed that she would be an excellent teacher. She also knew that the children would be good for Sheetal, helping her to learn more about herself.

Lucy had been searching for a teacher to take over the dance program since Ila had left to be married. On Sheetal's recommendation, Maher hired Satish Rajaram Sakinal, a professional master dancer who

Ritual blessing dance with candles.

performs and teaches Kathak Indian classical dance. Satish happily accepted the position. He did not have the same personal challenges of overcoming high family and societal status that Ila and Sheetal had to go through. His background and upbringing aligned more closely with that of the Maher children and women.

Satish is a man of incredible dedication and commitment—both to his art form and to his students. In the four years since becoming Maher's dance teacher, he has gotten up at 4 AM six days a week to catch a bus and travel more than two hours across the city of Pune to reach Maher by 7 AM so he can conduct dance classes for the children before they go to school. He then takes the bus back to the city, where he continues teaching Kathak dance to other youth.

Developed in North India, Kathak is a dance form characterized by fast and precise footwork (*tatkar*), spins (*chakkar*) and innovative use of *bhav* (spiritual emotions) that are transmitted from performer to audience. There are three major schools of Kathak, developed in Jaipur, Lucknow, and Benares. The name Kathak is derived from the

Sanskrit word *katha*, meaning story, and *katthaka* in Sanskrit means s/he who tells a story, or something that has to do with stories. The dance is thus often narrative in form, depicting specific stories through the medium of dance. Important components of modern Kathak include expressive motion, rhythmic accuracy, graceful turning, poised stances, technical clarity, hand gestures (*mudras*), and subtle expression (*bhava-abhinaya*).

Satish dove into his teaching work in earnest, and Sheetal began choreographing a series of dance sequences for the Maher dancers. Satish was putting the children through their paces—refining their technique and style—every morning, with the girls and the boys alternating days. Sheetal was organizing the dance steps into coherent artistic stage performances. She also refined the scenes in the Gandhi drama, and began rehearsing both the dances and the drama—scene by scene—with the children. It was intensive work, and became all the more absorbing as the time of the performance approached and the pressure mounted. Sheetal felt a tremendous responsibility, knowing that the children would be performing before a few thousand people. Yet she found a whole new strength within herself that she had never known before. For the last month before the performance, she left work every day at 5 PM, drove straight to Maher to get there by 6 PM, ate a quick dinner, and began rehearsing with the children. Rehearsals lasted until 9—sometimes 10—PM. It took everything Sheetal had to keep up the intensity. But the performances were coming together. Lines were forgotten less and less often, and the dance steps all started to fall into place.

Finally the big weekend of Maher's tenth anniversary arrived, and the dance performances came off exquisitely, as described in chapter 13. This was the beginning of a whole new era for the Maher dance troupe. Having performed so beautifully before thousands at such a large venue, invitations to perform elsewhere began pouring in from many sources. The troupe was invited to dance at corporate functions, festivals, and schools throughout the region. They performed at Wadia College, Sangam World Guide Center, and the Pune Festival. Other performances were held in both Pune and Mumbai at corporate functions for HSBC Bank and John Deere. It was a triumph for Maher, for Satish and Sheetal, and most of all for the Maher children who were inspiring audiences wherever they went.

"My life has changed so dramatically," Sheetal said, reflecting back on a time before she came to Maher. She never could have imagined how inspiring it would feel to watch the children perform, and how gratified she would feel to have had the opportunity to help them reach this level of quality performance. "Before coming to Maher, I was very selfish, always thinking about my needs first. Since coming to Maher, I have learned how to truly give to others. And in the process I've realized how much I have been given!"

At the time of this writing (September 2008), Sheetal has just submitted her resignation to the bank where she has worked as a

Maher dancers performing at a conference.

senior financial analyst for many years. The work of Maher has pulled on her heart too much for her to remain in her bank job, despite the financial benefits. She is joining Maher as a full-time volunteer, and she will take a part-time job somewhere to support herself. "We are so happy and grateful to God to have Sheetal with us," Lucy said. "I told her that she will miss a lot of worldly pleasures, but she is not concerned about that. She is a seeker, and Maher has slowly become her passion."

Like all those who commit themselves to Maher, Sheetal will gain far more than she will give up.

CHAPTER 13

Ten-Year Triumph for Maher

Whatsoever you do unto the least of my people, that you do unto Me.
—Matthew (25:40)

Five village schoolgirls were playing jump rope together after school. When they finished, they said goodbye to one another and went on their separate ways. One of the girls was walking through the woods by herself when suddenly a group of five boys appeared, as if out of nowhere. The boys approached the girl in a threatening manner, slapping and ribbing one another with rowdy and aggressive gestures. The girl kept on walking, determined to get home without being bothered by these irksome hooligans.

The boys began to taunt the girl, calling her names and demanding to know where she was going in such a hurry. She refused to talk to them, and kept walking swiftly on her way. But the boys continued to pester her, laughing and joking with each other as they jeered at her. The girl set her jaw firmly, and stepped up her pace with staunch resolve.

The boys' heckling escalated, and they continued to sneer and jibe at her. Suddenly, one boy's arm shot out and pulled at the girl's blouse. Then another yank came at her dress from behind. The boys' gestures toward the girl became increasingly invasive and violent as they egged each other on. The girl's face became visibly distraught, but she kept moving ever faster and began using her arms to fend off the boys' increasingly aggressive advances.

More than 2,500 people were watching—riveted—as the distressing scene unfolded on stage. The girl and the five boys were Maher actors, performing on the occasion of Maher's tenth anniversary, February 2, 2007. Maher's board of trustees had gone all out to put together this gala celebration for the purpose of introducing Maher more widely to prominent citizens of Pune, and India.

The event was held at the Corinthian Club in Pune, a grand and elegant conference center with a large, fully equipped outdoor stage on which the Maher dances and theater performances were held. This magnificent venue was surely expensive—far beyond anything Maher would ever have considered on its own—but the use of the conference center and its professional stage was fully donated for this special occasion by local offices of British and German corporate sponsors of Maher. Visitors and guests came from all over India, and from sixteen foreign countries, including Austria, Australia, Bangladesh, Belgium, England, France, Cambodia, Canada, Germany, Holland, Italy, New Zealand, Pakistan, Scotland, Spain, Sri Lanka, and the United States.

The dramatic enactment on stage continued with the boys stepping up their harassment of the girl. One of the boys seized her schoolbag, wrenched it from her shoulder, and hurled it to the ground. Another yanked off her *dupata* (Indian shawl), tore it in two, and threw down the pieces. In desperation, the girl clenched her fists and began swinging her arms to block the multiple hands grabbing at her. At one point she managed to break free into an open run to make her escape, but one of the boys caught her arm as she fled. He whirled her around and threw her to the ground. The boys then circled around the girl, who was now on her back with arms and legs flailing. They moved slowly around her, wildly gesticulating with their arms and hands. Thus was the gang rape of the girl discretely enacted symbolically.

When the boys were finished with the girl, they tore her sari in half, threw the pieces on her, and departed in a huff, leaving her lying there in agony. She lay still for several moments before sitting up and begin-

Symbolic enactment of gang rape, performed in one of Maher's theater performance skits portraying the violence against women in Indian society.

ning to pull herself together. Wobbly and quivering, she struggled to stand. Picking up the articles of torn clothing and her schoolbag, she began to hobble homeward.

Upon reaching home, the girl blurted out what had happened to her parents, in desperate need of their healing love and care. But her father burst into a screaming rage. "How could you let this happen?!" he thundered. "What will our friends and neighbors say? What will the townsfolk say?" he bellowed. "You have destroyed the family's honor! How will your sister ever get married? You must go! Leave this home at once, and never come back! Never!"

"But where will she go?" asked the girl's mother meekly. "I don't care!" the father roared. "It doesn't matter! She can go anywhere. Or better, she can jump in a well!" The girl's mother and sister were crying bitterly but were unable to do anything to stop the ruthless banishment. The girl was pushed out the door, which was slammed shut behind her. This scenario is actually a common family response in India to girls being raped.

Doubly betrayed—first by the brutal gang rape, then by cruel banishment from her own family—the girl departed the only home she had ever known. She had woken up that morning an innocent, happy girl of fourteen, and gone off to school like any other day. Now, just hours later, her very identity was shattered to the core—from the stabbing violation of the gang rape, to the wrenching rejection by her own parents, to the banishment forever from her home and community.

Utterly devastated, in a state of shock, she sat down on the road crying. As she continued to sit, the girl slowly became aware that several loving women and nurturing girls began to gather around her. They seemed almost like angels from heaven to her as they wiped her tears, put their arms gently around her, helped her stand up, then led her off with a guiding hand. The girl followed them, having no idea where they were taking her, and was led to a wonderful new community of healing and love, which was of course Maher. The drama concluded with the Maher women welcoming this new arrival, taking in the girl with the love and healing nurturance she had not found anywhere else.

The stage lights dimmed slowly, and there were several moments of deep, poignant silence before the applause began. The clapping continued enthusiastically, and the emcee finally stepped forward and thanked the audience, then briefly explained that this tragic scenario, difficult as it was to watch in this brief theatrical drama, is tragically played out in reality in the lives of untold thousands of Indian girls and women every year. And most are never so lucky as to find a Maher to take them in after such a shattering experience.

RAPE IN INDIA

According to several recent media articles (e.g., *Hindustan Times*, Jan 14, 2008), rape is the fastest growing crime in India. The latest (2006) crime statistics released by the Home Ministry's National Crime

Records Bureau (NCRB) show that every hour, eighteen women become victims of crime. The number of rapes a day has increased nearly 700 percent since 1971—the year that rape statistics were first compiled by the NCRB—growing from seven cases per day to fifty-three per day in 2006. In comparison, all other crimes have grown by 300 percent since 1953 when the NCRB started keeping records.

These figures take account only of the cases that have been reported; the number of unreported rapes is far higher. According to some estimates, only one in sixty-nine rape cases in India is reported. Approximately 20 percent of those reported result in convictions for the accused.[1] One reason for the low reporting rate is the tremendous shame and humiliation involved for both victim and perpetuator, so rapes are often hushed up. In the majority of cases, the rapist is a personal acquaintance or family member of the victim, which adds greatly to the pressure to conceal these cases.

According to NCRB figures for 2006, among thirty-five Indian cities with a population of more than a million, Delhi topped the list of crimes against women, with 4,134 reported cases (nearly one-fifth of the total crimes against women).[1] One-third of the rapes and a fifth of the molestations took place in the city. Hyderabad was second most dangerous for women, with 1,755 cases. Among the states, Andhra Pradesh had the highest number of crimes committed against women—21,484, or 13 percent of the total cases, in 2006. Uttar Pradesh was a close second, with 9.9 percent of such crimes. Madhya Pradesh reported the highest number of rape cases, 2,900, and also molestation cases.

Understandably, Indian women who have been victims of rape do not generally speak about it because of the painful stigma of shame and dishonor. At Maher, numerous women and girls are rape victims, and in most cases the rapist was one of their own family members

---

[1]   *http://www.dancewithshadows.com/rapes_india.asp*

or acquaintances. At least twelve girls currently living at Maher were raped by their own fathers.

Given the devastating scale and impact of rape and sexual violence, it is vitally important to find skillful ways to raise awareness about these crimes, not only in India, but in all countries. Rape is a worldwide phenomenon. Wherever it happens, it carries the same crushing shame, anger, and shattering emotional trauma. Shying away from facing this painful reality head on—in the name of social propriety or dignity—can easily become a kind of unwitting complicity of silence that only further perpetuates the brutality of rape. As Martin Luther King, Jr., emphasized, corruption and social injustice can never be transformed by keeping them hidden, but only by bringing them into the open and confronting them with the power of love.

Maher's stage drama about rape does just that—it brings the horror of rape into the light of day with great power as well as sensitivity and discretion. The drama depicts the shattering impact on the rape victim of a tragically common scenario in India in which the rape victim is violated as much or more by her own family and the society as by the rape itself.

The following documented case is a clear example of the pattern. A thirteen-year-old girl in Rajasthan was married in an arranged marriage, and a few weeks after she moved in with her husband, her father-in-law brutally raped her. Totally devastated, she turned to her own parents for healing and justice, but they ruthlessly rejected her for bringing shame upon the family. Her "impurity" would not only permanently stain the family's honor, but it would prevent her sisters from getting married because they would not receive marriage proposals. So her own father demanded that she commit suicide, to save the family honor.[2] In this case, the girl was saved at the last minute by local women activists. But few are so lucky.

---

[2]   Mary Anne Weaver, "Gandhi's Daughters," *The New Yorker*, January 10, 2000.

Mahatma Gandhi was abhorred by these one-sided attitudes about women's purity. "Why is there all this morbid anxiety about female purity? Have women any say in the matter of male purity? We hear nothing of women's anxiety about men's chastity. Why should men arrogate to themselves the right to regulate female purity?"[3] Yet many a young woman's death in India is the direct consequence of having been raped, and then either being killed or forced to commit suicide to save the family's honor. In other cases, if the girl acquiesces to hushing up the rape, her reward is often to be raped repeatedly over time by the same perpetrator.

On top of the grief caused by the actual incident and her family's reaction, the rape victim also has to face ruthless treatment from society. She is typically looked upon as if she is at fault and somehow asked for it. She may be treated as some sort of alien, and is subjected to lecherous and curious looks. If she is unmarried she will usually remain so, because it is very difficult to get a marriage proposal. In the villages, rather than prosecuting the case through legal channels, the girl is often married off to the rapist! If the rape victim is married, her fate depends entirely upon her husband. If he is somewhat broad-minded, he will stay with her; if not, he abandons her. Not only the men, but women too have similar attitudes. There are many women who would not hesitate to defame another woman's character, just to portray themselves as "good" girls.

For the relatively few rape cases that are prosecuted, only a small percentage reaches conviction. The woman is typically bombarded with all manner of humiliating questions, and the cases are withdrawn midway through the legal process. If the perpetrator is influential and rich, it is almost guaranteed that justice will be circumvented. Until recently, there was a provision in the law which said that if the

---

[3]   Usha Thakkar, "Breaking the Shackles: Gandhi's Views on Women," *www. gandhi-manibhavan.org/activities/essay_breakingshackles.htm*

woman were proved to be of a "loose character," the case was automatically dismissed.

According to a UN Population Fund report in 2005, more than two-thirds of married women in India between the ages of fifteen and forty-nine have been beaten, raped, or forced to provide sex. The same report also found that 70 percent of Indian women believed wife beating was justified under certain circumstances, including refusal to provide sex—or preparing dinner late.

Clearly, much work remains to be done. As observed recently in a Punjabi court of law:

> Of late, crime against women in general and rape in particular is on the increase. It is an irony that while we are celebrating woman's rights in all spheres, we show little or no concern for her honor. It is a sad reflection on the attitude of indifference of the society towards the violation of human dignity of the victims of sex crimes. We must remember that a rapist not only violates the victim's privacy and personal integrity, but inevitably causes serious psychological as well as physical harm in the process. Rape is not merely a physical assault—it is often destructive of the whole personality of the victim. A murderer destroys the physical body of his victim, a rapist degrades the very soul of the helpless female. The Courts, therefore, shoulder a great responsibility while trying an accused on charges of rape. They must deal with such cases with utmost sensitivity.[4]

◊ ◊ ◊

---

[4]   *www.thewip.net/contributors/2008/06/understanding rape in india.html*

When the applause died down, the emcee announced the next segment, a speech by one of the Maher benefactors. This was followed by a Kathak classical dance performed by thirty Maher dancers in their colorful attire, swirling all around and stamping their feet as they wove their way among one another.

The evening as a whole was comprised of a beautiful tapestry of dances, inspiring speeches, and anecdotes—punctuated with two performance dramas. The opening ceremonies included spiritual readings from different religions and a prayer dance by the children of Maher that brought home the message that all religions teach respect for human dignity. The Chief Guest for the evening was Mrs. Anu Aga, a prominent businesswoman from Mumbai and leading activist for abused women and slum children. Mr. Lalit Kumar Jain, a senior real estate developer in Pune, was the guest of honor. In her rousing inspirational speech, Anu Aga outlined the impressive achievements made by Maher and stressed the fact that India today needs many more Mahers. Dr. Hamir Ganla and Mrs. Anuradha Karkare, previous and current presidents of Maher, presented the goals and programs of the project.

The speeches were followed by more dances by the Maher troupe. These dances must be experienced in person to be fully appreciated. No words can do justice to the impact and nameless beauty of the divine energy that shines through them. The very spirit of India in its profound splendor and mystery comes pouring through them. With each dance the audience was moved and uplifted ever higher as the energy and radiance of the dance was transmitted through the performers to the audience. Witnessing the grace and skill of the dancers—people who only a few months or years prior were immersed in unimaginable suffering in their personal lives—was deeply moving.

Earlier in the evening, another mini-drama had been performed, illustrating another major aspect of the suffering of women in India. In brief, this drama unfolded on stage as follows: A mother is feeding her young daughter in the kitchen, and her husband suddenly bursts into

Dance performance at Maher's 10th anniversary celebration held at the Corinthian Club in Pune, 2007.

the room, staggering across the floor. Waving an empty bottle around in his hand, he demands money from his wife to buy more alcohol. His wife shakes her head, pointing to the child's mouth, indicating the need to save their money for food. This enrages the man, and he starts hitting his wife. She ducks his blows and backs away, but he comes at her again ferociously, knocking her down. The young daughter tries to intervene, pulling at the leg of her father's pants, but the father viciously yanks the child off, sending her careening across the floor. He then resumes beating his wife. The woman defends herself by pushing him away, and in his drunkenness he loses his balance and falls to the floor. This only infuriates him further, and he gets back up and charges at his wife, seething with rage. She sidesteps him and he crashes into the wall. The husband leaves the stage shaking his fist, and returns a few moments later. Now he comes at his wife with a bucket, which he pours over her head. He steps back, makes a gesture of lighting a match, and throws it on her. The daughter shrieks as her mother bursts into flames.

A dramatic skit in Maher's theater performance, depicting a scenario of bride burning. Here the woman's drunken husband wants to buy more alcohol, and he is threatening to kill her because she is refusing to give him money that was set aside for food.

Five more young Maher actors appear silently on stage a few feet away, moving their arms in vigorous rhythmical vertical circulation, creating an uncanny theatrical depiction of leaping flames. The burning woman is shaking and stumbling about with an expression of excruciating agony on her face. The man flees, and the daughter freezes in terror, watching her mother burn to death. The woman whirls about in a desperate but futile attempt to escape the unrelenting flames, then falls to the ground writhing. Her thrashing about on the floor slowly subsides as she succumbs to the fire and dies.

The lights dim, and the emcee steps out and explains to the audience in a sober tone that this scenario depicts the actual fate of literally thousands of women in India every year. She goes on to say that Maher is one place where many women who had been abused and/or threatened with murder have taken refuge, and that Maher is doing everything it can to raise public awareness about these issues and mobilize public support for practical solutions that will one day put an end to these tragic scenarios.

The evening's performance concluded with a rousing final dance for which a unique theme song entitled "Maher" had been composed especially for the occasion by a talented composer in the city of Pune. The music filled the air and the stage became a flurry of swirling color as the dancers crisscrossed the stage in a grand crescendo and powerful finale. The audience roared with applause for several minutes afterward while the dancers did their curtain calls. Lucy, Hira, and various Maher board members and staff were pushed to join the dancers up on stage. It was a triumphant moment, and the enthusiastic response from the audience was ample reward for all the hard work and preparation that had gone into it.

After the performance, the crowds were inspired and charged with enthusiasm as they gathered for dinner at the banquet-style tables, enjoying a delicious and plentiful Indian meal donated for the occasion by the Mayfair Corporation in Pune. It was a major moment for Maher, and for the authors, who had visited the community repeatedly over several years and had witnessed its magnificent evolution during that time. There were many tears of joy on that gala night.

◊ ◊ ◊

"Absolutely magnificent!" beamed an elegant middle-aged woman impeccably dressed in a flowing dark green sari, with jewels glistening around her neck. She and her husband had come up after the performance to congratulate Lucy, Hira, Anuradha and Dr. Ganla. "What a wonderful show this was!" she exclaimed. "And it powerfully illustrates the real challenges facing Indian women!"

"Thank you so much," Lucy replied, with shining eyes.

"Thank you!" the woman responded. "It is all conveyed so beautifully with the dances, music, and theater pieces. I was deeply moved."

"I'm very gratified that you liked the show," Lucy replied. The woman and her husband were a prominent couple in Pune, he a wealthy businessman and she a leader in the arts and social projects in the city.

"How beautiful the dancing is!" the woman continued. "It obviously took a lot of hard work to bring this all together so exquisitely."

The woman's husband had been curiously silent, looking on intently and becoming fidgety. Finally he could contain himself no longer. "The show was well done, to be sure!" he blurted out. "But, with all due respect, I must object to the one scene. You should not be showing that!"

"Which scene is that?" Lucy asked, squinting in puzzlement.

"You know the one," he replied tersely. "The others were fine, it's just that one."

"Forgive me, but I'm afraid I don't know which part of the show you're speaking of," Lucy said.

"Well, if I have to spell it out," he stammered, "it's the rape sequence. That is not appropriate to show in public!"

"Why is that, dear?" his wife queried.

Quickly masking his irritation with his wife for interjecting this question, the man continued. "First of all, there are many youth and young girls here. It's not appropriate for them to see this. Second, it's too private and personal a kind of thing to bring forward in a public gathering like this. It's just not proper. It shows very poor taste, and I'm surprised that you would allow such a thing, especially as a nun!"

"I appreciate your feelings, sir," Lucy replied, "but if I may ask, how should we bring proper public attention to address these crucial matters? How shall we communicate about these issues to the people living in interior villages, the majority of whom are illiterate? We can't give them books and magazine articles—they can't read. Theater performance is one of the few practical ways we can do it."

"Well, it could shock innocent girls, who should be protected from having to witness such a thing. And it could even encourage boys to be more promiscuous, almost like giving them permission!" he stammered, shifting uncomfortably on his feet.

"Let me assure you, sir, the vast majority of young girls you are concerned about—yes, the very girls and women right here at this gathering—are already painfully aware of these horrific realities," Lucy responded. "They live with the very real threat of rape every day. And I can say with confidence, sadly, that a significant portion of them have already experienced rape. And the boys are well served by witnessing the devastation and horror that rape causes in a girl's life—as well as the dynamics that happen in groups of boys that can unwittingly lead them down this kind of path. So the youth—girls and boys both—are acutely aware of these issues. What harm is done for them to witness on stage what they face in their lives every day? I rather think it helps them, and gives them permission to talk about these things in a constructive way that perhaps they haven't been able to do before." As you and I are doing now, Lucy thought, but she held her tongue. Her eyes softened as she spoke with this man, who was clearly struggling mightily with his own discomfort.

"I know it's a terrible thing! And I certainly don't claim to know how to fix it," the man retorted with evident discomfort. "But that part of the show is in poor taste, and it should be removed. The rest of your show is fine, and worthwhile."

"If I may ask you, sir," continued Lucy, "can you tell me why it is in poor taste?

"Well, I just don't think it's appropriate. It's outrageous, actually! Rape should not be exposed like that in public! It's too intimate an affair, or I don't know what," he said, looking confused as he fumbled for words. "It just shouldn't be paraded about in public!" he concluded adamantly.

"If we keep it hidden, as you recommend, isn't that part of the very denial that enables rape to keep happening?" Lucy asked.

"I'm not in denial," he protested. "I'm talking about ethics and decency here. The rape scene was inappropriate."

"What about the scene of the bride-burning? Was that inappropriate?" Lucy asked.

"That's different," the man replied, "because those cases are in the paper all the time, and we know all about them. But it shows very poor taste to depict rape in a public performance like this."

"So it is in poor taste to depict a girl being raped, but it is not in poor taste to depict a woman being burned alive by her husband?" Lucy asked. "Can you explain to me the logic of that?"

The man scratched his head slowly, and his wife jumped in to the rescue. "I think we have to be going now. You've certainly given us some food for thought, and again I want to say how moved I was by the whole program. Keep up your wonderful work!"

"One last thing . . ." Lucy said, as the couple was leaving. "I understand that the rape scene made you feel outraged and uncomfortable, sir. But I wonder if you can redirect your outrage from rape symbolized in a theater play to outrage at the rape that is rampant in society? As you say, it is a terrible thing. Please come and join our efforts, and know that you are always welcome to visit Maher—at any time!"

"Thank you," the couple said in unison as they departed.

◇ ◇ ◇

The tenth anniversary celebration was the beginning of a whole new chapter for Maher. It garnered a high visibility for the project among the prominent citizenry of Pune many of whom were previously unaware of Maher. Actually, Lucy and Hira and several other Maher staff members had been concerned beforehand that the whole event was overly high profile—held in an excessively posh venue for a Maher function—and they were concerned about the relatively high cost of the gala event, even though all financial expenses were donated by supportive organizations. By her nature, Lucy naturally goes for simplicity and modesty in all things material, and excels rather in the intangibles of love and integrity and spirit. Yet many people came to this event who would not have heard about Maher otherwise, and certainly would never have visited, because it is located in such a remote village region.

Many prominent executives from large companies and IT (information technology) firms in the Pune region attended the anniversary celebration, and they left very inspired and wanting to help. As a result, several CEOs and company executives have since come forward to sponsor various programs at Maher. Numerous professionals in the Pune district have also stepped forward to offer their help, including doctors, psychologists, nurses, and psychotherapists. Today Maher receives frequent calls from corporations and professionals in the Maharashtra region inquiring what kind of help Maher requires—calls that never came prior to this event. Several local companies as well as international corporations have become increasingly involved, some in support of a particular project, such as one of the children's homes or the project at Vatsalyadham, and some by giving grants for general support. The corporate sponsors are listed in appendix E. The publicity and support it is receiving as a result of the celebration event is helping Maher to take the next steps in its evolution.

The day after the celebration, back in Vadhu Budruk, the Maher troupe put on the same program from morning to night—performing the full three-hour sequence three times over the course of the day. More than 7,000 people from the surrounding region came to see the performance and join in the festivities, and Maher provided a delicious meal to every one of them.

The day opened with a prayer service led by Maher women and children, followed by the ceremonial lighting of the oil lamps and spiritual readings from the Bhagavad Gita, the Qur'an, and the Bible. It was one of those large-scale spiritual festivals that Indians are so skilled at putting on, and everything came off without a hitch. People came

Dance performance for Maher's 10th anniversary weekend festivities held for local villagers at Vadhu Budruk. More than 7,000 people from surrounding communities attended.

in droves and waves throughout the day—those nearby on foot and those from further away in every kind of vehicle imaginable. People on bicycles and auto rickshaws came peddling in from all directions. Bullock carts rumbled slowly in, wheels creaking with every rut and bump, packed with people hanging off the sides. Families of four or five arrived on a single motorcycle. Jeeps that were nominally eight-passenger vehicles came stuffed with upwards of twelve adults and eight children inside—often with another five or six people riding on the roof rack. This is India, after all!

At the end of the long day, the children of Maher honored "Lucy Didi." "How do you feel after these ten years?" they asked her. Smiling from ear to ear, Lucy replied, "I feel so happy now that Maher has grown into what it is today. I give thanks and praise to God, who makes all things possible, and for all the help He sends through good people from India and abroad!"

CHAPTER 14

Against All Odds— Dancing in Britain!

The law of love could be best understood and learned through little children.

—Mahatma Gandhi

"No! They're orphaned children! You cannot take them to England," the officer said firmly, staring intently at Sister Lucy as he leaned across his desk at the passport office. "It's not possible!"

Lucy moved back, reacting to the force of refusal she felt coming from this man. "But, sir," she said, speaking in a soft, clear but strong voice, "we filed all the necessary paperwork with your office, and the children are already scheduled to perform in many UK schools and organizations. What are we to do?" Lucy laid copies of the documents on his desk.

"I've gone through these already," the officer said as he picked up the papers and handed them back to her. "Most of the children have no birth certificates, and those who do have no idea where their parents are in order to get their signature. How are we to issue passports without proper identification and a permanent address for these children?" he asked. "It can't be done."

Lucy didn't have an answer in that moment. She knew only one thing for certain. She was not going to let the words "No!" and

"Impossible!" and "It can't be done!" block her from seeing this dream come true. As had happened so many times in the past, she would find a way, if God willed it to be so.

Traveling back to the office, the conversation among Lucy and two of the Maher staff, Salim and Manju, quickly turned from any feelings of disappointment to a strategic meeting as they began brainstorming how to move through this problem. Together they settled on a plan of immediate action: appealing to higher authorities. As soon as they reached the office, they each got on the phone and began calling some of Maher's most influential supporters in India, specifically political ministers. They explained what they were up against, and asked if there were any way to get around the problem.

The passport officer was not wrong in his assessment. Under normal circumstances, any person applying for a passport had to furnish, at the very least, a valid birth certificate and a permanent address. However, this was not a normal situation. Unlike most citizens, the majority of Maher children had no birth certificates, no permanent addresses, and for those who had deceased parents, no death certificates had been issued in most cases. Some children who had been abandoned on the streets at a young age did not even know their mother or father.

Even in cases where the parents were known and alive, they were often very difficult to locate. Ayanna's mother, who was an alcoholic and worked as a prostitute in the slums of Bombay, was one such example. She lived on the streets, moving from place to place, job to job, never settling for very long. For Ayanna to go on the UK tour her mother had to give permission and sign her passport application. This meant that Maher had to send someone to search the streets at night to find her; not an easy task.

Two female Maher social workers accompanied by a male driver made the five-hour journey by car from Pune to Mumbai to begin combing the city's red-light districts looking for Ayanna's mother. Like skilled detectives, they probed every possible nook and cranny until finally, on the third night, they found her. She was happy to see them, and excited to hear about her daughter's opportunity to perform in the UK. However, convincing her to leave her steady work as a prostitute, even for a few days, and come to Maher to sign the papers in person was challenging. Ayanna was thriving at Maher—excelling in her school studies, enjoying her friends, and flourishing as one of the key performers in the dance program. For her mother, however, Maher felt like a prison. There were specific rules at Maher that everyone had to follow: no smoking, no drinking, no soliciting sex—behaviors which Ayanna's mother was not willing or able to give up. After some time and a lot of bargaining, she finally agreed to return to Maher just long enough to see her daughter and sign the papers. Thus, Ayanna was able to go on the UK tour.

That was one child, but what about the other thirty children who still needed passports and had birth no certificates, home addresses, or even parents who could prove their existence? Because Maher was an institution, the passport office could not accept its address as the home address for the children. Yet, it was the only address that many of them had—Maher was their home, after all! There was no time to waste, so the Maher staff contacted their attorney and got him working on affidavits for each of the children. The staff began compiling records to prove that the children in question were registered in and attending school. Submitting these documents along with the ministers' endorsement would hopefully be sufficient. There was no guarantee, however.

The decision hung in limbo for several weeks, with phone calls and letters back and forth to the passport office. Then one day Mr. Suresh Kumar Menon, the chief passport officer, showed up in person at Maher. Lucy and Hira showed him around and he was impressed by what he saw. "I have good news for you," he said finally, beaming with joyful assurance. "The ministers, along with several of our passport officials, have created temporary passports for your children, good for five years." As it happened, there was an obscure clause in the passport regulations that allowed, under special circumstances, temporary passports to be issued. This was the first time that the policy had ever been enacted. "In fact," said Mr. Menon, "this is the first time in India's history that street children have been given passports to travel abroad. Congratulations!"

This had been a big hurdle, and everyone felt tremendous relief and joy. Yet, with only five months to go, there was no time to lose. Another potentially major hurdle lay ahead: applying for the visas.

BEYOND INDIA—FIVE MONTHS TO GO

Some 4,400 miles away, in York, England, an entirely different group of people was focused on other details of the tour. Rosemarie Temple, John Armstrong, and Wendy Dickenson, members of the UK Friends of Maher and the primary tour coordinators, were busy scoping out dance venues, ground transportation, and lodging in preparation for the arrival of the Maher dance troupe. They were also working to raise the necessary funds for this big endeavor. To their surprise, they discovered that obstacles related to the tour were not limited to the Indian government. Western friends and supporters in Europe and the UK began raising several questions that sparked quite a discussion.

"It's not a good idea to take these Indian children out of their native environment," one woman who had been a longtime Maher supporter exclaimed. "I'm concerned that when they see how nice it is here, they'll just want to have more money, more freedom, more things to buy!" Other concerns were raised. "I wonder how the other children at Maher will feel," another woman mused, "the ones who don't get to come to the UK. Won't they be jealous? How will Maher handle the apparent discrimination?" A man from the European Friends of Maher raised a question that was also on the minds of several others. "Wouldn't all this money that will be spent on costly airfares be better used on food and shelter for more women and children in need?"

The questions and deliberations continued for several weeks, stimulating lively discussions and debates both within and outside Maher. "I understand all the concerns," asserted Roswitha Ertl shortly after returning home to her native Austria from Maher, "but has anyone considered the incredible learning experience this will be for the children, not only for the Indian children, but also for the British children? It's a wonderful opportunity." Roswitha and another university student, Johanna Ober, both twenty-four years old, had just completed four-month social work internships at Maher. "And why shouldn't the Maher children be given the same chance to see the world that any of our children might have?," Roswitha mused, "I can't imagine what I would have done if someone in India told me I couldn't visit there because seeing India might change me!" Roswitha sat back, her face a bit flushed with indignation. She and Johanna were meeting with the authors who were visiting them in Vienna.

"I agree with Roswitha," chimed in Johanna. "I need to tell you about an experience I had the other night when I went to a concert. There was a Japanese children's choir and a full youth orchestra performing—125 young people from ten to nineteen years old on stage. The concert was free and open to the public as part of a cultural exchange program between Japan and Austria. It was held here in Vienna at the Musikverein, one of Europe's leading concert halls. Sitting there enjoying the music, I wondered to myself, what's so different about these children who traveled from Japan and the Maher children? Why couldn't the Maher children have the same opportunity—without question—as these young people were getting? Is anyone in Japan or Europe concerned about whether these children will be changed if they visit Europe? I doubt it. Probably no one asked whether the money slated for airfares couldn't be better spent elsewhere. It's sad to me to think that the Maher children may not get this opportunity, simply because they are poor!" Johanna sat down feeling a bit vulnerable with all she had just expressed, but glad she had spoken so passionately on behalf of the Maher children.

Thousands of miles away, in the small village of Vadhu Budruk, Sister Lucy began hearing the concerns raised among some of the Westerners. She talked through the issues on the phone with Rosemarie Temple, met with the Maher trustees, and then, as she so often did, took the questions and concerns into her meditation and prayer. She listened deeply for guidance and the best course of action. As always, she trusted the process, knowing that she would be led in the proper direction toward whatever would be of greatest service to the Maher community, and ultimately to God.

Lucy could not deny the validity of some of the criticism. She understood the questions and tried to alleviate the fears that some people were feeling. She was not overly concerned about exposing the children to the ways of the Western world; in fact, she felt that seeing some of the differences would be an overall positive and enriching experience for them. The fact that both she and Hira had recently been on a fundraising tour to the United States and Europe was proving beneficial as well. They were able to prepare the children first-hand for many of the experiences and feelings that would most likely come up, especially those cultural differences that might seem odd or strange, or perhaps attractive and desirable. Hira was particularly helpful in preparing the children, as this had been her first trip outside of India and her mind and heart were fresh with the differences between East and West. Of most importance, Lucy and Hira knew their children well, and both were confident that they would not fall into wild desires for more of what the West offered. Rather, they anticipated that the children would bring home valuable learnings they could share with everyone at Maher and important memories they would treasure into their adult lives.

ENDLESS BLESSINGS—TWO MONTHS TO GO

Of course, other things were happening at Maher during this time as well, including the inauguration on February 2, 2008, of the new building at Vatsalyadham, Maher's home for mentally disturbed women. This date was special because it was "Maher Day," the celebration of Maher's eleventh birthday. Mr. Shri Sharad Pawar, India's Minister of Agriculture, was the keynote speaker. Mr. Pawar had been instrumental in helping Maher get the children's passports, and he had vowed to help Maher however he could.

On the day of the inauguration his words proved to be as good as gold when he saw the children perform their exquisite dances and dramatic rendition of Mahatma Gandhi's life. Noticing Mr. Pawar's appreciation as the youngest Maher girls performed an Indian blessing dance, Sister Lucy leaned over and whispered, "These children performing are the ones who will be going to the UK if we can raise the funds for their airfares." The minister nodded to Lucy, and his face lit up with delight in seeing the next act: ten teenage boys dressed in brightly colored shirts of blue, pink and yellow spun across the stage to a high energy hip-hop song. The cheering audience clapped in rhythm with the music as three of the boys did back-flips, cartwheels and one-leg swipe breakdancing. With gleaming eyes and wide smiles, the boys concluded their dance, bowed, and exited the stage. "Excuse me just a moment," Mr. Pawar said to Sister Lucy as he took his cell phone from his coat pocket and quickly dialed a number before the final dance began. Lucy nodded and inhaled deeply, taking full advantage of a moment of rest from all the exciting activities of the day.

Finishing his phone call, the minister smiled at Lucy and whispered, "I have good news to announce." Just then the music came pouring through the PA speakers again, drowning out any further conversation as fourteen teenage girls entered the stage, each dressed in traditional *lehenga-choli* outfits with full ankle-length skirts of various colors—magenta, blue, orange, and green—draped with golden sashes. Their hair was tied up neatly and laced with sweet-smelling jasmine flowers. What radiant beauties these young girls are, Lucy thought, saying a silent prayer for them and their futures as young women. Slowly the girls began stamping their feet in rhythm with *keharwa*, the eight-count beat of classical Kathak Indian dance. A chorus of ringing *ghungroo* bells accompanied each precise step. (*Ghungroos* are small metallic bells strung together and tied to the ankles of classical Indian dancers.) The girls' hands gracefully flowed in unison, first in single-hand gestures known as *asanjukta hasta mudra* and later in combined gestures called *sanjukta hasta mudra*. The musical sound of the tabla drums filled the room—*ta, thei, tat, ta ta, tigda, digdig*—as the girls picked up their pace, matching the ever-increasing rhythm, their colorful skirts fanning out as they spun faster and faster. Mesmerized, the audience sat in silent awe of these girls whose incredible grace and refined poise disclosed the beauty of their

Maher dancers attaching *ghungroo* bells to their ankles before a performance.

emerging womanhood in what could only be described as divine. The music stopped as suddenly as it had begun and the dancers finished on the first beat of the time-cycle known as *sam* in the Kathak tradition. The room was utterly silent—time was suspended for a few moments and the girls held perfect balance before the audience broke out in resounding applause.

After the performance, Mr. Pawar took the podium, his hands held high in applause for the Maher dancers. The children's faces beamed with delight as the minister congratulated them on the excellence of their dance performance. He then turned to the audience. "Many of you are aware that these beautiful dancers that you've just seen perform today have been invited to perform in England. I have some good news to share with you about this. I just now spoke on the telephone with executives from Air India, and I am pleased to announce that Air India has offered to donate more than half the cost of the airline tickets for the Maher dance troupe to fly to London!"

"Hooray!" shouted the children with glee as they began hugging and slapping one another on the back. Sister Lucy could not believe her ears. Could this possibly be true? she wondered. She walked up to the stage, her face glowing with incredulous gratitude. As she shook Mr. Pawar's hand in appreciation amidst the resounding applause, she leaned over and whispered, "Sir, did I hear you correctly?" Moving back slightly, Mr. Pawar tilted his head from side to side several times enthusiastically. "Yes, you did, Sister," he assured her, smiling widely. "Oh, thank you so much! " Lucy responded. "You have made our children and everyone at Maher so happy."

Airline sponsorship for the Maher UK tour was a major boost to the fundraising campaign that Rosemarie was spearheading in the UK, and it virtually eliminated the moral question that some people had posed of why precious resources were being spent on airfares rather than shelter and food for more women and children. Moreover, joint support from an Indian corporation and UK funders was important for balancing the financial investment and fostering harmonious relationships among all parties involved from both countries.

ON THE ROAD TO MUMBAI—ONE MONTH LEFT

The afterglow of the big celebration and Minister Pawar's announcement was short-lived, however, as another major hurdle suddenly reared its head. "Sister, Sister," Manju called out, looking distressed as she rushed over to Lucy's desk at the Pune office. "What is it, Manju?" Lucy asked, looking up over the reading glasses that were perched halfway down her nose. "You must look at this immediately," Manju insisted. "It's a letter from the UK Border Agency Application Centre in Mumbai. They're rejecting all the children and staff's visa applications!"

Lucy's eyes narrowed, causing the wrinkle lines between her eyebrows to deepen as she read over the letter Manju had just handed her. Rosemarie and Wendy, who happened to be visiting from the UK at the time, stood up quickly from the desk where they were working and came to Lucy's side. "What is it now?" Rosemarie asked, letting out a slight groan characterized by mixed feelings of concern and frustration. "What does it say?"

Lucy sighed a long breath and proceeded to list all the items the visa office was requiring for the visa applications to even be considered. These items had not been required in the original visa application guidelines, which Maher had followed meticulously. The application office now wanted letters of invitation from each performance venue (schools, organizations, churches, etc.) addressed to each individual child and adult traveling to the UK. With thirty-seven people on the tour, this requirement alone would require at least a few hundred letters. They also wanted bank statements documenting ample funds to cover the entire tour costs and documentation verifying accommodations and guaranteeing that the children would all be staying together in the same location.

Lucy looked up at Rosemarie and Wendy with single-minded determination. She stood up and, gathering papers in her briefcase, began rapidly giving instructions in Hindi to her staff. "We have to leave—now!" she announced, switching back to English as she directed the two British women out the door to the Maher jeep.

"Where are we going?" Wendy asked, leaning over to grab her bag as Rosemarie slipped on her sandals, which had been placed neatly next to many other pairs just outside the front door. "To the visa office in Mumbai," Lucy told her. "We don't have much time before you both leave to go back to the UK. It's very good that you're here right now. You'll be able to explain everything about the tour to the British visa authorities much better than we can."

Lucy picked up her cell phone and called Hira to explain the situation and to say that she and the two English women would not be coming home that night. "We'll have to travel all night," she said, putting her phone away as she turned to look at the women in the backseat. "The office opens at 8 AM and we need to be there early before the lines get too long." Yuvaraj, the Maher driver, started the jeep and took off down the bumpy dirt road into the thick rush-hour traffic of cars, scooters, cows, bicycles, goats, auto rickshaws, and the immeasurable swarms of pedestrians in Pune City.

Compiling all the necessary documents in order to resubmit the visa applications was going to take time—which was running short, with less than two months before the April tour was scheduled to begin. Fortunately, Sister Lucy was correct in her decision to travel to the Mumbai UK Border Agency. Showing up in person with two British hosts along added clout and credibility to Maher's case with the British passport authorities. Rosemarie and Wendy were able to provide proof of certain items on the spot, including sufficient bank funds from the UK Friends of Maher account to cover tour expenses, something Maher was unable to vouch for. Verification of the accommodations and provision of invitation letters—both of which the

Maher's dynamic dance troupe honed their performance skills in multiple venues in India, while hoping to take their message and dances abroad someday.

visa office required to safeguard against any possibility of child trafficking—could be expedited by volunteers back in the UK who were already working on other tour details.

Rosemarie and Wendy returned home to York with plenty of follow-up work. Over the next two weeks the visa office in Mumbai was flooded with the necessary documents—sent by international air courier as soon as they were completed. Just a few weeks after their long overnight trip to Mumbai, Rosemarie and Wendy received the happy news from Lucy: thirty-day visas had been issued and received for all the children and staff. The Maher dance troupe was coming to the UK!

SIX HOURS REMAINING

Everyone was packed and ready to go. The children were giddy with excitement, with less than six hours remaining before they were due to leave Maher on a chartered bus for the Mumbai airport. Although tears welled up in Lucy's eyes from time to time, rarely had anyone ever seen her actually cry—but the new twist of events on this day literally brought Lucy to her knees. Early in the afternoon she had received a summons to appear immediately before the Women and Child Welfare panel of officers for failing to submit to their office the required paperwork to take the children out of India. Immediately, Lucy and two Maher staff had rushed to the office in Pune, where Lucy had pleaded with the officers for hours—explaining that she had not known about this requirement.

But it was to no avail. The welfare office was adamant in denying Maher permission to take the children out of India. Lucy returned home to Vadhu Budruk—empty-handed and broken-hearted. "How were we to have known?" she lamented, as her mind reviewed all the different applications and processes Maher had been through over the past year of organizing this tour. No one had informed her about this requirement. The passport office had never mentioned it, nor had the visa office. Working with orphaned children was new for all of them, and they did not know all the procedures themselves.

Lucy glanced up and looked around the room at Athena, Hira, Sheetal, and Shirley—members of the Maher staff who were sitting with her, their faces shadowed with dismay and sorrow. How sad Lucy felt at the prospect of telling the thirty-one children who were all set to leave that they could not go. They had all worked so diligently over the past year with their teachers, Sheetal and Satish, learning new dances and perfecting the dramatic play of Mahatma Gandhi's life. Indeed, over the previous few weeks the children had eagerly gathered every evening to practice their performances, often right up until bedtime. How could Lucy go to them now, a few hours before they were supposed to leave, and announce that everything they had worked so hard toward was suddenly canceled? This tour was the chance of a lifetime for anyone, and such an opportunity for orphaned and street children in India was exceedingly rare and unprecedented.

All the months of preparations and the seemingly insurmountable challenges that the Maher staff had faced and successfully overcome now seemed moot as the entire trip was virtually dissolving before their eyes. Lucy's hands were tied; she could either cancel the trip or take the risk of defying the child welfare office.

Sitting around the table at the Vadhu Budruk office, the women began recalling the numerous obstacles they had faced and surmounted over the past year. "First, getting the passports approved and the affidavits submitted for the children without birth certificates," Athena said, as she leaned over the table to pick up a cup of freshly brewed masala tea that Maia had just served.

"Then, the difficulty that the UK Friends of Maher had in raising funds," Shirly added, "and the questions and long discussions about whether or not the children should even travel to the West. And then the blessing that Mr. Shri Sharad Pawar gave us in securing the Air India donation!" Maia shuffled around the table, offering cookies and making sure that everyone had a cup of tea.

"And then, of course, the visa applications were rejected," Hira contributed. "Remember, Didi, how you had to travel all night to Mumbai with Rosemarie and Wendy?" Hira's eyes sparkled as she giggled and leaned into Lucy, resting her head momentarily on her shoulder at the thought of the English women and Lucy sleeping in the jeep. Lucy chuckled as she gave Hira two short pats on the shoulder. "Ah, we are so blessed for the support of all our Maher friends and for all that God has given us," she said as she shifted into several moments of reflection. The room grew quiet as everyone sat in the silence.

"It is true," Lucy said softly, gently breaking the tranquil stillness. "We have faced many obstacles, but this could be the biggest so far." She sighed deeply. There was another poignant silence, and then she added, "But we can't stop now—we cannot. We have to take the risk. So we will go to the airport tomorrow, and let God's will be done. We need to pray now," she said, taking the last sip of her tea and closing her eyes. The four other women followed. This was an unusual request from Lucy, who did not typically ask for prayer outside of the daily morning and evening community meditation time.

This was a time of crisis, and Lucy knew that prayer was the most important thing to do. After a few moments of centering silence, she began. "Dear God," she appealed, pausing a moment to allow her call to be heard. "We are so grateful for all You have bestowed upon us here at Maher. Tonight, we ask for Your help once again. Help us face our challenges with courage. We pray that You protect Maher from any harm or wrongdoing, both from our own accord, and from others. We pray also for the officers at the Women and Child Welfare office, for they, like us, are Your divine children. Father, forgive them, for they do not know what they are doing. If it is Your will, we pray that the way will be made clear and safe as we travel to the airport and board the plane to England tomorrow."

Lucy remained in silent prayer for a few more moments and then she ended with, "Peace." Opening her eyes and pushing her chair away from the table, she stood up and moved over to the computer. "We must go forward," she said calmly, with renewed resolve. "Athena, draft the statement that the officers ordered. Be certain to write the letter as they instructed, stating explicitly that we are proceeding at our own risk to take the children out of the country, without their permission."

Lucy then went into the community room and gathered the children in the dance troupe to explain the situation to them. "We are leaving at 2 AM, as planned," she said, speaking in Mahrati to the children, who all instantly let out a cheer of excitement. "Hush, hush." Lucy puckered her lips as she waved her hands slowly downward toward the floor, prompting them to be quiet. "I have something to tell you, children. There is a chance that we may not be allowed to board the airplane." The beaming smiles faded quickly, and faces turned sad and disheartened as Lucy told them that some of the documents had not

Excited Maher dancers at the Mumbai airport on the day of departure for London.

been completed as required. She shared just enough information with the children to prepare them for possible disappointment without instilling undue fear. Like any loving mother who cares for her children, Lucy held the burden of concern for everyone—not knowing for sure whether they would face a barrage of police who would physically block their departure at the airport.

It was a long final several hours. The children and staff boarded the bus and made the five-hour journey to the airport, where everyone went through check-in, passport control, and security screening without a hitch. Lucy and the other Maher staff remained calm and measured throughout, acutely aware that they might be suddenly deterred at any moment. Not until the airplane lifted off from the Mumbai runway with everyone securely aboard did Lucy breathe easily.

REACHING THE OTHER SIDE

"Long live Didi! Long live Didi!" The chanting of the Maher children filled the small church community room as they lifted their voices in gratitude for Sister Lucy. Outside, the weather was cool and damp, not unusual for England in late April but a stark contrast to the far warmer climate of Pune, India. At long last the Maher dance troupe and staff had triumphed against the many odds and arrived safely in this bucolic wonderland of quiet, rolling green farmland that felt galaxies away from their familiar rural surroundings of dirt roads, bullock carts, wandering cows, blaring Tata truck horns, and the smell of outdoor dung fires from nearby huts.

"They have something to share with you," Sheetal, the dance teacher, said to Sister Lucy, offering her a chair as the children stood with bright eyes and big smiles eagerly waiting to present their gift. Lucy's smile widened and her eyes softened as she realized what the children—all thirty-one of them—had been up to all afternoon. "Nadira and Ubaidah have each written a song for you on behalf of all the children to express their love and gratitude for all you have done for them," Sheetal announced. Feeling shy and slightly embarrassed with all the attention, Lucy sat down and prepared herself to receive the offering.

Aarti, a short-haired petite eight-year-old moved to the front of the children, closed her eyes, and began reciting a prayer in Marathi, her mother tongue. Earlier that day she had specifically approached Sheetal to ask if she could lead the opening prayer. Impressed and pleased with Aarti's determination, Sheetal readily consented. Only later, during the prayer, did Sheetal realize Aarti's full intention for making such an offer. After giving thanks on behalf of everyone, Aarti then turned to face Sister Lucy and offered her heartfelt apology for having caused trouble earlier that day, and she asked for God's forgiveness. Tears welled up in Lucy's eyes as Aarti concluded the prayer and the children began singing the first song.

A STRANGE NEW LAND

The children were fairly well acquainted with the ways of England and its peculiar sights by the time the authors arrived in Yorkshire on April 28. After all, they were international travel veterans now, having been away from home for twelve days! We knew most of the children reasonably well, having visited Maher periodically over the past five years, so it was especially exciting to be with them as they were discovering and broadening their worldview. The entire trip was an ongoing adventure of new and unusual experiences for the children, beginning with the airline flight, during which they had quickly stolen the hearts of all the passengers on board singing songs and performing a few dance steps in the aisles.

After landing, the bus trip from Heathrow airport to the city of York and the days that followed marked many stark differences between their homeland of India and the English lifestyle.

"There are no people on the streets!" Ambu said with a puzzled look, as she and the other children began describing their impressions to us.

"Yeah," Darshan piped in, "where is everyone? It feels so lonely." All the children's heads nodded in agreement.

"And all the cars drive together in straight lines," Mangesh said. "Not like India, where the cars go every which way." The children giggled as Mangesh waved his arms round and round in a haphazard way, mimicking the traffic in India.

"Everything is so *cleeeean!*" Chandrakala exclaimed. "I would like India to be this clean," she said, smiling softly and gazing out the window onto the pristine, empty street of Wheldrake, the small village seven miles southeast of York where the Maher group was staying. "I now understand what Didi has been trying to teach us about picking up trash at Maher," she added.

Vicki, a sixteen-year-old boy, quickly added, "Yeah, it's a pretty place, but I wouldn't want to live here. I would get lonely with no people around." The room went quiet while the children sat still for a moment, as if reflecting on what it must feel like to be alone. "I think," Sayali began meekly, "that everyone here is very hard-working, and that work comes first." Darshan perked up again, saying, "Time is very important! In India everything runs late. When Auntie Rosemarie and Auntie Wendy ["auntie" and "uncle" are endearing terms used for honorary friends and elders] say that the bus will leave at eight o'clock, we cannot be one minute later. And yesterday, at the school, the teacher stopped the performance before it was over," he continued, with a look of puzzlement, "because all the students had to leave exactly at three o'clock." Several of the children sighed with disappointment.

"It was okay," Vaibhav, one of the Maher staff and a performer in dramatic plays, said to us on the side, wanting to ease any feelings of misunderstanding. "The culture is very different here than in India, and the children were just confused."

Suddenly three skinny twelve-year-old Maher girls scurried around the corner, giggling and chattering away in Marathi, clinging to the arms of Zoe, a stout thirteen-year-old English girl. Zoe lived in a row house across the street and had ventured over out of curiosity to meet these children after seeing some of them playing outside. Zoe towered over the three girls by at least six inches, and her fair skin, green eyes, and red hair were a dramatic contrast to the Indian girls' darker skin, brown eyes and hair. Several more of the children surrounded Zoe, quickly befriending her and pulling her into another room to dance together. Lucy, Prakash, and Shirly (two other Maher staff) simultaneously let out a big belly laugh as they watched the children so easily embrace one another with love.

Later that evening, when dinner was served, Zoe sat on the floor Indian style eating dal, rice and chapatis with the entire Maher family. She even joined in singing the prayers in Marathi with the children, and when she could not figure out the words, she swayed back and forth, clapping her hands in rhythm.

Maher dancers perform at Leeds Civic Hall in an invitational program for dignitaries hosted by the Mayor of Leeds in northern England, April, 2008.

"This was so much fun!" Zoe said as she approached Sister Lucy, who was sitting on the sofa talking with a local Indian family who had graciously provided the evening meal. "Thank you so much! May I come back tomorrow?" she asked, bouncing a bit with excitement as a broad smile spread across her face, revealing two rosy pink cheeks. "Certainly, you may!" Lucy said, reaching out and taking her hands. "You are welcome anytime."

THE PERFORMANCES

"Wow! That was really cool!" nine-year-old William exclaimed as he sat on the gymnasium floor of his primary school in the city of Leeds with his friend Ethan and two of the Maher boys. Over three hundred students had just watched the Maher children perform a variety of dances, plus a thirty-minute dramatic rendition of Mahatma Gandhi's life. "That fellow sort of even looks like Gandhi!" William continued, his eyes sparkling with admiration as he nodded toward Gaus, who was still dressed in his costume of a white loin cloth, sandals, and round wire-framed spectacles. "I didn't even know who Gandhi was," Ethan said. The young Maher actors had just portrayed the life of Gandhi, beautifully weaving in many of his teachings, including the spiritual principles of *ahimsa* (nonviolence) and *satyagraha* (clinging to truth).

In his fervor William began recalling several of the scenes: Gandhi's life as a lawyer and how he was thrown off the train in South Africa; the Salt March; India winning its independence from Britain in 1947.

"Why were the Indian men fighting each other?" Ethan asked. "You know, when Gandhi wouldn't eat or drink anything for so long." He looked up inquisitively at Mangal and Vinayak, two of the Maher boys.

Scene from Maher's theater performance of the life of Mahatma Gandhi, performed in the United Kingdom.

"They were fighting because of their different religions," Vinayak said. "One group was Hindu and the other group was Muslim. Gandhi fasted until they stopped fighting." Mangal smiled, then added, "At Maher, we all live together, even though we have different religions. Like, Rosie is Christian, and I'm Hindu," he said, looking across the room at Rosie. Ethan and William nodded their heads. "I thought it was nice when Gandhi took off his shirt and gave it to the man who didn't have one," Ethan said. Mangal and Vinayak tilted their heads back and forth, smiling at Ethan and William. "Boy!" said William, "I have a lot to tell my mum today!"

During their stay the Maher dance troupe performed in many venues throughout Yorkshire, including more than twenty elementary and senior high schools, and at a large public event with several hundred people hosted by an area physician, as well as private performances for the Lord Mayor and First Lady of Leeds.

AMBASSADORS FOR INDIA

"My life is my message!" Mahatma Gandhi called out from the window of the departing train to a journalist on the platform below who had asked him for a message to take back to the people. "Have you ever heard this story before?" Cynthia asked, after she finished telling the famous story about Gandhi. Two or three heads nodded in the small group of Maher teenagers who had gathered in a circle on the floor with her and Will (the authors). Will and Cynthia had called this meeting with the six older children at Maher to give them an opportunity to share something of their lives, their hopes, and their dreams, and also to hear what they were learning and feeling in visiting this foreign country for the first time. "I believe that your life is your message," Cynthia continued, "not only for India, but also for the world! You came to the UK, all the way from Vadhu Budruk, to spread a message of love."

"You are ambassadors!" Will asserted, like a proud parent who was uplifting his teenagers into their role as young leaders. "Through your dance performances, the story of Maher and of Gandhi and India is being shared with many people here in the UK." The children giggled shyly as they listened to "Will Uncle," as they call him. "You have much to share about your lives," he continued, softening his voice. "Both the pain you've experienced, and now the love of Maher you feel, and how it has helped you to heal. Your dances are bringing a message of love to the British people."

The children were settling in, becoming more inward and reflective. "Would any of you like to say something about your own story?" Cynthia asked gently. The room was very quiet and still for several moments. Some of the children sat with their heads slightly bowed. Cynthia scanned the circle with her eyes. "Sonali, do you want to say something?" she asked one of the girls with a nudge of gentle encouragement.

Sixteen-year-old Sonali smiled shyly and began to speak. "I never thought I'd get love from anybody," she said, her voice soft and hesitant at first. "I gave up hope from the time my mother died. More than anything else, I got love from my mother. That's what I want to share with others." Sonali looked up at Cynthia with a heart full of longing. She had been at Maher since she was seven years old. "When I was small, I didn't realize what it means to miss my mother; as I grew bigger, I started to understand it. Now, I console myself saying that Didi gives me love." Sonali gazed at Cynthia and Will for a moment, then bowed her head. The room drew quiet again except for the occasional rustling of someone repositioning themselves to get comfortable. "Thank you, Sonali," Will said softly. Sonali looked up, tilting her head gently from side to side, large tears starting to roll down her face. Will reached over and handed her a tissue.

"It isn't easy to tell our stories," Will continued, "especially when they're painful. But telling the stories of your life—and the pain you've experienced—can help other people who are also in pain." Looking around the circle, Will knew that his words were beginning to evoke some difficult memories as he saw the sad faces of these sweet children who were normally so cheerful and bubbly. Cynthia, also, felt the despair. They were both holding a silent prayer as they sat with the children, listening to the truth of their pain. "There are so many people living in painful situations," Cynthia continued compassionately, "some similar to what your lives have been like—living on the street, hungry, without their mother or father. And as Sonali said, many of them feel like they'll never be loved. But all of you know that love is possible." She smiled tenderly at the children. "You know that through the love you've received at Maher your lives have totally changed. That's why you're the messengers of love." The children giggled as the painful emotions lifted and the feeling in the room lightened.

◇ ◇ ◇

"It's like a dream—not real—to come to the UK," said Gaus, a young man of seventeen who had lived at Maher since he was ten. "If it wasn't for Maher, I wouldn't be here, or have any education." Gaus is one of several Maher teens who have just entered college. "My father was an alcoholic. He ended up paralyzed and in the hospital. He couldn't work. It was very difficult for my mother. We were very hungry—only eating chai tea and a little bit of bread. I began working in the hotel and on the street begging." Gaus looked up with tearful eyes. "We were so hungry," he said, trying to explain. "I wanted to stay in school, but I couldn't pay the fees. I finally had to leave."

Sister Lucy had heard about the family and the situation, so she visited Gaus's house. When she arrived, the father was in bed incapacitated and the mother was exhausted from working all the time. Lucy brought Gaus back to Maher.

"My life is so different now, and full of opportunities," Gaus said joyfully. Two years earlier he had been invited to speak at the 2007 World Social Forum held in Nairobi, Kenya. It was a unique opportunity and honor, and Gaus had been one of only two youth from India who were invited to speak at the Forum. It was very exciting and inspiring for everyone at Maher that Gaus had received the invitation. Sister Lucy had fully supported him in going and worked hard to make all the necessary preparations. Sadly, due to some bureaucratic complications at the passport office in Delhi, his passport did not come through in time, and at the last minute Gaus was unable to attend. Yet he seemed to take it all in stride, and felt honored that he had been invited to speak at such a distinguished international gathering.

Like most young people, Gaus has many aspirations for his life, although he was a bit shy in sharing his deepest dreams. To encourage him and all the children to share, Cynthia explained that dreams are important and should not be diminished by boundaries and doubts. "If Sister Lucy hadn't followed her dream, and if she hadn't shared her dreams with others, Maher would never have existed," she told them. "Can you imagine your life without Maher?" With that, Gaus listed his dreams of what he hopes to become: "an aeronautical engineer, an astronaut, a cricket player, and a social worker—just like Didi!"

◇ ◇ ◇

Najuka, a confident seventeen-year-old who had just begun her college education, decided to tell her story next. "If it wasn't for Maher, I wouldn't have done any dance, or education. I had a dream to be a dancer, but nobody was there to help," she said. Najuka portrays Gandhi's wife, Kasturbai, in the dramatic play, and she is one of the principal performers in many of the dances.

"When I was three, my mother died from a kidney problem. The doctor asked my father to give blood to help my mother, but my grandmother told him to run, or else they'd take his blood. So he ran away, and my mother died." Najuka's voice trembled as tears began to roll down her face. She paused for several moments to recompose herself. "There was nobody to take care of us," she said, her voice shaking as the tears continued. "Finally, my other grandmother [her mother's mother] took us in. My father and my grandmother [her father's mother] found out, and came to take us; they were going to sell me and my sisters. My uncle came with a knife and finally made them let us go." Najuka took a tissue out of her pocket, removed her glasses, and wiped the tears from her eyes.

"Then," she continued, "I worked as a servant in a man's house for three years, but he never gave me any money for the school fee. I realized that he was cheating me. So I went back home and my father put me in an orphanage. When my uncle found out, and saw that I was not getting proper food, he came and got me, and brought me to Maher. That was four years ago, when I was thirteen. Now, because of Maher, I'm a dancer, and I've gotten to go and perform in Bombay, Delhi, and now the UK," she said, looking up, her eyes sparkling again. "I don't know how I can be grateful enough."

Najuka's dream is to dance. She wants to teach dance to the Maher women and children like Sheetal and also work another job part-time.

◊ ◊ ◊

Rosy came to Maher two years ago, when she was fifteen. "I never thought I'd be educated. Now I feel there is a lot of hope for my life," she told the group, her voice filled with conviction. "My father married my mother, but before that he was already married, and he had children that he never told us about. We came to know much later. My mother's family threw us out, because she had married a man who was already married. We went through so much difficult time. My mother had no education and there were three children. We didn't know where to go. We finally went to my grandmother's house. Meanwhile, my father died, and then my mother." Tears welled up in her eyes as her voice grew softer. "After that, we ended up with my auntie, but she had three children of her own. I thought, where will we go? What will we do? No one would take us, not one single relative." Rosy began to sob. Several of the other children in the circle began crying too.

After a few moments, Rosy continued. "We had no clothes, no food. We lived on the street. No one would even look at us. Everyone thought of us as a burden," she said, bowing her head and wiping the tears as they fell onto her cheeks. "That's when I ended up at Maher and my life changed." Rosie looked up, gently smiling, her eyes still wet with tears. "My dream is to work with children who are like me, children who are suffering. I want to work for them," she said. "I don't want the same suffering for others."

Rosy's ambition is to continue in college, and then she would like to train as a professional dancer. Her dream is to come back to Maher and work as a dance teacher, following in the footsteps of Ila Tiwari, the founder of Maher's dance program.

◇ ◇ ◇

"Sonali, what are your dreams?" Will asked, realizing she had not spoken in a while. Sonali looked down, smiling shyly. "I would like to start an organization like Maher," she replied softly. "Maybe I'll become a doctor and work for the poor," she added with a giggle. "And I want to keep dancing, and teach the children at Maher."

◇ ◇ ◇

The hopes and dreams of these young people capture just a few reflections of what shines in the hearts of the nearly four hundred children at Maher. These children's lives are being transformed through the power of love, and their worldview is radically changing. The hundreds of children who have passed through the nurturing arms of

Maher—and those yet to come—are future leaders, whether they end up in the household baking bread and tending babies or as political leaders guiding a country or as social workers counseling the needy. Mahatma Gandhi said, "If we are to reach real peace in the world, we shall have to begin with the children." The truth of his words resonates deeply in these beautiful children, and through them shines brilliantly into the world.

CHAPTER 15

The Eternal Drama of Draupadi

Abandon all dharmas, and take refuge in Me alone.
I shall purify you from all sins, do not grieve.
—Krishna, Bhagavad Gita (18:66)

The two great Sanskrit epics of India are the *Mahabharata* and the *Ramayana*. Both are foundational texts of Hindu scripture focusing on the battle between forces of good and evil, and both are replete with profound stories, teachings, and spiritual wisdom. The Bhagavad Gita (or "Song of God") is the most celebrated scripture of Hinduism, and is contained as part of the *Mahabharata*.[1] Often called "India's favorite Bible," the "Gita" has inspired some of the deepest spiritual masters East and West, and was the scriptural foundation of Mahatma Gandhi's life and work. Albert Einstein said of it, "When I read the Bhagavad Gita and reflect about how God created this universe, everything else seems so superfluous."[2]

The *Mahabharata* is a vast and profound scripture, one of the longest epics in any language, with a total of some ninety thousand verses. As Western students of the Indian tradition, the authors make no claim to be experts on the *Mahabharata*, or any other Indian

---

[1] Among many excellent English translations of the Bhagavad Gita, some of the most accessible include the translations by Eknath Easwaran, Juan Mascaro, Swami Prabhavananda, and Barbara Stoller Miller.

[2] see *www.hinduism.about.com/od/thegita/a/famousquotes.htm*

scripture. Nevertheless, we have gleaned powerful insights and inspiration from the story of Draupadi recounted below that seem to offer a unique symbolic perspective on the work of Maher and its mission to support Indian women in freeing themselves from the oppressive patriarchal structures of contemporary Indian society. These insights are articulated in this chapter.

By way of context, the core story in the *Mahabharata* is a struggle for the throne of the kingdom of Hastinapura, ruled by the Kuru clan. Two collateral branches of the Kuru family are pitted against each other: the one hundred Kaurava brothers, led by Duryodhana, and the five Pandava brothers, among whom Yudishthira is the eldest. Both Duryodhana and Yudishthira claim to be first in line to inherit the throne. The struggle culminates in a devastating war in which the Pandavas are ultimately victorious, despite being vastly outnumbered. Krishna, an incarnation of God, does not fight in the battle but serves as charioteer for Arjuna, the chief warrior among the Pandavas. The profound dialogue between Arjuna and God (incarnated as Krishna) recorded in the Bhagavad Gita takes place on the Kurukshetra battlefield just prior to the start of the war.

There is a key turning point in the *Mahabharata* when the war becomes inevitable. This point of no return takes place when the beautiful princess Draupadi is gambled away by her husband Yudhisthira in a high-stakes dice game. Yudishthira is fond of gambling, but he is no match for his opponent, who is very experienced and given to trickery. Yudhishthira keeps losing one round after another, and he loses his entire kingdom and gambles away his four brothers and himself into slavery.

Finally Yudhisthira puts up his wife Draupadi as a stake in the game, and loses her as well. One of Duryodhana's henchmen then drags Draupadi by her hair from the women's chambers, where she was in retreat because it was the time of her menstrual period, and where no man is allowed to enter without permission. She is dragged into the Royal Court, dressed only in a single "wearing cloth," as was the women's custom at the time of menstruation. The Kuru elder statesmen, senior military leaders, and high priests are all assembled, including the king, Dhritarashtra, who is blind (significant symbolism in itself).

Draupadi is in shock and outraged. She asks Yudhisthira whether he gambled himself into slavery before or after he wagered her in the dice game. Discovering that he had lost himself beforehand, Draupadi speaks out and makes a bold appeal for justice. She turns to address the wizened elders who are empowered by both legal and religious authority to administer justice. "How can a man who has lost himself claim any authority over his wife?" she demands to know. "My husband, having first lost himself, had no authority to put me up as a stake in the dice game!"

The leaders to whom Draupadi appeals are frozen in a crippling and devastating silence. Subservient to a "code of honor" that upholds the dictates of an indulgent dice game as paramount—overruling all considerations of justice, ethics, responsibility, dignity, and basic rights—the elders of the society are paralyzed in inaction. Vidura, a brother of Duryodhana, stands up and makes a passionate appeal to the assembled elders to do their duty and intervene to protect the royal daughter-in-law, but not one of the leaders makes a move. Bishma, the senior statesman, normally a man of the highest ethical standards, offers Draupadi a pitifully inadequate response, saying that "morality is subtle."

The Kuru elders' silence bespeaks a profound betrayal of Draupadi, and symbolically the betrayal of the feminine, and the betrayal of every woman in any age or culture who has ever been violated and then yet further violated and humiliated when her appeals for justice fall upon the deaf ears of the patriarchal institutions of society.

Draupadi continues her appeal, arguing that the dice game was unfairly structured since the opposing party did not likewise put up his possessions and his wife as stakes in the game. Draupadi is clear and forthright, her arguments brilliant and articulate, her logic impeccable. Nobody can refute her. Yet not one of these esteemed leaders sitting in the highest positions of power and authority in the land steps forward to take the only righteous course of action, which is to defend an upstanding and innocent woman who is being flagrantly violated and humiliated by depraved scoundrels—in plain sight for all to witness.

Unprotected by the very pillars of society who should have jumped to her aid, Draupadi is now utterly defenseless against the tyranny of her captors. The inevitable consequence follows forthwith: a jubilant Duryodhana proclaims Draupadi to be his property and his slave. As such, she has no right to own anything, not even the clothes she is wearing. "Let's disrobe her!" he guffaws triumphantly, "and have a closer look at what we've won!" He orders his deputy, Dushasanna, to strip Draupadi naked before the assembled multitudes in the Royal Court hall.

Once again, not one of the venerated elders or assembled spectators in the Royal Court lifts a finger on Draupadi's behalf. Instead, they cast their eyes downward or turn to the side, as if not directly gawking at this reckless humiliation will somehow render it less outrageous and injurious. The situation is becoming more desperate by the minute. Draupadi has nowhere to turn; she has already appealed to the highest court of the land, and it responded with paralyzed impotence—allowing her humiliation to proceed unimpeded before the masses. Dushasanna triumphantly starts ripping Draupadi's wearing cloth off, as Draupadi cries out in desperation to Lord Krishna.

At this juncture in the *Mahabharata* story, a miracle saves Draupadi's honor. As her single cloth is pulled off, another one appears in its place, and then another and yet another. Dushasanna keeps pulling off her cloth, becoming frantic in his determination as he keeps pulling off one after the other. A huge heap of multicolored clothes is piling up on the floor, and Dushasanna finally collapses in exhaustion.

Draupadi cannot be stripped. The assembly of lords and kings applauds, simultaneously awestruck and gripped with fear because of the invisible power that has miraculously protected Draupadi. The miracle is due to Draupadi's beloved, Lord Krishna, who intervenes on her behalf. In her moment of crisis, Draupadi fulfills one of the most important teachings of the Bhagavad Gita, which is to abandon all forms of support whatsoever, and in absolute faith take refuge in the Divine alone, symbolized here by Krishna.

The story continues, with Draupadi commanding a new respect and awe from the elders. The blind king grants her three boons—anything she wishes. Draupadi avails herself of only two, the first to free her husbands (Draupadi is the wife of all five Pandava brothers), and the second to reclaim their weapons. She chastises the Royal Court for its unconscionable betrayal of her, proclaiming that "where righteousness and justice do not exist, it ceases to be a court; it is a gang of robbers. Why else do these foremost of the Kuru elders look silently on this great crime?"

THE "MAHABHARATA" OF CONTEMPORARY SOCIETY

The haunting scene of violation and humiliation of an innocent woman in the "supreme court" of the Kuru elders, and the devastating war that results from it, is one of the most enduring images from the *Mahabharata*. Symbolically, it remains highly relevant in contemporary society. The Kuru society is evidently one that has lost the integrity of its masculine elders, and is therefore not able to protect itself against the corruption and aggressive domination from younger, immature masculine energies within its own ranks. This seems to be the condition of many contemporary societies as well—with masculine elders either absent or ineffective—and the results are just as devastating today as they were in the time of the *Mahabharata*.

Whenever a woman—anywhere in the world—is unjustly oppressed or abused or violated and turns to the authorities only to find justice thwarted or denied by patriarchal institutions, she is symbolically reliving the disturbing drama of Draupadi. And just as Krishna stepped in where the Kuru elders failed, it is at this same point—where contemporary elders and laws and society fails—that a project like Maher is needed to step in.

Symbolically, Maher intervenes at precisely the point where the institutions of society have betrayed the feminine—either by choosing to look away or by standing idle in frozen impotence, thereby allowing the outrageous violation of women to proceed unabated. In the case of Lila, for example, whose story was told in chapter 10, just when her husband's family was about to burn her alive, Maher stepped in as "Krishna" and provided the "miraculous sari" of protection that ultimately saved her life.

Over the years, Maher has served in precisely this role for many an imperiled "Draupadi" who would otherwise be dead today because contemporary society has betrayed them in precisely the same manner as the Kuru elders betrayed Draupadi. Maher thus takes up the cause of today's unprotected Draupadis and becomes the symbolic sari that saves their dignity, protects them from further violation, and sets them back on their proper course. Maher could also be viewed symbolically as the voice of empowered women who step up to the plate in the Royal Court of Kuru elders—standing up for justice where the patriarchal leadership is failing to provide it and advocating for the just cause of the multitude of violated Draupadis who turn up at Maher's door every week.

The prominent businessman in chapter 13 who challenged Lucy after Maher's tenth anniversary—vehemently and "righteously" insisting that the rape scene be expunged from Maher's theater performance—was unwittingly standing in the place of the Kuru elders. Like the blind king Dhritarashtra and the other Kuru elders, he was exhibiting the same complicit denial—determined to keep the crushing and debilitating horror of rape hidden from himself and others so he could justify his refusal to take responsibility for it. It's not that he approved of the rape, any more than Bhishma or Drona approved of Drapaudi's violation. They were abhorred by it. It's just that he did not want to face it because then he would have to take responsibility in some form or another, which would in turn require him to participate somehow in challenging the prevailing societal order that permits this level of outrageous injustice to go on.

The role of Krishna in this story bears some similarity to the role of Jesus when he intervened to protect the woman accused of adultery. Had Jesus stood idly by, as the Kuru elders did, she would have been murdered on the spot, and those who stoned her would have gone away scot-free, reinforced in their self-righteousness.

◊ ◊ ◊

Draupadi speaks truth to power—brilliantly. Yet, not only does she represent the voice of the feminine speaking truth to patriarchal power, she is something much more profound. When patriarchal power refuses to listen to Draupadi and stands idle while she is violated, divine power itself steps in and overrules worldly power—working a miracle to protect her. The fact that Draupadi is not herself a full incarnation of the Divine makes this story all the more powerful, because she is human, like the rest of us, yet because of her deep closeness with God (Krishna), divine power works through her and on her behalf.

The story of Draupadi is remarkable in scriptural literature as a woman who manifests divine power to overcome unjust worldly power. There is nothing quite like it, for example, among the women in the Bible. In the New Testament, Mary alludes to God scattering the proud and bringing down the powerful from their thrones in the "Magnificat," but she herself never confronts the worldly powers directly. Draupadi's story is more akin to that of Jesus confronting the Pharisees and Sadducees for their spiritual corruption. In the Tanakh

(Hebrew Bible), the stories of Judith and perhaps Esther or Ruth come to mind, but God never intervenes directly on their behalf. The story of Susanna in the Book of Daniel (canonical in the Catholic and Eastern Orthodox Bibles but omitted from the Tanakh) bears some similarity to Draupadi's story in terms of Susanna's plight. However, despite Susanna's deep faith and trust in the Lord, it is a man (Daniel) who receives "inspiration from the Lord" and steps in for the rescue, rather than Susanna championing her own cause. It is only in an apocryphal text such as the *Acts of Paul and Thecla* that we find a story analogous to Draupadi's. When Saint Thecla is about to be burned at the stake or devoured by wild beasts or gang raped, she prays to her Lord Jesus Christ, who performs a miracle each time to save her.

Draupadi is unique as one of the most complex and admittedly controversial female characters in Hindu literature. Certain sects of Hinduism, particularly in South India, worship Draupadi and reenact the *Maharbharata* drama as a part of their religious festivals.[3] Draupadi's character is compassionate and generous on one side; on the other, she is brilliant and courageous and wreaks havoc on those who do her wrong. She is never willing to compromise either her own rights or the rights of the Pandavas, and she remains ever ready to fight back in the face of high-handed injustice. Draupadi combines a powerful blend of willful determination that befits *kshatriyas* (warriors) and loving forgiveness characteristic of pious devotees. Draupadi has five husbands, which is of course unthinkable in contemporary society, but the reasons for this are clear enough in the epic story, and not of her own making. Her unusual martial status is ultimately quite irrelevant to who she is and what she stands for.

The great Bengali writer and poet Bankimchandra Chattopadhyay, author of "Vande Mataram" (the national song of India), drew an

---

[3]   Alf Hiltebeitel, *The Cult of Draupadi* (three volumes), University of Chicago Press, 1991

illuminating distinction in 1887 between Draupadi and Sita of the
Ramayana. He observed that Sita is chiefly a wife in whom the softer
feminine qualities are expressed, whereas Draupadi is preeminently a
tremendously forceful queen in whom woman's steel will, dignity, and
brilliant intellect are most evident. He also pointed out that Draupadi
performed all her household duties flawlessly, yet with complete
detachment. In Draupadi he sees exemplified the Bhagavad Gita's pre-
scription for controlling the senses by the higher self.

Gandhi often presented ideal models for women drawn from the
Indian traditions, such as Sita, Draupadi, Damayanti and Mirabai. He
visualized Indian women as the new Sitas, Draupadis and Damayantis,
"pure, firm and self-controlled." He viewed Draupadi as an inspiring model who was not dependent on men and saved herself by an
appeal to Krishna when the Kurus failed to protect her. Interestingly,
Gandhi did not advise a woman to be an ideal wife or ideal mother.
Deviating from the traditional framework, he advised women to be
sisters. Pointing out the greatness of a sister over a wife, he maintained
that a sister is to all the world, whereas a wife hands herself over to
one man.

Hindu women in India today generally model themselves after
Sita, the divine incarnation (*avatara*) of the goddess Lakshmi and
obedient wife of her husband Lord Rama (who is an incarnation of
Vishnu, as is Krishna). Sita sets the standard for wifely and womanly
virtues for most Hindu women. Very few Hindu women model themselves after Draupadi, perhaps because of her unusual marital status,
or because she is not a full divine incarnation, as Sita is, or because she
is vengeful at times (she vows to wash her hair in Dushasanna's blood
for revenge, and does so toward the end of the epic). Nevertheless,
Draupadi provides a powerful female precedent within the spiritual heritage of India as a woman who has no qualms standing up to
injustice, has God (Krishna) backing her up, and is quite prepared

to rebuke men when necessary, regardless of their social or political standing in a patriarchal society that has gone terribly out of balance.

The implications of this legendary tale in the life of Draupadi are far-reaching, and they raise a larger question for contemporary women in India: How might the lives of Indian women be different today if they were to draw more strength and inspiration from the spirit of Draupadi in their struggle for equality and liberation from an unjust patriarchal society?

CHAPTER 16

Longing to Serve

I slept and dreamt that life was joy.
I awoke and saw that life was service.
I acted, and behold: service IS joy!
                    —Rabindranath Tagore

"This is something larger than me!" Chaya exclaimed with enthusiasm. "It is what gives me happiness inwardly. Taking care of my family, my career—all that is just about me," she continued, her eyes shining. "It's fine, I love my family very much. But somehow, what gives me the greatest satisfaction is this project for these less fortunate children in India."

Chaya Pamula was speaking passionately about the project for homeless children and women in India she founded in 2005, inspired by Maher. Chaya and her husband, Mohan Pamula, are highly educated IT professionals who relocated to the United States in 1997, joining the growing ranks of Indian professionals emigrating to the West. They settled in New Jersey with their daughter, and Chaya works in senior management for a leading international pharmaceutical company, heading up their IT strategic planning department. Mohan works in software development and analysis for a major bank. Chaya holds an MBA and Mohan has a Masters in engineering.

Like the growing number of Non-Resident Indians (NRIs) or Persons of Indian Origin (PIOs) living in the West, Chaya and her husband came to the United States to realize their aspirations, and by any external measure they are now fully living the American dream.

They own a spacious, elegant, newer home in a manicured, upscale neighborhood that bears little resemblance to the dusty crowded neighborhoods where they grew up in Hyderabad, India. Speaking Telugu at home and impeccable English outside, Chaya and Mohan have become US citizens. Their daughter, Anusha, is a brilliant and highly motivated teenager who just graduated from high school and left home to begin her studies in international affairs at Georgetown University in Washington DC. Because her parents' income was too high, Anusha was ineligible to receive financial aid based on need, but she landed a hefty merit scholarship to support her studies.

By any measure, Chaya and her family have "made it" beautifully in the West. They live in comfort and affluence that would have boggled the minds of their parents or any earlier generations of their family. Yet, throughout her years in the United States, Chaya was inwardly conflicted by the vast economic disparity between her newfound affluence and the extreme poverty of her own people back home. From the time she was a young woman she had always yearned to do something for those less fortunate than herself.

"I lost my dad when I was fourteen, and my mother when I was eighteen," Chaya explained. "They were such a beautiful pair—truly an ideal couple—always giving and serving others, including people outside our family. I missed them *soooo* much, even till today. So I longed to give some kind of help or support to others who also had no parents, because I knew firsthand the deep pain and emptiness of this condition."

When Chaya returned to India for holiday visits, she began to visit projects and homes for destitute women and children. She was generally very disappointed by what she found. "At one home, the very first moment we arrived the director said he was looking to raise five lakhs [500,000 rupees, or about 13,000 US dollars], and he wanted to know if I could help. As we proceeded with the visit there was a bad smell throughout. Many of the rooms seemed like dungeons. The children were craving attention, and were dressed in torn and tattered clothes. Happiness and joy were missing altogether. The kids under five years of age were given somewhat better care because, as the director explained to me, they had a better chance of being adopted. I left the place feeling very sad."

Chaya continued to visit other homes, but "each place felt mechanical," she lamented. "I began to feel disheartened, and if this was all there was, I didn't want to get involved. Nothing inspired me." She began to lose hope.

Against this background, when Chaya arrived at a new home called Maher for yet another such visit, she was understandably very skeptical. Her host, Dr. Anuradha Karkare, had introduced her to Sister Lucy Kurien that morning in Pune, and the three of them drove out to Maher's main facility in Vadhu Budruk. "From the moment we arrived there, everything was totally different!" Chaya told us. "As we drove up, hordes of children came running, almost out of nowhere, and piled themselves all over Lucy as we got out of the jeep—showering her with love and affection. It was amazing to see, and that was just the beginning." Chaya visited five of Maher's homes that day, and Lucy invited her to sit in several meetings in which various issues were being hashed out with the housemothers. "I saw how Lucy did not spell out answers for them, but gave them the courage to manage things on their own. She also showed me the records of Maher—everything was very clear and out in the open."

Chaya returned to her home in New Jersey very inspired, and she and Mohan decided to make a financial contribution to Maher. Over the next several months, Chaya came to realize that beyond helping Maher financially, what she really wanted to do was to start her own new home in Hyderabad.

Chaya and Mohan took the steps to register a charitable trust in Hyderabad, and gave it the name SOFKIN (Support Organization for Kids in Need). Chaya decided initially to start the organization as a project for children only, and she is now in dialogue with Maher about expanding the project to include battered women. She organized the first fundraiser for SOFKIN in New Jersey in 2005, and in August 2006, the home opened its doors with three children. Four more children came within a month, and soon it became ten. Chaya capped it at twelve in order not to grow too quickly and to gain experience with the operation.

Chaya's biggest concern was how she could manage such a project from halfway around the world. At times it seemed utterly preposterous, and she agonized over the question, What if something goes wrong, and I am not there? Many close friends and relatives tried to discourage her. "Are you absolutely sure you want to take on this responsibility?" they asked. "How can you possibly run this project in India from your home in the United States?" These were legitimate concerns from well-meaning friends, and the discouraging doubts and questions almost stopped Chaya from going forward with the project. She prayed deeply about these questions, and continued to feel the inner prompting to keep going. So she kept going.

Chaya put several measures in place to ensure the smooth operation of the project, including contingencies to cover problems that might crop up in her absence. Some of her family members in Hyderabad joined in to help her and have played an important role in the business. Her father-in-law keeps the main accounting books for the project, and her two brothers help in various ways, such as completing legal documents when needed and assisting Kalyani, the main housemother, with emergencies that need immediate attention, like a recent plumbing repair.

Chaya talks on the phone over the Internet with SOFKIN staff in Hyderabad twice each day, every morning and evening. The purpose is twofold: first, to support Kalyani as the housemother in charge—to give her an ear and sometimes an outlet, which provides a safety net for Kalyani and keeps Chaya closely informed on what is happening with the project. The daily phone contact also enables Chaya to keep a close connection and bonding with the children and with other staff members.

The process was bumpy at first, with one problem after another cropping up as the project got up and running. But now it is operating quite smoothly, and Chaya is enjoying the project greatly. "When people praise me for doing a 'great' thing, I am always so aware of how little I'm actually doing. Still, I do feel satisfied with the project inwardly. I'm very content to help these twelve children come up in their lives; I don't need this project to be more. But if it grows, that's OK too."

Another big gift of SOFKIN is the impact on Chaya's daughter Anusha, who has grown to love the project. Anusha founded a youth group to support SOFKIN at her high school in New Jersey. The group generated lots of enthusiasm, as young Indian teenagers living in the United States are interested in the conditions under which their

Chaya Pamula (center) and her daughter Anusha and husband Mohan share a moment of celebration with Sister Lucy Kurien and Maher's associate director Hirabegum Mullah (far left).

counterparts halfway around the world are living. Anusha's group has conducted several fundraisers, raising two thousand dollars in one case—a substantial sum when converted into Indian rupees. When the group gets together, the kids talk about values and how to care for those who have less than they do—so it raises the conscience of the youth involved.

"I had never planned or expected this to happen," Chaya says, "but this has been a wonderful benefit of the project." It has drawn Anusha and Chaya closer together and given Anusha a new respect for and understanding of her mother. "Anusha is very attentive to the times when I'm talking to India," explains Chaya. "Sometimes, if I'm tired or discouraged, she is there for me. She will prompt me or encourage me, telling me it's time to call Kalyani, or she will offer to do the dishes while I call. It has affected her greatly in a positive way, and also our relationship, which has been a wonderful thing."

EXPANDING MAHER IN INDIA

On the other side of the world, thousands of miles away from Chaya's home in New Jersey, Sister Lucy and Dr. Anuradha Karkare (the president of Maher's board of trustees) had just visited Ranchi, the capital city in India's state of Jharkhand. With the board's approval, they were there to begin laying the groundwork for the opening of another Maher.

Jharkhand, popularly known as *vananchal* (meaning "land of woods"), is recognized as one of the richest areas in India for both its mineral wealth and forestry production. Juxtaposed with the abundance of natural resources is the severe poverty in Jharkhand, which has some of the worst conditions in all of India.[1] In certain areas, poverty and consequent malnutrition have given rise to diseases like tuberculosis,

---

[1] Jharkhand Medical Journal, Dr. N.K. Singh, MD, FICP, Editor, *http://www. jharkhandmedicaljournal.com/hfact.htm*

which has assumed epidemic proportions in certain places.[2] Although several public and private health facilities are available, the overall infrastructure for dispensing health-related services is limited.

Another serious condition in Jharkhand is the high number of women dying in childbirth. The maternal mortality ratio is 23 percent higher than the national average.[3] According to Sister Lucy, who has been concerned for years about the grievous conditions, there are several reasons for this situation, including extreme poverty, poor education, a substandard literacy rate, and a social system where girls marry and become pregnant at an early age. Nearly 40 percent of pregnant girls and women do not receive antenatal care.[4] The majority of deliveries occur at home by an untrained midwife, who cannot handle crisis situations, ultimately risking the life of the woman. Many women die, and subsequently very few infants survive due to insufficient food and a dearth of proper nourishment. Those who do survive are often neglected. The children run away from home and end up on the streets or living in railway stations. Consequently, there is an increase in juvenile delinquency.

"Ranchi, in particular, is an area where women suffer tremendously," Lucy told us. "It is inhabited primarily by a tribal population, and the thoughts and ideas are very backward and superstitious. Most of the men are alcoholics and have bad health habits. As a result, they die earlier, leaving behind a widowed wife and many children. The women are not left with any support."

---

[2]   Revised National Tuberculosis Control Programme Jharkhand, Government of Jharkhand website, *http://www.jharkhandonline.gov.in/depts/healt/ Web%20Site/HEALTH%20WEBSITE/html/tb/tuber.htm*

[3]   Ministry of Health and Family Welfare, SRS Report, *http://mohfw.nic.in/ NRHM/State%20Files/jharkhand.htm#hp*

[4]   Sinha, Kounteya, India reports maximum no of childbirth deaths, Oct 16, 2007, The Times of India, *http://timesofindia.indiatimes.com/article-show/2461713.cms*

The initial focus of this new project will be to establish a home for street children and orphans, providing shelter, nutrition, counseling, education, and discipline. Working with the children will enable Maher to get a foothold in the area and over time build on this foundation a project that serves both women and children.

Maher's other new project is in Ratnagiri, in the Konkan area of southern Maharastra, and is implemented in collaboration with Jesuit priests. Father Tony Da, the current Jesuit provincial, is a visionary and he is very supportive. After initial surveys were completed by Hira, Anand, and Meera of the Maher staff, the new project opened its doors in October, 2008.

◇ ◇ ◇

Uplifting people with innovative and inspiring visions is something that Sister Lucy does extremely well. From the moment Chaya arrived at Maher over five years ago she has felt Lucy's encouragement and support. Whenever there have been barriers to overcome, she has contacted Lucy, who has always given her moral and practical support. "Lucy had lived through so many different obstacles and challenges, and it was so helpful when she'd just tell her experiences to me," Chaya said. "She'd give me the courage I needed to keep going."

Developing and documenting the procedures and rules by which the SOFKIN home is to be run has been an important organizational aspect. Chaya's experience of having managed a franchise where she set up the office for an IT training center has been very valuable. She has applied some of the same organizational principles in developing her strategy for SOFKIN. Collaborating with Kalyani, she has created a daily schedule and a weekly menu that the housemothers follow. Kalyani maintains the daily accounting records for the household as well.

Providing a high quality of life for the children, despite very modest resources, is vital to Chaya. "SOFKIN must be an improvement in overall quality of life for these children," she said. "Otherwise, the project is not worth doing. The children must have not only the basic necessities—shelter, safety, nutritional food, clothing, education—but especially important is the love and affection they need and deserve." This requires trustworthy staff, which Chaya is fortunate to have with her current housemothers.

Chaya herself loves to be with the children, and she looks forward to the day when she can spend more time with them. However, at this point she devotes most of her time to fixing problems. "After the first year, the children started to call me 'Amma.' I asked them why, and two of the older ones explained, 'You are the one who is taking care of us and keeping us happy and safe, so we want to call you by a name that says who you are to us.' So I said 'Fine,' and in fact I was very happy. I did check to ensure that my own daughter, Anusha, was OK with it, because I didn't want to pass on a wrong message, and she was totally fine with it."

SOFKIN is funded by a growing circle of Indian friends and colleagues in the IT industry in the United States, most of whom are Chaya's friends and associates within the Indian community in the New Jersey area. Chaya organizes a major event every year to raise funds for both SOFKIN and Maher. A few corporate sponsors have stepped forward, including one that has been donating twelve thousand dollars. Chaya has been careful not to raise more money than is needed. "I don't want more funds than are required to run the project, because we aren't trying to expand at this time, and we don't want to be sitting on extra resources that aren't going directly to the current needs of the project."

The SOFKIN project has transformed Chaya's life. The project funders have been inspired by SOFKIN and Maher for achieving something they had believed was impossible. Thus, SOFKIN is affecting their lives as well. Yet, few want to get more involved than this. "It's easy for them to write a check, and to participate in that way, but they don't want the larger responsibility," Chaya said. "They are glad that someone is doing it. They often tell me they don't have the time, or the 'guts,' to do something like that."

Chaya can't imagine doing anything less. "My career fulfills the promise I made to my mom before she died," she said. "Mom wanted me to get educated and trained so that I would never be dependent on anyone else for my livelihood. I have done that in my career, but it didn't really fulfill me. But with SOFKIN, I am more fulfilled inwardly," she said, gently touching her heart. "I started to respect myself in a way that I had not done before, despite my success with the MBA and my corporate profession."

Chaya's story is a powerful illustration of what one person can do. There are approximately 3.2 million Non-Resident Indians living in the United States and Canada, and 2.5 million in Europe and other affluent countries.[5] Millions of these people are highly educated and well-to-do, and by choice have left their homeland behind except for occasional visits. Chaya's example shows what is possible, and provides inspiration and encouragement for innovative ways in which a Westernized NRI can take practical action that makes a real difference back home, while also continuing to live a life in the West. (For more information about SOFKIN, visit *www.sofkin.org*.)

---

[5]   Dr. Thomas Abraham, NRIs/PIOs–A Catalyst for Development, GOPIO: Global Organization of People of Indian Origin, *http://www.gopio.net/ publications.htm*

CHAPTER 17

Goodbye to *Chalta Hai!*— Keys to Maher's Success

A nation is not free until its women are free.
—Nozizwe Madlala Routledge, former Deputy
Minister of Health and Defense, South Africa

When Dr. Hans Hisch and Dr. Christine Hisch from Vienna, Austria, first met Lucy Kurien in 1994, she was just finalizing the purchase of the land for the first Maher project. As long-term benefactors of Maher, they summarize what they have witnessed since that time:

> The story that followed seems like a miracle. The original seed has grown into a mighty plant nurtured by love, commitment, and flexibility to respond to whatever challenges might appear. When visiting India in 2005, we were overwhelmed by what had become of Maher in just a few years. It could serve as an example for huge business concerns—perfect management, excellent teamwork, most efficient use of all resources, immediate and profound response to new situations, openness to new ideas—all embedded in a deep love and care for the individual, who is treated with deepest respect.

Dr. Hamir Ganla of Maher's board of trustees has observed that "Maher has a remarkable absence of major conflicts and struggles, compared to most organizations and communities." Over the years, Dr. Ganla has served on many boards of different organizations and seen all manner of difficulties, many of them because people don't listen, either to themselves or to each other. "But on the Maher board, people do listen, and it makes such a difference. And if they don't listen, they don't last."

Other leading businesspeople have made similar observations about Maher. Paul Arzt, of the One World Group Buermoos in Austria, observes that "the spirit of Maher is not only unique for the Pune region and India, it is an encouraging spirit for many partnership groups in Europe, too—and our company is one of them."

Why is this? What is the secret to Maher's success? What are the key elements and factors that help Maher function so smoothly? Maher Trustee Dr. P. K. Sharma has reflected on this question:

Many people from various walks of life reach out to help Maher. I asked myself why, when there are so many other options. What is that "something" that touches the right chords in people?

On one of my visits there I came close to what could be one of the answers. I saw the children playing, smiling, laughing and generally enjoying themselves. There was no leg pulling or putting anyone down. One child fell and the game stopped immediately and everyone rushed to help the child back to his feet, and with all smiles, the game resumed. There was no trace of the so-called killer instinct essential to modern-day sports and sports persons.

It was then that I stepped back and looked at the children of Maher. They have come from broken homes and from severely deprived families. They have seen more violence and bitterness in their few years than most of us see in our entire lives. Given the circumstances, one could expect they would be filled with rancor and bitterness to the brim, with naked hatred flashing in their eyes.

Yet here is the surprise: the healing power of Maher works. The entire team is so well geared that any institute could learn [from Maher] the art of soul and mind healing. The bitterness is replaced by love, compassion, and genuine feelings for everyone.

Now replace these innocent children with battered women, and you can, to some extent, visualize the efforts put in by the Maher team in restoring the women's dignity, self-esteem and self-confidence. Even in my fanciest noble thoughts, I could never have envisaged such a forum/help center that could contribute in so many ways to help these unfortunate victims of circumstances. I would never have been able to learn so much about the harsh realities of life, and the forgotten fellow citizens of mine. Maher is a godsend. I think it is the healing touch of Maher that brings out the best in everyone.

Thus, the key to Maher's success is—in a word—love. This is the true "magic of Maher." "When it comes to food and shelter," says Lucy, "people eventually figure out a way to fend for themselves. They can sleep under a tree. They can beg, borrow, or steal to meet their requirements. What they cannot get through such means is unconditional love and attention."

Yet, the love at Maher is something far beyond "good feelings." It is a love born of profound faith, deep devotion to the Divine, and the inherent goodness present in human beings. It is a love that manifests itself in myriad ways: as careful planning and implementation, as deep caring and concern, as discipline and organization, as prayer and meditation, as laughter and frolic, as healing and holding, as deep listening and sensitivity, as attention to innumerable details. It is divine love in active service.

WHAT MAKES MAHER WORK SO WELL?

It's all well and good to recognize that love is the foundation of Maher's success. Love is indeed the root, the means, the pathway, and the goal of Maher. But, in practice, how does this love translate into practical reality and form? What makes for the magic of Maher? What are the specific features, characteristics, and structures that help Maher function so well? Here are perhaps the key factors:

Maher is a vibrant community of women healing women. Though initially drawn together by a shared need for refuge, the women of Maher have created something quite beyond a mere shelter. The feeling of Maher is unlike an institution, and much closer to a very large family. Maher is not just a project, but an inspired community of women, children, and men bound together by shared dreams and commitments. It has the ambience and security of a loving home, not only for the children but for the adults as well. There are struggles and conflicts, to be sure, but these are constantly ground down in the face of something much larger—the vision of a dignified, safe, and healthy life for all women, men, and children of Indian society—regardless of their past, economic situation, or any other limiting characteristics.

All the housemothers and many of the female staff were themselves formerly battered women who sought refuge at Maher. Knowing the harsh realities firsthand, they are especially skilled and compassionate in their caregiving and healing support. This principle of empowered women healing women in distress has been integral to the success of Maher.

The women at Maher know their rights and responsibilities, and for the most part they exercise them with dignity and quiet determination, without indulging in male bashing or excessive self-pity. They care for and support one another in all aspects of their lives, and they give each other strength and courage to grapple with the often daunting challenges they face.

Children play a crucial role, as do the men at Maher. Caring for the children is very healing for the women, and helps to move them out of their painful past. The children are genuinely happy—bringing tremendous joy and levity to the entire Maher community. The men at Maher provide stable and solid grounding for both the children and women that aids in reestablishing safe and trusting relationships with emotionally healthy male figures.

Maher serves others beyond itself. As a force for healing, Maher serves not only its residents, but also the surrounding villages and society of which it is a part. Maher's satellite homes in other villages in the region are bright lights that radiate love and healing into the larger community. Through its outreach programs, Maher catalyzes a healing effect that reaches beyond its own boundaries—into the outlying villages, to Pune and Mumbai and India at large, and now stretching to other countries as Maher dancers have recently begun to perform internationally.

By tapping the wellsprings of love in the human heart, Maher provides a powerful healing atmosphere that has been dubbed "the magic of Maher." The results are palpable in the children's shining eyes and the spirited laughter of residents and staff. These healing effects also extend to the staff, board, and volunteers who serve there, several of whom have remarked that Maher has given them more than they gave to it. One of the Maher staff tells a story that illustrates this principle of love in action, and how it transformed her:

I was very touched and shocked when I first saw Sister Lucy hug a madwoman on the road. The woman was stinking, unbelievably foul! In the beginning, I could never imagine

that Lucy could touch and hug someone like that. But Lucy
went right up to her and hugged her! And brought her with
us to Vatsalyadham. It gave me goose bumps, and I thought,
My God, how can she touch her?! Lucy could get bad diseases!
But why doesn't she get these diseases? It is something to do
with being so pure—so pure your body doesn't matter. Lucy
really broke it—untouchability. When I saw her doing that, it
was such a shock. And then, after I saw it two or three more
times, something changed in me. And before long, I also started doing the same thing myself.

Senior staff are fully committed to Maher. The key senior staff at
Maher are fully committed to the vision, goals, and practical implementation of Maher's projects. They are giving their lives to this
project. Several of them have families, which means they have their
personal lives and responsibility, and still they are giving their very
heart and soul to the project. Their level of commitment exceeds what
would most often be found in a more typical employment position.
The Maher mission and implementation is so compelling that the staff
remains inspired by the work, and they give everything they have to it.
Several of the core staff who have been there since the beginning practically live and breathe Maher. To find staff like this is not easy, and
Maher often looks long and hard to find the right people to occupy
key positions within the organization. Lucy has often commented that
the primary constraint in Maher's future growth and development is
finding the right people who are truly committed.

Maher is a successful interfaith spiritual project. The interreligious
spiritual foundation of the Maher project is alive and real, rather than
being just empty rhetoric or philosophical aspiration. The senior staff
and trustees all engage in spiritual practice of one kind or another,
covering several traditions, including Hindu, Buddhist, Christian,
and Islamic. The overarching guidance for the project is grounded

in a deep trust of the spirit and its ways of working that often baffle human ways of understanding. This interfaith foundation gives the community a spiritual depth, openness, and flexibility that inspires everyone who experiences or visits Maher. Silent meditation and prayer time are an integral part of life for the women and children at Maher. Maher demonstrates the feasibility of an interfaith project that operates smoothly and effectively—upholding universal spiritual values without being beholden to any particular religious philosophy, church, or sect.

Maher is a caste-free zone. The tragedy of India's caste system can only be healed in practice by groups and communities of people from different castes collaborating, or better yet living together in harmony—thereby transcending these destructive divisions. Maher is a place where even people with deeply ingrained and socialized habits of prejudice in relation to caste have been able to shed these limitations and move to a place within themselves where caste truly does not matter anymore. Maher is thus an oasis of unity in a desert of division. It is not the only such oasis in India, but Maher's work to transcend caste distinction is something needed all across the nation.

Maher tackles fundamental causes of poverty and oppression. Maher has grown into a multidimensional project that skillfully addresses a complex spectrum of problems within the social fabric of the Pune region. Committed to redressing not only the symptoms but also the causes of social oppression and poverty, it has developed effective programs in surrounding villages aimed at the education of children, adult literacy, sound ecological practices, and economic self-reliance for local villagers. While many projects focus on one or two key issues only, or serve narrowly defined populations such as those of a particular religious faith, Maher seeks to address a wide range of social, economic, psychological, educational, and environmental needs in an integrated manner. Taken together, Maher's programs provide its residents with a high-quality, dignified life—despite living on very meager financial and material means.

Maher serves vulnerable and outcast populations. Maher's mission has expanded to include serving the needs of the Untouchables—tribals and Dalits—living in the region, people below the lowest rung of India's caste system who are not even recognized by the local or national governments. Maher provides water wells, schools, and basic medical services—utterly transforming the lives of these people.

Maher operates with integrity of principles and practice. Maher operates with a high degree of integrity in all its administrative and service operations. Corruption is rampant in Indian society, and Maher stands out as an exemplary organization in its adherence to ethical business practices. Bribes are commonplace in Indian commerce and government, where they are widely regarded as part of the routine costs of doing business. Maher has refused to pay bribes for any purpose. This policy has significantly delayed implementation of several practical goals, such as obtaining building permits or connections to utility services. Maher has developed a unique reputation among local authorities for its adamant refusal to yield to pressures for bribes. It has also turned down offers of major funding from specific religious denominations that came with strings attached requiring Maher to teach the children the scriptures of a particular religion, an example of which was given in chapter 4. Maher has thus maintained independence from various religious, political, and economic agendas of outside institutions.

Although the above are probably the key factors that determine the success of Maher, there are several others as well:

Group homes are no larger than twenty children and two housemothers. This structure helps to keep Maher from feeling like an institution and guarantees much interpersonal contact between the children and the housemothers. It helps to provide an atmosphere like a home, rather than an institution.

A self-help group in a village near Maher, facilitated by Anand Sagar, who joined Maher in its infancy as the first social worker.

Attention is given to detail. Every operational and procedural detail is carefully considered at Maher. To give just one example, as we mentioned previously, no alarm clocks are used to wake up the children. Instead, the housemothers put on bhajans (Indian spiritual songs), and then go to each child individually and wake them with a gentle hand on the shoulder.

There is long-term follow-up. When it comes time to leave Maher, women are tracked carefully by Maher's team of social workers and counselors to ensure smooth reintegration into society. The frequency of follow-up visits and contacts depends on the particular circumstances of each case and the nature of the situation the woman is entering. Special care is taken in cases where there has been a history of severe abuse or life-threatening conditions. In the case of a woman who is not going back to her family—for example, if she is getting a divorce and becoming a single mother—Maher allows her to stay longer in order to build an appropriate financial base before leaving. Typically, the woman leaves Maher when she has built up a financial base of around 50,000 rupees (1,065 US dollars), which is sufficient for her to make a new start.

Maher provides vocational counseling and training in practical economic skills for women, which helps them to develop their own sources of income when they leave. Some are trained extensively in the crafts production unit, learning skills that allow them to develop a steady income stream after they leave Maher. Each woman's particular skills and capacities are assessed on an individual basis, and a number of women are placed in employment positions with the help of Maher's network of colleagues and friends in the larger Pune region.

Dance and cultural programs are part of the Maher experience. The program in classical Indian dance and music has provided a powerful rejuvenating force at Maher. In any healing community there is a need for group activities that lift the spirit, help people heal and move beyond their troubled past, and bond with one another in shared goals and new activities that bring renewal and draw out the best in people. The dance program at Maher has done just this, and the beauty is that it draws upon the deep roots of India's own dance and musical heritage. Thus, through Maher, a tiny portion of India is healing itself through its own dance traditions.

"THE HARVEST IS PLENTIFUL, BUT THE LABORERS ARE FEW"

"Lucy Kurien's motto is 'love all.' She follows the dictates of her heart," write the editors Jo and Vinod of *Frozen Thoughts*, an international magazine that interviewed Lucy. "And she detests the *chalta hai* attitude, and prays that everyone who practices it deletes it from their vocabulary."[1] "*Chalta hai*" is a vernacular term in Hindi that originally meant "It will do," but according to the Dictionary of Indian English, it has come to mean "Anything will do; the typical careless Indian attitude." One hears chalta hai frequently in India, and the "chalta hai attitude" refers to an irresponsibly unconcerned or lackadaisical attitude among people in India that is often cited as the reason for India's poor state of affairs. Lucy would love to see India bid a permanent goodbye to chalta hai, because the attitude is diametrically opposed to the high standards of caring, integrity, diligence, ethics, and loving concern that Maher is founded upon.

"It was a humbling experience to meet Sister Lucy," continue Jo and Vinod. "We learned from her that we would find happiness in following our heart; and if we believe we can do it, we can turn our dreams into reality. The love and happiness we felt at Maher Ashram was overwhelming. We pray that it continues to reach out to people longing for unconditional love and care."

The authors once asked Lucy, "What is your dream for the future of Maher?" We close this chapter with her response:

> I would love to see many more people come forward and truly commit themselves to the vital work of building communities of healing and love. It is such fulfilling work—you can't imagine! And the need is so great! Not only in India, but everywhere. One of my favorite lines from the Bible is "The harvest is plentiful, but the laborers are few." Sadly, this is so true. Here in India, despite the poverty, our scarcest resource for expanding Maher is not money; it is finding deeply committed people. The money will always come, but where are the

---

[1]   Jo and Vinod, *Frozen Thoughts*, July 2007, p. 42. *www.frozenthoughts.com/ pdf_simply/july_07.pdf*

truly committed souls? So my prayer for the future is that the fire of real Love will ignite more people's hearts, and inspire them to join this vital work. It can be done anywhere, and it is needed everywhere.

CHAPTER 18

Expanding the Maher Vision

My life is in the hands of the Buddha, dharma, and sangha—literally. I've handed it over. Whatever is necessary for me to do benefit to all beings, let me do it. I don't care . . .
                                        —Tenzin Palmo

"How magnificent! I'm so moved by this project!" exclaimed Tenzin Palmo, beaming from ear to ear. She had just learned about Maher for the first time from Sister Lucy. The two had met briefly in March of 2008 in Jaipur, India, where they had both attended an international conference of women leaders entitled "Making Way for the Feminine" (sponsored by Global Peace Initiative of Women). Lucy summarized the various projects of Maher and showed pictures to Tenzin Palmo, whose eyes grew ever wider as she took in the magnitude of what Maher was doing.

Jetsunma Tenzin Palmo is a well-known Buddhist nun from North India who secluded herself in a remote cave at thirteen thousand feet in the Himalayas, where she lived in spiritual retreat for twelve years. She meditated for twelve hours a day, accomplishing a depth of spiritual renunciation that most Tibetan lamas believed was utterly impossible for a woman. She faced unimaginable cold, wild animals, floods and rockfalls, and almost died twice. When she came down from the mountain, she founded the Dongyu Gatsal nunnery in northern India to train Tibetan nuns in the spiritual practices that had been denied women for centuries, and to revive the Togdenma lineage. Today her nunnery is thriving, and she has successfully over-turned the entrenched patriarchal prejudice that systematically barred women from rising to spiritual mastery and enlightenment within the Tibetan Buddhist tradition. She leads retreats around the world, and is widely recognized as a highly realized spiritual master.[1]

Before she departed, Tenzin Palmo took Lucy's face into both of her hands and gently moved her head forward until their foreheads were touching. She whispered a blessing prayer for Lucy, and for Maher. It was an intimate and auspicious moment for the few of us present, wit-nessing these two spiritual leaders embrace one another. Both women have directly challenged the long-standing patriarchy within their respective contexts, overcoming tremendous obstacles while remain-ing true to their hearts. Both have founded inspiring communities of women in India that are manifesting their respective missions in pro-found and impactful ways. Both faced entrenched opposition to their work that would have stopped most others. Both were forced to stand utterly and painfully alone—particularly in the early years. Both are fulfilling the highest teachings of their respective spiritual traditions. And both share the same utter abandon of themselves—handing their lives over completely to the Divine, in service of others.

"MAY EVERY BRICK AT MAHER SHIMMER WITH GOD'S INFINITE LOVE"

The Indian saint Ramakrishna teaches that "those persons are truly free, even here in this embodied state, who know that the Divine is the sole true agent, and that they by themselves are powerless to do anything." This spiritual secret is one that Lucy Kurien and many of the Maher staff are living out. "God is my strength," Lucy confides. "He led me from the ignorance of life to the reality of people's lives. He leads me on to the unknown. With Him I keep walking. My faith

---

[1]   For an engaging and inspiring account of Tenzin Palmo's life, see *Cave in the Snow*, Vicki Mackenzie, London: Bloomsbury, 1999.

and conviction have helped turn my dreams into reality," she affirms. "I am happy and peaceful. I have made my life as simple as possible. God could not have been any kinder to me. It is the women and children who are giving me everything in life—happiness and a purpose to live for. Earlier I used to ask myself, what can I do for them? Now I ask, what more can I do for them?"

In her own way, Lucy lives up to the scriptural teaching that "Greater love hath no woman than this—that she lay down her life for her friends" (John 15:13 [edited for gender]). Lucy's closest friends are God and her fellow human beings, and she has totally given her life to both—thereby fulfilling the two greatest commandments of her religious faith. Total faith in God—grounded in prayer and meditation—has been the foundation of Lucy's commitment, guidance, and inspiration. In this manner, Lucy and her "heart child" Maher have been carried through every impasse and challenge, despite many extremely daunting moments. Lucy's life has been threatened on a number of occasions. One night early on, an angry mob came and informed Lucy that they would destroy Maher. Yet such things have not deterred Lucy in the slightest.

The oasis of love and visionary spirit at Maher is contagious, and everyone who visits is moved by the beauty, joy, and peace of the place. This is all the more remarkable given that every week three or four new women show up, bruised or bloody, on Maher's doorstep. Yet the joy and laughter there never cease, and the grace and inspiration keep flowing. "My deep prayer is that every brick, every speck of dust at Maher, shimmers with God's infinite love," declares Lucy with conviction. For anyone who visits, it is evident that Lucy's prayer is answered.

WHAT FUTURE FOR MAHER?
"The goal of Maher is to create a society that does not need a Maher," affirms Father Francis D'Sa. The wisdom of his vision speaks for itself. The long-term goal of Maher is to help transform society so thor-

Two Maher girls offering *aarti* blessing to visitors.

oughly that no such refuge project is needed. Lucy articulates a similar perspective. "The ultimate goal of Maher is to reach out to more and more communities in need, and eventually to effect change throughout the whole of India. Our sincere dream is to see an end to the kind of violence and discrimination that has driven the women and children in our care to seek refuge. We are devoted to working toward the prevention of injustice and cruelty, while at the same time providing a sanctuary for those who have been touched by unkindness."

But how do we create a society that does not need a Maher? What is the future of Maher? What are the larger implications of its pioneering vision and work? What is the potential for implementing similar projects elsewhere in India? Elsewhere in the world?

MAHER'S SUCCESS IS NOT UNIQUE TO INDIA

Reflecting on the key factors behind Maher's success as listed in the previous chapter, it quickly becomes evident that these factors are not unique to India. With the exception of the caste-free zone, which applies specifically to India, the keys to Maher's success are not unique either to Maher alone nor to an Indian social context. Rather, they represent a practical implementation of universal principles of integrity and the human spirit—love, healing, commitment, diversity, service, ethics. With appropriate adaptations and augmentations, these keys can be applied to the creation of similar projects in oppressive societies elsewhere. The example of Maher is therefore vital not only as a practical project in India, but as a pragmatic inspiration for anyone who seeks practical ways to help oppressed women and children rise up from the ashes of entrenched social and patriarchal injustice.

In saying this, we are by no means suggesting that the factors contributing to Maher's success can be simply copied or transferred haphazardly anywhere. Nor are they sufficient by themselves to guarantee successful implementation of a project. Great care and sensitivity will be required in any attempt to found a similar project elsewhere, with judicious modification and augmentation applied as appropriate. A women's community project in any country must necessarily be created with sensitivity and skillful attention to that culture's specific characteristics, social norms and values. Just as the caste system imposes certain characteristics unique to the Maher project, other cultures will have specific considerations that require unique adaptations for projects in those countries. Thus Maher cannot be simply transplanted to another country, or even to other parts of India, without suitable and potentially major adjustments and modifications.

Nevertheless, Maher is a shining beacon of hope for all, and its remarkable success provides a sound basis for inspiring similar projects elsewhere. Maher demonstrates how much a small group of deeply committed women and men can accomplish, even in one of the most patriarchal societies on Earth. Social conditions for women and the low-caste populations of India are among the most oppressive for any population anywhere on the planet. As Lucy once remarked, conditions for women and the poor in many parts of India are essentially no different from the barbaric conditions that prevailed in Biblical times. In light of this, Maher's achievement in implementing such a successful women's community project in such an exceedingly challenging context is a remarkable achievement indeed. While recognizing that no single project is a panacea and that the scale of women's challenges in India is enormous, nevertheless Maher serves as a powerful inspiration to all those who seek practical solutions for healing and uplifting downtrodden peoples.

Ironically, perhaps the path to creating a society that does not need a Maher anywhere is to create Maher-like projects everywhere. Maher itself has started new projects in the state of Jharkhand in north-central India and in the Ratnagiri district of southern Maharashtra. The new Maher homes were inaugurated on October 10, 2008, in Ratnagiri, and on November 1, 2008, in Jharkhand. Other people and organizations will be inspired by Maher's success to start their own projects. SOFKIN, founded by Chaya Pamula (see chapter 16), is one such project already in existence, and another is being started in Velhe Taluke near Pune by Dr. Kashinath and Angela Chitte. Other projects are in the planning stages.

Beyond this, Maher is certainly not alone in working to uplift conditions for women in India. There are many different kinds of important projects throughout the country, far beyond the scope of what can be reviewed here. A few representative examples of related or similar projects elsewhere in India are summarized briefly in appendix D.

MAHER TRAINING CENTER

To support its current and future initiatives, Maher has begun to train social workers, clergy, religious nuns, and other clinical professionals in its model. Trainees visit Maher for periods ranging from a few months to two years, during which time they learn the details of daily operations, are exposed to the overarching philosophy and spirituality of the Maher model, and engage in specific practical service to some aspect of the project. After the training period, they take these lessons back to their home communities and begin to apply the learnings there.

The training dimension of Maher will be expanded significantly in the future. Plans call for a staff training center that will develop and refine the training program and make it available on a larger scale. The goal of the training center is twofold: to broaden the scope and effectiveness of future Maher staff, and to train others to apply Maher principles or practices in new or existing projects of their own.

EMBRACE PEOPLE AS PEOPLE, NOT AS PEOPLE OF A PARTICULAR RELIGION

Social workers and health professionals are coming to train at Maher in growing numbers. Religious sisters and priests are also coming, and they in turn often send other sisters and clergy for training. Most religious trainees typically stay for one or two years. Currently there are three Catholic sisters at Maher—two from the Holy Cross congregation and one from the Carmelite missionaries. "Personally this makes me very happy, as we are creating interreligious and interfaith community together," says Lucy.

Yet, sadly for Sister Lucy, significant institutional barriers are preventing more extensive training of religious sisters at Maher. Several Church authorities and congregations, including Lucy's own Sisters of the Cross, have reservations about sending Catholic sisters to Maher. They are concerned that there is no structured daily mass or prescribed timetable followed, which they deem to be an essential part of religious life. "The Church is not very pleased with our way of religious life because we aren't living in a traditional structured community," Lucy said with chagrin.

"What I would like the Church to understand," she continued, "is that, living within the traditional congregation, it is very difficult to associate with people of other faiths. We are not able to mix with them, so how can we serve them?" Lucy's face displays a great sadness whenever she speaks of this discrepancy. She went on to explain that in the convent she found it impossible to live in the way she felt was necessary to truly serve those people whom the congregation was ostensibly serving. "My conviction was to live with people of all faiths, without concern for people of a particular religion. The Church authorities told me this was too much for them to understand." Yet Lucy was simply expressing the same deep conviction that Mahatma Gandhi expressed in a similar way when he proclaimed, "I am a Muslim and a Hindu and a Christian and a Jew—and so are all of you."

"In an organized religious community, there are lots of rules," Lucy continued. "For example, we can't leave at prayer time. We cannot reach out to people except at certain times and under certain conditions. We are beholden by the rules of the community. Yet the Spirit calls us to respond—on its terms—to the need of the moment. So it is important to take risks, and to go beyond rules. At certain times it is necessary for people to go beyond established rules. We have to take the risk." And Lucy has done just that. Indeed, a number of her superiors within the Church structures counseled her early on against striking out on her own to create a new project. If Lucy Kurien had followed their advice rather than take the risk to follow her own heart, Maher would not exist today.

Lucy is ever more convinced of the crucial importance of the interfaith spiritual foundation of Maher. Personally, she is deeply devoted to Jesus Christ as her "personal guru," and at the same time she profoundly honors all religions. For Lucy, like Father Thomas Keating, upholding the truth of all religions is a powerful expression of her love for Jesus and her own Catholic faith tradition, rather than a threat to it. Maher effectively constitutes a new form of interreligious or spiritual community that crosses traditional religious (and secular) boundaries, yet maintains spiritual integrity, depth, and commitment. Once, when asked to which church she belongs, Lucy replied with a big smile, "the church of humanity."

Maher demonstrates that interfaith religious community can work in practice without diminishing the seriousness of the religious life, and without compromising a deep devotion to the Divine or the life of prayer and meditation. In Lucy's words, "Religion is a valuable tool, but we must not get attached to any particular religion. Because then, for me, I'm convinced that we are closing our mind to others. I am a Catholic, and a religious nun, but if I stay confined within those boundaries, then I'm closing my doors to others. We must embrace and include all people as people, and not as people of particular religions. Suppose, for example, that there is communal violence [religious conflict]. How can I stand apart from this and condemn it as wrong if I myself belong to one particular religion? And if I myself am living only with people of one religion? Am I not then part of the communalism, even if not in its extreme forms? When I am independent, then I can speak courageously as an advocate for love between all people and all faiths."

SYNERGY AMONG COMMUNITIES

Maher's goal is not to franchise itself widely and grow into some huge, unwieldy mega-project. Rather, its vision for the future is to grow steadily and organically—initially expanding its programs and scope to other parts of India—and to serve as a training and resource center for other pioneers who may wish to start similar projects, either in India or elsewhere in the world. Toward this goal, Maher is just now beginning to compile detailed operations and training materials— both to document and streamline its own operations, and to serve others who are in training.

The finale of Maher's dramatic theater performance of the life of Mahatma Gandhi.

In the long term, if the Maher example continues to grow and inspire others as a leading model, there may be motivation to create a loosely structured association of such communities. Such a step would be premature at this time, but at an appropriate point down the road such an association could foster mutual learning, quality control, sharing of effective practices, and innovative exchange programs, while at the same time leaving each project free to develop on its own.

BEYOND MAHER: RISING TO NEW LIFE

The lessons of Draupadi's story in the *Mahabharata*, recounted in chapter 15, can be extended symbolically to a societal level. In any patriarchal society that has spiraled out of balance and in which the Masculine has lost itself—to domination, injustice, corruption, greed—the Masculine has no true authority and no legitimate claim over the Feminine. If the Feminine then steps forward and stands for what is right and true—in genuine love and humility and with courage—the Divine itself will step in, and work miracles.[2] This is the profound teaching—or rather, divine promise!—that is conveyed in the story of Draupadi in Hinduism, in Saint Thecla in Christianity, or in any of the saints in any tradition who have served as the instruments through whom the Divine performs its work for justice in the world.

Patriarchal power in any of its forms—political, religious, economic—no matter how strong and formidable it may appear, is paltry and impotent in the face of divine power. There may be struggles and defeats along the way, but in the end the Divine will always prevail—whether symbolized by God, Allah, Buddha, Yahweh, Krishna, Tara, the Great Spirit, or simply Love and Truth. This is what Mahatma Gandhi was speaking to when he said, "Whenever I despair, I remember that the way of truth and love has always won. There may be tyrants and murderers, and for a time, they may seem invincible, but in the end, they always fail."

In her groundbreaking research on the cross-cultural origins of patriarchy, historian Gerda Lerner was astonished to discover a striking pattern in the rise of women's oppression that was replicated in every ancient culture she examined: "The most important thing I learned was the significance to women of their relationship to the Divine, and the profound impact that the severing of that relationship had on the history of women."[3] Lerner concludes that the beginning of women's oppression was directly coupled with the decline of women's

---

[2]   In this example, of course, the "Feminine" can work through men as well as women, just as the "Masculine" also works through women as well as men.

[3]   Gerda Lerner, *The Creation of Feminist Consciousness: From the Middle Ages to 1870* (New York: Oxford University Press, 1993), cited in C. Flinders, *At the Root of this Longing, Reconciling a Spiritual Hunger and a Feminist Thirst* (San Francisco: HarperSanFrancisco, 1999, p. 126). See also Gerda Lerner, *The Creation of Patriarchy* (New York: Oxford University Press, 1986).

direct connection with the Divine. The logical implication is that the end of women's oppression may be intricately tied to women reclaiming and taking full responsibility for their innate connection to the Divine—directly, rather than mediated by priests, swamis, lamas, or religious institutions, whether of the East or West. This would create a fundamental link between feminine spirituality and the emancipation of women that has yet to be widely recognized or embraced. And this is precisely the essence of the teaching so powerfully illustrated in the story of Draupadi, for without her direct connection to the Lord (Krishna), nothing would have saved her.

Maher is a shining example of these teachings. A small number of five or six deeply committed souls in twelve short years has been the instrument through which a vibrant healing community has been created that has provided refuge and rehabilitation to nearly 2,000 people (1,350 women and 600 children total). Maher is a wonderful example of Margaret Mead's famous aphorism, "Never doubt that a small group of thoughtful, committed citizens can change the world. Indeed, it is the only thing that ever has." In Maher's case, this has been accomplished against all odds in an exceedingly patriarchal society—a miracle in its own right. The story of Maher is a story of one miracle after another—from the innumerable healing stories of the women and children to the many critical moments in Maher's evolution when major challenges or obstacles blocked the way forward or threatened to destroy the project altogether. In every case, something unexpected happened—often unbidden and seemingly coming out of nowhere—that turned things around and kept the project going.

Yet projects like Maher can also be created elsewhere. The principles of love, courage, service, truth, and integrity that underlie the Maher project can be manifest anywhere, and are needed everywhere. There is a profound, untapped potential in every society across the globe for women (and men) to join together and begin working with love to effect the needed changes and to provide refuge to their sisters and brothers and children. For anyone who aspires to create such a project, the key requirement is articulated succinctly by the great German mystic, Meister Eckhart, who tells us that we need only get ourselves out of the way and "let God be God in us."

Maher, and projects like it, are magnificent flowers in the garden of humanity—fragrant blossoms of love that point the way forward to the only future that will ever succeed on this Earth, which is to live together in harmony across all divisions of religion, caste, gender, nation, and race—as one human family.

Let us close this book with the words of one of India's greatest women saints, Sri Anandamayi Ma:

> I find one vast garden spread out all over the universe.
> All plants, all human beings, all higher mind bodies
> are about in this garden in various ways,
> each has its own uniqueness and beauty.
> Their presence and variety give me great delight.
> Every one of you adds, with your special features, to the
>   glory of the garden.
>
> Who is it that loves, and who that suffers?
> The Divine alone stages a play with Himself.
> Individuals suffer because they perceive duality.
> Find the One, everywhere and in everything,
> and there will be an end to pain and suffering.

Acknowledgements

First and foremost, we thank the wonderful women residents of Maher who opened their hearts and told us their stories with tremendous courage and sensitivity. It is not an easy matter for Indian women to open up and disclose sensitive personal information, particularly to foreigners, and we are deeply grateful for their candor and friendship.

We also thank the Maher children and youth who shared their stories and dreams with us, and who are such a joy and inspiration to all who meet them.

How can we even begin to thank Sister Lucy Kurien, and the Maher staff and Board of Trustees, who are stewarding such a profound and beautiful project? Sister Lucy has thrown open the doors of Maher to us, and our gratitude is boundless. Hirabegum Mullah has been extremely gracious and supportive since the day we first set foot at Maher. Salim Xavier has been a constant source of unwavering technical support for many years, and Manju Devarapalli has been quick to respond to our every need and question during the extended editorial process. John, Yuraj and the other Maher drivers took us wherever we needed to go, sometimes driving through the night to meet a flight or other deadline.

We are grateful to the Maher Board of Trustees, who graciously invited us to participate in several of their meetings. In particular, we thank Fr. Francis D'Sa for introducing us to Maher, and to Dr. Hamir Ganla, Dr. Sharma, and Dr. Anuradha Karkare for in-depth interviews.

We wish to express our thanks to Regina Sara Ryan, our editor at Hohm Press, for her impeccable editorial skills, and to Dasya and Bala Zuccarello for their excellent support. Nancy Lewis did a thorough job of copyediting.

We thank the following individuals for graciously contributing their photographs: Christine Lendorfer (p. 58), Roswitha Ertl and Johanna Ober (p. 151), Royda Crose (p. 175), and Mikaela Keepin (p. 124, 211, 219, and 224). The remaining photos were taken by the authors, or by Maher staff. If we have inadvertently omitted a photo credit, we beg the photographer's forgiveness.

Deep thanks go to Father Thomas Keating for his spiritual mentorship and sustained encouragement on this book, and for his permission to reproduce the Snowmass Conference principles of interfaith spirituality in Appendix B.

We are grateful to Chaya, Mohan, and Anusha Pamula for opening their home to us on several occasions, and providing a quiet space to complete some of the writing. We are similarly grateful to the Medical Mission Sisters in Pune and to Lori and Bob Warmington and Michael Abdo of Aspen, Colorado for providing writing retreat space.

Finally, we are grateful to the many individuals who have given generously of their time and skills to contribute to this book in one way or another. We wish to thank several Maher interns and volunteers for writing about their experiences of Maher, several excerpts of which are quoted in the text. These include Andrea van der Leeuw, Dinesha Hoekstra, Johanna Ober, Roswitha Ertl, Alexandra Gramps, and Mikaela Keepin.

We thank Rosemarie Temple and her colleagues for hosting our visit to the UK. We are also grateful to Christine Lendorfer, Roswitha Ertl, and Johanna Ober for hosting our visit to Vienna. Our thanks to Ravi Ravindra for allowing us to borrow the title for Chapter 12.

So many other people have helped us in this project in so many ways, it would be impossible to name them all, but you know who you are, and we offer our sincere thanks to all. In particular, we wish to thank our families for their love, encouragement, and patient support throughout the four years of writing this book. If we have inadvertently neglected to thank anyone else who deserves an explicit acknowledgement, we ask for your understanding and forgiveness.

APPENDIX A

Rainbow of Services at Maher

Maher is a whirlpool of diverse projects serving the needs of both women and children. There are more than 100 women and nearly 400 children at Maher, reaping the benefits of the exposure, training, and vocational programs of Maher. Maher has twenty-two projects in total. Brief summaries of each project are given below.

Mamtadham: a home for women in distress. Maher provides safety, shelter, health and nutritional needs, counseling, and vocational training to help the women gain self-confidence and wellbeing, with an overarching goal to reunite them with their families.

Aashai: a home for the unwed mothers. While at Maher these women and girls participate in all the activities and help in the ongoing work. Once they have delivered, they are reunited with their families.

Kishoredham: a home for children. These children come from broken families. When they come to Maher they receive the basic needs—shelter, nutritious food, clothing, counseling, education. The children are also trained in yoga and meditation, dance, karate, computer usage, and music. The overarching goal is to reunite the children with their families.

Vatsalyadham: a home for mentally disturbed women. There are fifty-one women who have been rescued from various places—most of them off the street. Psychiatric treatment, counseling, medication (prescribed as needed), and different healing therapies are given to the women with the goal of supporting a better quality of life and wellbeing.

Sukh Sandhya: a home for destitute aged women. Currently (2009), there are twenty-three elederly women, living adjacent to Vatsalyadham. They participate in all the activities, including gardening and the daily operations of the house. The positive role they provide for the Maher children as grandmothers is an added blessing for the program.

Parishram: a vocational training workshop. As part of Maher's multidimensional, healing and therapy program, the women residents participate in vocational training to help them become economically self-sufficient. The women learn to make several different items including, greeting cards. candles, incense, gift bags, jewelry, crochet bags, curry and henna powder. These products are sold to companies and to the friends and well-wishers of Maher. The women earn a percentage of the sales.

Swavalamban: a project of self-help groups in villages throughout the region. There are 237 self-help groups working in different villages. Every month several more are added. Most are for women, but Maher is unusual in creating more than thirty self-help groups for men. The specific work being done by the self-help groups includes: establishing tree plantations, offering street plays, conducting seminars, building toilets in the villages, micro-financing and self-financing at the village level. These self-help groups have become agents of unity and cooperation in the villages and in the community.

Dhyanganga: a project to establish libraries in the rural areas to foster reading habits that will help improve the literacy rate in children and in adults.

Premalaya: a day care centre. The purpose of this project is to care for the children who are left alone at home when their parents go to work.

They are provided a safe environment, nutritious food, activities, as well as given periodic check-ups by a nurse at the primary health center.

Vidyadham: a project for "outstation" children (that is, not resident at Maher). Children are sent here, according to their interest, for professional training. The goal is for them to eventually assist their families economically. They are able to manage their lives.

Ushalaya: a project of kindergartens. There are currently (2009) seventeen kindergartens in different villages. This is one of the ways that Maher can establish a presence in the villages and have regular contact with the children and women.

Pragati: a project to raise awareness about health and sanitation in the villages, to abolish the dowry system, and to eradicate superstitious beliefs that are harmful to the health and wellbeing of the community.

Swachata: a project about vermiculture pits to support the farmers in the villages. Training is given in the villages about the usefulness of vermiculture pits.

Kalasagar: a project of open school for people who have dropped out of school. Guidance is given to support people in their studies, and also to help them expand and develop their skills and talents.

Vidyalaya: a project for "tuition" (tutoring) classes. Maher offers tutoring classes twice a day for students whose parents are illiterate and unable to help their child.

Tantragyan: a vocational training program for youth who remain at home after their education. They are provided training as *balwadi* (kindergarten) teachers, social workers, computer technicians, caters etc.

Ekta: a project to help keep families united. Maher provides assistance with educational materials, food, clothing, shelter, medical support, etc., to families in need.

Lokmangala: a project for general outreach during acute crisis. Maher provides support in a variety of forms to people and communities during times of natural disasters—tsunami, earthquakes, etc.

Aadhar: a project for job placements for women and youth.

Karyamandal: a project to look after the administrative work of the organization—coordination with others, accounts, projects, public relations, etc.

Adivasi Kalyan Kendra: a project that caters to the needs and welfare of tribal people who are landless and are being economically exploited by the landlords.

Gamat Shala: a project that cares for the slum children and the children of brick kiln workers by providing daycare and nutrition. Its literal meaning is "Play and Learn."

Interfaith Spiritual Principles

Thomas Keating, O.C.S.O.
St. Benedict's Monastery
Snowmass, Colorado

In 1984 I invited a group of spiritual teachers from a variety of the world religions—Buddhist, Tibetan Buddhist, Hindu, Jewish, Islamic, Native American, Russian Orthodox, Protestant, and Roman Catholic—to gather at St. Benedict's Monastery, Snowmass, Colorado, to meditate together in silence and to share our personal spiritual journeys, especially those elements in our respective traditions that have proved most helpful along the way.

As our trust and friendship grew, we felt moved to investigate various points that we seemed to agree on. The original points of agreement were worked over during the course of subsequent meetings as we continued to meet, for a week or so each year.

Our most recent list consists of the following eight points:

1. The world religions bear witness to the experience of Ultimate Reality to which they give various names: Brahman, Allah, Absolute, God, Great Spirit.
2. Ultimate Reality cannot be limited by any name or concept.
3. Ultimate Reality is the ground of infinite potentiality and actualization.

4. Faith is opening, accepting, and responding to Ultimate Reality. Faith in this sense precedes every belief system.

5. The potential for human wholeness—or in other frames of reference, enlightenment, salvation, transformation, blessedness, nirvana—is present in every human person.

6. Ultimate Reality may be experienced not only through religious practices but also through nature, art, human relationships, and service of others.

7. As long as the human condition is experienced as separate from Ultimate Reality. It is subject to ignorance and illusion, weakness and suffering.

8. Disciplined practice is essential to the spiritual life; yet spiritual attainment is not the result of one's efforts, but the result of the experience of oneness with Ultimate Reality.

For more detailed information, see *The Common Heart: An Experience of Interreligious Dialogue*, Netanel Miles-Yepez. Editor (N.Y.: Lantern Books, 2006).

Maher Housemothers' and Children's Daily Schedule

MORNING SCHEDULE

5:45	Rising
6:00	Prayer (entire community)
6:30	Exercise
7:00	Bath
7:00 – 8:00	Tabla and Dance classes
8:00 – 8:30	Breakfast
8:30 – 9:00	Children's community chores/duties
9:00 – 10:00	Study
10:15	Snacks
10:30	Children go to school
11:30 – noon	Housemothers' meditation and prayer

AFTERNOON SCHEDULE

12:30	Lunch
3:00 – 4:30	Women's classes (cookery, values training, health and cleanliness, etc.)
4:30 – 5:30	Personal time for women (bathing, cleaning, washing, etc.)
5:30	Children return from school

5:30 – 6:30	Watering the plants /Snack/Games, etc.
6:30 – 7:30	Study for children and Literacy class for women
7:30 – 8:00	Prayer (entire community)
8:00 – 8:30	Supper
9:00 – 10:00	Study
10:30	Sleep

Until 10:30 A.M., the housemothers are caring for the children (preparing breakfast, giving baths, helping with studies).

When the children leave for school at 10:30, the women either go to the production centre centre or to the kitchen.

Upon the children's return from school, the housemothers' primary responsibility is again caring for the children—preparing and serving food, cleaning, washing, etc.

Other Indian Organizations with Missions Similar to Maher

India has a long and vibrant history of women's movements and projects. Throughout the country there are many organizations doing similar or related work to Maher's, although in most cases not embedded within a larger explicitly interfaith and inter-caste community, such as Maher is creating. This Appendix briefly summarizes three examples of other women's projects, and these are by no means exhaustive or representative, but they give an idea of related efforts in India.

1. Vimochana is a feminist organization based in Bangalore that advocates justice for women and provides counseling and legal guidance for women in distress. Founded some twenty-one years ago, the organization began as an "office-based counseling service," but the staff soon realized that they needed to personally investigate the cases coming to them. This entailed moving beyond the office and "into the field," where they began to discover many things that were disturbing, such as witnessing the sight of burnt bodies of girls and women. They learned how families often dismissed the death as the girl's "fate," and often had no interest in investigating what had actually happened to her. This is an example of the chalta hai attitude that is prevalent throughout India, which is a laxidasical attitude that anything goes. Vimochana staff also experienced firsthand that "the police and courts provide very little relief." The police are frequently uncooperative, and often do what they can to cover up the death as an accident or suicide. Of course it is true that many a woman does resort to suicide in India, but typically because she is forced into "the decision through bigamy, sexual harassment, or an uncaring husband."

Vimochana staff face innumerable challenges when they help women who have been abused. For example, a woman who survives an attempted murder will usually be very angry and prepared to seek justice initially, but then when they file her case to take legal action, the woman often backs out suddenly and returns to the abusive environment. Another problem is that both the men and women tend to lie about what really happened. The men are often outraged that Vimochana is coming into their homes—"interfering in a personal matter." The women frequently tell lies owing to embarrassment about what they have endured. Women tend to share more openly in private sessions, when other family members are not present. Finally, the Vimochana staff need to be constantly aware of possible misuse of the organization by women who give false stories to take revenge on a man. Despite these occasional attempts to misuse their services, Vimochana continues to operate because of the massive need.[1]

2. Another organization of women slum-dwellers in Delhi have established a Non-Governmental Organization (NGO) founded in 1979 with a "unique model of self-governance." The organization provides counseling for abused women and holds the "perpetrators accountable through a feminist variant of an indigenous form of resolving conflict known as *mahila panchayats*, or women's courts." The

---

[1]   Interview with Celine Suguna of Vimochana, in *Urban Women in Contemporary India: A Reader*, Rehana Ghadially (Ed.), Sage Publications, 2007

project resembles Maher in the manner of women healing women, and women taking authority where men have failed to do so. Beyond a few part-time attorneys who provide law courses and counsel for specific cases, the organization is staffed and coordinated by women from the slums, often survivors of violence themselves. In marital conflicts adjudicated in the women's courts, men are held accountable and must work with their wives toward resolution, including providing financial maintenance. Women are required to understand their legal rights in order to make an informed decisions—often for the first time—on their own behalf. Most of the time, reconciliation between the couple is achieved. When this not possible, the NGO provides support through training, education and legal counsel for the woman so that she is able to economically sustain herself and her children. Through their work, the NGO staff provides a public model for everyone in the community to witness a new way of viewing the role of wife, daughter, mother, and mother-in-law. It is vital however that the women's court council understands women's oppression and empowerment, otherwise a backlash against the woman can occur in which the council unjustly sympathizes with the husband. This has been a problem at times in practice. This grassroots, community-based, NGO "continually challenges deeply ingrained attitudes [in the patriarchal culture] reflecting gender inequality." In this way, these women are working to change the root-cause of gender violence that goes far beyond the symptoms of sexual abuse, dowry deaths, and a host of other violent acts against women that manifest in the daily life of Indian women.[2]

3. The last example we explore here is **The Banyan** project in Chennai. In 1992, a crazed, nude woman ran up and down a Chennai street under the midday sun. As people either gawked or walked on, two

---

[2]   Veronica Magar, article in *Urban Women in Contemporary India: A Reader*, Rehana Ghadially (Ed.), Sage Publications, 2007

young women were appalled by what they saw and approached the woman, hugged her, and took her back to their college nearby. There they cleaned her up, clothed her, and calmed her down. Then they tried to find an organization in the city that would take this woman in, and discovered there was virtually nothing available. So the two young women, Vandana Gopikumar and Vaishnavi Jayakumar—close friends who were both twenty-two years old at the time—founded a refuge project for mentally disturbed street women, called The Banyan.

Within a decade, The Banyan had its own modern centre in a suburb of Chennai, where today about 275 women are sheltered and treated for mental disorders. Like the story of Maher, The Banyan story is full of challenges, grit, and long hours of tireless service. "While men in India tend to be cared for better, women are set adrift. Literally. They wander about losing their moorings," says Vandana Gopikumar. "They get on a bus or a train, and being ignored by the sea of people, they arrive wherever the train takes them." Like Maher's Vatsalyadam project, The Banyan takes these women in off the street, and provides them with basic needs and mental health and psychiatric treatment.

As reported by The Banyan's trustees, "The Banyan is an organization that cares for and rehabilitates homeless women with mental illness found in the streets of Chennai. At its home, Adaikalam, The Banyan provides the women a safe shelter, care, medical attention, and a supportive environment to enable them to recover and to take responsibility for their lives again. The Banyan also supports the women's return to their families and communities and when this is not possible, supports the women in setting up new lives for themselves. Over the past 14 years, The Banyan has reached out to more than 2000 women and reunited over 1000 women with their families all throughout India."

Maher Organizational Data

MAHER OPERATING BUDGET 2007

Sr. No	Name of the Projects	Amount Approximately
1	Aadhar	183391.00
2	Aashai	142256.00
3	Dnyan Ganga	63370.00
4	Ekta	202361.00
5	Kalasagar	74072.00
6	Karyamandal	942234.00
7	Lokmangal	209904.00
8	Mamtadham	947228.00
9	Parishram	423082.00
10	Pragati	100602.00
11	Premalaya	158133.00
12	Sukh Sandya	219464.00
13	Swachata	98264.00
14	Swavalamban	214348.00
15	Tantragyan	224125.00
16	Ushalaya	255065.00
17	Vatsalyadham	1335800.00
18	Vidyadham	113401.00
19	Vidyalaya	110627.00
	Kishoredham	
21	Aboli	532956.00
22	Anand Balsadan, Kendur	244755.00
23	Chayadham - Avalwadi	255256.00
24	Dayasagar - Bakori	328681.00
25	Jai - Vadu	380238.00
26	Jaswandi - Vadu	313867.00
27	Kamal - Vadu	521139.00
28	Khabia Balsadan - Shirur	384015.00
29	Krupa Balsadan - Apti	229539.00
30	Mogra - Vadu	265919.00
31	Navjeewan Balsadan - Takarvasti	319450.00
32	Premankur - Keshnand	295500.00
33	Premsagar - Pune	304344.00
34	Sadabahar - Pune	326667.00
35	Zendu - Vadu	287278.00
36	Champa - Vadu	225073.00
37	Chameli - Vadu	262390.00
		11494794.00

All figures in Indian Rupees
(One US dollar = approximately 38 Rupees)

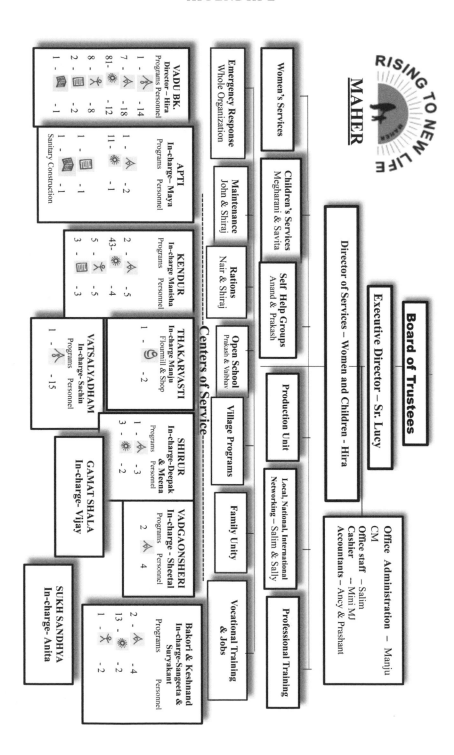

RISING TO NEW LIFE

MAHER

Board of Trustees

Executive Director – Sr. Lucy

Director of Services – Women and Children – Hira

Office Administration — Manju
CM
Office staff — Salim
Cashier — Mini MJ
Accountants — Ancy & Prashant

Local, National, International
Networking – Salim & Sally

Women's Services

Emergency Response
Whole Organization

Children's Services
Megharani & Savita

Maintenance
John & Shiraj

Self Help Groups
Anand & Prakash

Rations
Nair & Shiraj

Open School
Prakash & Vaibhav

Production Unit

Village Programs

Family Unity

Vocational Training
& Jobs

Professional Training

Centers of Service

VADU BK.
Director – Hira
Programs   Personnel
1 -   - 14
7 -   - 18
81-   - 12
8 -   - 8
2 -   - 2
1 -   -1

APTI
In-charge– Maya
Programs   Personnel
1 -   - 2
11-   - 1
1 -   -1
Sanitary Construction

KENDUR
In-charge Manisha
Programs   Personnel
2 -   - 5
43-   - 4
5 -   - 5
3 -   - 3

THAKARVASTI
In-charge Manju
Flourmill & Shop
1 -   - 2

VATSALYADHAM
In-charge– Sachin
Programs   Personnel
1 -   - 15

SHIRUR
In-charge–Deepak
& Meena
Programs   Personnel
1 -   - 3
3 -   - 2

VADGAONSHERI
In-charge - Sheetal
Programs   Personnel
2 -   4

GAMAT SHALA
In-charge– Vijay

Bakori & Keshnand
In-charge–Sangeeta &
Suryakant
Programs   Personnel
2 -   - 4
13-   - 2
1 -   - 2

SUKH SANDHYA
In-charge- Anita

MAHER – Where the women end up after coming to Maher

Year	Back to Home	In Maher	Working outside	Married / Other Institute	Training	Shelter in Maher	Expired	Total
1997	28	—	27	1	3	—	—	59
1998	31	—	14	—	6	1	—	52
1999	73	1	20	1	3	—	—	98
2000	58	—	6	—	1	1	—	66
2001	110	—	6	—	3	4	—	123
2002	79	10	14	—	7	5	—	115
2003	109	14	3	6	—	5	—	137
2004	129	13	3	5	1	17	—	168
2005	120	14	3	3	—	17	—	157
2006	133	7	2	—	1	11	1	155
2007	99	8	—	—	—	13	1	121
2008 Till 14th Aug.	52	8	2	—	—	27	1	90
Total	1021	75	100	16	25	101	3	1341

MAJOR DONORS TO MAHER

CORPORATIONS
Capgemini (formerly Kanbay)
Seco Tools Pvt. Ltd
John Deere Technology Centre
HSBC Bank
ZF Steering Gear India Ltd
Patni Computers System Ltd.
Hoganas
Patodia Glass Industries
Inner Wheel Club
Rotary Club, Pune Central and Riverside
Intervet India Pvt. Ltd
Lions Club, Pune downtown
ForbMarshall
LG Electronics
Bajaj Electricals

CHARITABLE FOUNDATIONS
Wereldkinderen - Netherlands - Dutch Group
Friends of UK - England and Scotland
Hartheim Institute - Austria
Foerderverein fuer MAHER - Germany
Vienna International School - VIS - Austria
Maharastra Foundation - USA
Tides Foundation - USA
Sister Fund - USA
Manos Unidas (Spain)
Give2Asia Foundation - USA
SOFKIN - New Jersey, USA

MAHER BOARD OF TRUSTEES
(October, 2008)

How Can You Get Involved with Maher?

There are several different ways to become involved with Maher, and to help support the women, children, staff, and projects of Maher. Four principal avenues are outlined below that offer a broad range of possibilities. You are invited to become involved in any or all of these ways which include: financial donations, joining the International Friends of Maher, visiting Maher, or serving as a volunteer or intern at Maher. Your loving support and participation in whatever form is deeply appreciated.

FINANCIAL DONATIONS

One of the most direct ways to help Maher is by providing a monetary donation, either as a single contribution, or on a monthly or annual basis as many Maher supporters do. There are two U.S. based foundations that receive donations for Maher—the Maharashtra Foundation in New York City and Give2Asia in San Francisco. Simple guidelines for making tax-deductable donations and the foundation addresses are given below.

Maharashtra Foundation
P.O.Box 2287, Church Street Station,
New York, NY 10008-2287

MF Tax ID: 22-2213611
www.indiancharity.org

Maharashtra Foundation accepts small and large donations. Make sure the address on your check is correct, and please add on the "memo" line "For Maher." Ninety-five percent of your donation goes directly to Maher, and the foundation will send you a receipt for your tax records.

Give2Asia Foundation
P.O. Box 193223
San Francisco, CA 94119-3223
www.give2asia.org

Give2Asia Foundation accepts donations of $150 and larger. Donations can be made on-line or sent by mail to the above address. Either way, please make certain that your donation is marked for Maher. Ninety-three percent of your donation goes directly to Maher.

JOIN THE INTERNATIONAL FRIENDS OF MAHER

"Once a friend, a friend for life." This is the motto of Maher. As Maher has gained visibility, people from around the world have increasingly wanted to become involved or reach out to help in various ways. Most give on an individual level, through donations, volunteering, or spreading the word. In recent years various groups have formed to actively raise awareness and provide support for Maher. Currently these support groups are operative in Austria, England, Germany, Holland, Italy, and the United States. These groups form the loosely affiliated International Friends of Maher.

Wonderful projects and events of different kinds have been achieved by the people in each of these countries as they have joined together to do what they can to help. For example, the UK Friends of

Maher organized the 2008 tour for the Maher dance troupe that was described in chapter 14. The Austrian Friends of Maher hosted Sally Samuel and Anand Sagar, senior staff from Maher, to attend a clinical training in Innsbruck at an innovative institute for the mentally disturbed. One of the Austrian Friends of Maher members, Christine Lendorfer has also been a leader in advocating Maher at the Vienna International School where she is a teacher. Under her leadership, the school has adopted Maher as their service project for over three years now. Students, parents, and teachers all participate in fund raising activities and many of the teachers have a small amount deducted from their monthly salaries to support Maher. They have raised several thousand euros and have funded one of Maher's satellite homes. These groups and the other European Friends of Maher, as well as the United States group, have organized major fundraising tours bringing Sister Lucy and Hira to their respective countries to share Maher's story more widely and raise funds for its vital work.

Finally, many people who volunteered at Maher have continued to work in innovative ways after going back home to help raise money and awareness. One twenty-four-year-old woman, Mikaela from the USA, started a "Sitting for Maher" project, donating 100 percent of the money she earned from babysitting to Maher. Andrea and Dinesha, from Holland who are both eighteen years old, raised 2000 Euros by canvassing their friends and families. A portion of this money was used to build a small playground in the tribal village of Takarwasti. Two older volunteers, Bernie and Tess, from the UK, helped when Maher was in dire need of an administrative office in Pune. As sisters, they purchase and donated a building for Maher's administrative office.

These are just a few small examples; there are many other forms of financial donation and innovative support that Maher's foreign friends and funders have provided. To learn more, and for a listing of a Friends of Maher group in your area, please visit www.maherashram. org.

VISITING MAHER

Maher has many visitors who come for all sorts reasons. Many want to experience what they have heard about Maher, others want to learn what can be done for the poor and oppressed, others want to do something to help, and others come because they are moved by the stories of the women and children, or by the dedication of Sister Lucy and her staff. People are often amazed to see Maher with their own eyes, and most come away very inspired by the atmosphere of love, compassion and good will at Maher.

VOLUNTEERING AND INTERNSHIPS AT MAHER

Opportunities for volunteering or internships at Maher are numerous and varied, and depend on the particular circumstances of the individual(s) involved. The program for volunteers at Maher is currently being developed and updated, and most people who wish to volunteer can be accommodated in some way. Internships are not organized by Maher itself, but numerous students, professionals, clergy, and others have conducted internships at Maher. If you are interested in an internship or volunteering, please write to Maher at the address below and explain your situation, and what you are seeking to do. All volunteer and internship positions must be approved by Maher and arranged before the person makes the journey to India. However, visits to Maher can often be schedule on relatively short notice.

If you are interested in visiting Maher, or if you would like to serve as a volunteer or apply for an internship, please contact:

Maher
Survey No. 1295, Vadhu Budruk
Tal. Shirur, Dist. Pune 412 216
Maharashtra (INDIA)
Telephone: 02137-252174 or 02137-253839
Email: maherpune@gmail.com

Index

About the Authors

William Keepin, PhD, has facilitated over fifty intensive gatherings in six countries for healing and reconciliation between women and men. He is the President of Satyana Institute (www.satyana.org), and founder of its Power of Reconciliation Project. An environmental scientist, he was a whistleblower in nuclear science policy, and his research on global warming influenced international energy policy. He leads retreats on interfaith spirituality, and is adjunct faculty at Holy Names University. Will is author of *Divine Duality: The Power of Reconciliation between Women and Men* (Hohm Press, 2007) and co-editor of *Song of the Earth: the Emerging Synthesis of Spiritual and Scientific Worldviews* (Permanent Publications, UK, 2009).

Cynthia Brix, M.Div, MA, is an interfaith minister specializing in international peacemaking, and spiritual direction for young adults. She is Program Director of Satyana Institute (www.satyana.org), and co-founder of its Women's Spiritual Mastery project. Cynthia co-directs with William Keepin the Power of Reconciliation project that facilitates intensive healing between women and men in South Africa, India, Canada and the United States. Formerly the Unitarian Universalist campus minister at the University of Colorado, she leads retreats on interfaith spirituality, and is adjunct faculty at Holy Names University. Cynthia is contributing author of *Divine Duality: The Power of Reconciliation between Women and Men* (Hohm Press, 2007).

Contact Information: www.satyana.org
Hohm Press website: www.hohmpress.com